1967

CLASSICS
IN
POLITICAL
SCIENCE

CLASSICS IN POLITICAL SCIENCE

edited by JOSEPH S. ROUCEK

PHILOSOPHICAL LIBRARY
New York

15 East 40th Street, New York 16, N.Y.

Library of Congress Catalog Card Number. 63-11485

Type set at The Polyglot Press, New York
Printed in the United States of America

To Glenn E. Dumke
Chancellor,
The California State Colleges

Contents

Preface

Wherever people live together in groups there arises the problem of liberty on the one hand and of authority on the other. There has been no end of theorizing about the complexity of politics, ranging from analysis of the operational aspect of public affairs to the formulation of philosophic systems and ideologies. Since political thinking is usually, if not always, done in the light of acute questions, the scope of political thought covers most trivial events of the day as well as fundamental principles.

The present volume attempts to feature the "classics" in the field, through selection of those thinkers who, in the editor's judgment, have made a basic contribution to the political science field.

Our thanks and appreciation to Dr. Dagobert D. Runes, Director of the Philosophical Library, for initiating the project and for his critical guidance. Special thanks also to Professor Lewis Ice, Director of the University of Bridgeport Library, for his help in securing widely scattered materials for this project, and to Mr. Angelo Cocco, my assistant, for devoting endless hours to the routine tasks needed to bring the project to completion.

University of Bridgeport

JOSEPH S. ROUCEK

JOHN ADAMS

(1735-1826)

Although remembered as the second President of the United States (1797-1801), was one of the most prolific political essayists of his generation—and one of the most astute. Unlike his doctrinaire contemporaries, he was little interested in abstractions and generalities (such as natural rights and social contracts), and in the revolutionary struggle favored the radicals in action but not in thought. Although not disputing the natural-rights-social-contract theory on the whole, he believed it had little bearing on the controversy between England and the colonies; he felt the real issue was one of practical constitutional principles since Great Britain had reached a point in her development where former concepts had to be reconsidered and adapted to new situations. The Empire could no longer be ruled on a parent-child basis, but must be viewed as a partnership of equals, which in fact it had become. The British constitution, therefore, should be conceived as the fundamental law of the Empire, determining the equal rights and duties of the partners.

Thoughts on Government Applicable to the Present State of the American Colonies (January, 1776)*

My dear sir,—If I was equal to the task of forming a plan for the government of a colony, I should be flattered with your request, and very happy to comply with it; because, as the divine science of politics is the science of social happiness, and the blessings of society depend entirely on the con-

* This excerpt taken from: Charles Francis Adams, ed., *The Life and Works of John Adams,* Boston: C. C. Little and J. Brown, Vol. IV, 1851, pp. 102-103.

stitutions of government, which are generally institutions that last for many generations, there can be no employment more agreeable to a benevolent mind than a research after the best.

Pope flattered tyrants too much when he said,

> "For forms of government let fools contest,
> That which is best administered is best."

Nothing can be more fallacious than this. But poets read history to collect flowers, not fruits; they attend to fanciful images, not the effects of social institutions. Nothing is more certain, from the history of nations and nature of man, than that some forms of government are better fitted for being well administered than others.

We ought to consider what is the end of government, before we determine which is the best form. Upon this point all speculative politicians will agree, that the happiness of society is the end of government, as all divines and moral philosophers will agree that the happiness of the individual is the end of man. From this principle it will follow, that the form of government which communicates ease, comfort, security, or in one word, happiness, to the greatest number of persons, and in the greatest degree, is the best.

All sober inquirers after truth, ancient and modern, pagan and Christian, have declared that the happiness of man, as well as his dignity, consists in virtue. Confucius, Zoroaster, Socrates, Mahomet, not to mention authorities really sacred, have agreed in this.

If there is a form of government, then, whose principle and foundation is virtue, would not every sober man acknowledge it better calculated to promote the general happiness than any other form?

Fear is the foundation of most government; but it is so sordid and brutal a passion and renders men in whose breasts it predominates so stupid and miserable, that Americans will not be likely to approve of any political institution which is founded on it.

Honor is truly sacred, but holds a lower rank in the scale of moral excellence than virtue. Indeed, the former is but a part of the latter, and consequently has not equal pretensions to support a frame of government productive of human happiness.

The foundation of every government is some principle or passion in the minds of the people. The noblest principles and most generous affections in our nature, then, have the fairest chance to support the noblest and also most generous models of government.

A man must be indifferent to the sneers of modern Englishmen, to mention in their company the names of Sidney, Harrington, Locke, Milton, Nedham, Neville, Burnet, and Hoadly. No small fortitude is necessary to confess that one has read them. The wretched condition of this country, however, for ten or fifteen years past, has frequently reminded me of their principles and reasonings. They will convince any candid mind, that there is no good government but what is republican. That the only valuable part of the British constitution is so; because the very definition of a republic is "an empire of laws, and not of men." That, as a republic is the best government, so that particular arrangement of the powers of society, or, in other words, that form of government which is best contrived to secure an impartial and exact execution of the laws, is the best of republics.

Of republics there is an inexhaustible variety, because the possible combinations of the powers of society are capable of innumerable variations.

As good government is an empire of laws, how shall your laws be made? In a large society, inhabiting an extensive country, it is impossible that the whole should assemble to make laws. The first necessary step, then, is to depute power from the many to a few of the most wise and good. But by what rules shall you choose your representatives? Agree upon the number and qualifications of persons who shall have the benefit of choosing, or annex this privilege to the inhabitants of a certain extent of ground.

The principal difficulty lies, and greatest care should be employed, in constituting this representative assembly. It should be in miniature an exact portrait of the people at large. It should think, feel, reason, and act like them. That it may be the interest of this assembly to do strict justice at all times, it should be an equal representation, or, in other words, equal interests among the people should have equal interests in it. Great care should be taken to effect this, and to prevent unfair, partial, and corrupt elections. Such regulations, however, may be better made in times of greater tranquility than the present; and they will spring up themselves naturally, when all the powers of government come to be in the hands of the people's friends. At present, it will be safest to proceed in all established modes, to which the people have been familiarized by habit.

A representation of the people in one assembly being obtained, a question arises, whether all the powers of government, legislative, executive, and judicial, shall be left in this body? I think a people cannot be long free nor ever happy, whose government is in one assembly.

CZAR ALEXANDER II

(1818-1881)

Has been called "the Czar-Liberator," "the White Czar," and even "the Abraham Lincoln of Russia." Actually, neither his training nor his temperament predisposed him to any of those roles. When he came to power at the age of thirty-six, like his father he saw himself as an autocrat whose duty it was to use the power given him by Providence, and he abhorred any movement which challenged his regime. He possessed, however, sufficient wisdom to discern what changes were unavoidable and the strength of character to see those changes through—even over the opposition of the nobility. With whatever distaste, he set resolutely about the task of finding a solution to the crippling burden of serfdom. Immediate emancipation of the peasants without land would obviously have produced enormous disorders. In this dilemma, he preferred to consult the nobility, whose elected "marshals" assembled at Moscow in August, 1856, for the coronation. Earlier, in March, 1856, in a speech to the local nobility of Moscow, Alexander had thrown out the famous propaganda warning "that serfdom cannot be continued forever, and it would therefore be better that this reform be effected from above than below."

The nobles, however, declined to take the initiative. Nearly five years passed before the first major legislative enactment affecting the peasants was signed. In its final form, the legislation consisted of seventeen articles plus special sections, was titled "Act on the Emancipation of the Peasants from Serfdom," and was signed on March 3, 1861. (This was followed, in 1866, by special legislation bringing personal liberty to the state peasants. In addition, much supplementary legislation was needed to deal with particular problems of emancipation.) Although the emancipation act ended the serf-landlord relationship, it did not sever the peasant-commune ties; in fact, emancipation increased the jurisdiction of the commune over its members, for to it were transferred many of the administrative and police powers which the nobles had formerly exercised. Although the peasants were free, they remained a class apart, at the bottom of the social hierarchy. Yet emancipation accelerated the ruin of the nobility in spite of their efforts to safeguard their prerogatives.

---

*Emancipation Ukase: The Emancipation of the Russian Serfs**

By the grace of God, we, Alexander II, Emperor and Autocrat of all the Russias, King of Poland, Grand Duke of Finland, etc., to all our faithful subjects make known:

Called by Divine Providence and by the sacred right of inheritance to the throne of our ancestors, we took a vow in our innermost heart so to respond to the mission which is intrusted to us as to surround with our affection and our Imperial solicitude all our faithful subjects of every rank and of every condition, from the warrior who nobly bears arms for the defence of the country to the humble artisan devoted to the works of industry, from the official in the career of the high offices of the State to the labourer whose plough furrows the soil.

In considering the various classes and conditions of which the State is composed we came to the conviction that the legislation of the empire having wisely provided for the organization of the upper and middle classes and having defined with precision their obligations, their rights, and their privileges, has not attained the same degree of efficiency as regards the peasants attached to the soil, thus designated because either from ancient laws or from custom they have been hereditarily subjected to the authority of the proprietors, on whom it was incumbent at the same time to provide for their welfare. The rights of the proprietors

---

* Text: *The Annual Register, 1861*, London: J. & F. H. A. Rivington, 1862, pp. 207-212, *passim.*

have been hitherto very extended and very imperfectly defined by the law, which has been supplied by tradition, custom, and the good pleasure of the proprietors. In the most favorable cases this state of things has established patriarchal relations founded upon a solicitude sincerely equitable and benevolent on the part of the proprietors, and on an affectionate submission on the part of the peasants; but in proportion as the simplicity of morals diminished, as the diversity of the mutual relations became complicated, as the paternal character of the relations between the proprietors and the peasants became weakened, and, moreover, as the seigneurial authority fell sometimes into hands exclusively occupied with their personal interests, those bonds of mutual good-will slackened, and a wide opening was made for an arbitrary sway, which weighed upon the peasants, was unfavourable to their welfare and made them indifferent to all progress under the conditions of their existence.

These facts had already attracted the notice of our predecessors of glorious memory, and they had taken measures for improving the conditions of the peasants, but among those measures some were not stringent enough, insomuch that they remained subordinate to the spontaneous initiative of such proprietors who showed themselves animated with liberal intentions; and others, called forth by peculiar circumstances, have been restricted to certain localities or simply adopted as an experiment. . . .

We thus came to the conviction that the work of a serious improvement of the condition of the peasants was a sacred inheritance bequeathed to us by our ancestors, a mission which, in the course of events, Divine Providence called upon us to fulfil.

We have commenced this work by an expression of our Imperial confidence towards the nobility of Russia, which has given us so many proofs of its devotion to the Throne, and of its constant readiness to make sacrifices for the welfare of the country. . . .

Having invoked the Divine assistance, we have resolved to carry this work into execution.

In virtue of the new dispositions [of the nobility], the peasants attached to the soil will be invested within a term, fixed by the law with all the rights of free cultivators.

The proprietors retaining their rights of property on all the land belonging to them grant to the peasants for a fixed regulated rental the full enjoyment of their close. . . . In this state, which must be a transitory one, the peasants shall be designated as "temporarily bound."

At the same time, they are granted the right of purchasing their close, and with the consent of the proprietors, they may acquire in full property the arable lands and other appurtenances which are allotted to them as a permanent holding. By the acquisition in full property of the quantity of land fixed, the peasants are free from their obligations towards the proprietors for land thus purchased, and they enter definitively into the condition of free peasants-landholders.

Although these dispositions, general as well as local, and the special supplementary rules for some particular localities, for the lands of small proprietors, and for the peasants who work in the manufactories and establishments of the proprietors, have been, as far as was possible, adapted to economical necessities and local customs, nevertheless, to preserve the existing state where it presents reciprocal advantages, we leave it to the proprietors to come to amicable terms with the peasants, and to conclude transactions relative to the extent of the territorial allotment and to the amount of rental . . . observing, at the same time, the established rules to guarantee the inviolability of such agreements.

Aware of all the difficulties of the reform we have undertaken, we place above all things our confidence in the goodness of Divine Providence who watches over the destinies of Russia.

We also count upon the generous devotion of our faithful

nobility, and we are happy to testify to that body the gratitude it has deserved from us, as well as from the country, for the disinterested support it has given to the accomplishment of our designs. Russia will not forget that the nobility, acting solely upon its respect for the dignity of man and its love for its neighbour, has spontaneously renounced rights given to it by serfdom actually abolished, and laid the foundation of a new future, which is thrown open to the peasants. We also entertain the firm hope that it will also nobly exert its ulterior efforts to carry out the new regulation by maintaining good order, in a spirit of peace and benevolence, and that each proprietor will complete, within the limits of his property, the great civic act accomplished by the whole body, by organizing the existence of the peasants domiciliated on his estates, and of his domestics, under mutual advantageous conditions, thereby giving to the country population the example of a faithful and conscientious execution of the regulations of the State. . . .

ST. THOMAS AQUINAS

(1225-1274)

Was recognized as the philosopher of the Roman Catholic Church when his authority was officially granted by Pope Leo XIII in the encyclical *Aeterni Patris* (1879). This Italian scholastic philosopher was also known as the "Angelic Doctor" (*Doctor Angelicus*) and "Prince of Scholastics" (*Princeps scholasticorum*); his school companions at Monte Cassino called him the "Dumb Ox." He entered the Dominican order and studied under Albertus Magnus at Cologne, where he also began his career as a teacher; after 1252 he also taught at Paris, Rome, Bologna and elsewhere (Dante, in the *Purgatorio,* suggests that he died by being poisoned). His major contribution is the *Summa Theologica.* His political ideas can be found also in his *De Regimine Principium,* of which only the first book and the first six chapters of the second are by Aquinas, the rest being the product of his disciple, Ptolemy of Lucca. Aquinas also wrote *Commentaries on the Politics of Aristotle,* but this contains little of his theory of the state.

His philosophy, currently called Thomism, is based on the axiom that knowledge springs from the well of reason and revelation (the field cultivated especially today by Jacques Maritain). In Thomas' theory of knowledge the essential point is that there are levels, especially two—that which deals with the facts of nature, and which reason is competent to comprehend; and that which deals with truth beyond nature, and which must be revealed by faith, e.g., the mysteries of the Christian doctrine. These two are not opposed to each other, but faith must be called in where reason reaches its limits. Philosophy is knowledge of ultimate things by way of reason. Theology has two divisions: (1) natural, which can be understood by reason, and (2) revealed, which must come through faith, which reaches beyond reason. Knowledge is attained when human ideas fit exactly their objects, as the impression on wax fits the object which imprints it. Thomas concurred with Aristotle's belief that the soul is the "form" of the body and is incomplete without it. Soul, being immaterial, is immortal. Since the process of knowledge is fundamentally inductive, there is nothing in the intellect which was not present first in the senses. In metaphysics Thomas maintained that the most universal notion is being; this ranges all the way from God, the highest form, to matter, the lowest form. Since man by nature is a social animal, he inevitably lives in social groups. The rules for living together are formulated in the laws of the state, the aim of which is to maintain conditions for the highest welfare of men. He explained that the will of the people counteracts tendencies to tyranny. Although monarchy is most "in accord with nature," an acceptable form of government is that which performs well the functions of the state, including the education of the citizens and the maintenance of freedom from economic want. In support of his doctrines, Aquinas accepted Aristotelian philosophy because it was compatible with the doctrines of Christianity and met the needs of human society; many of his pronouncements were directly influenced by Jewish thinkers (especially by Maimonides and Bahya ibn Pakuda). His ideas were developed more fully by his follower, Aegidius Romanus (in his *De Regimine Principium*). St. Thomas and Aegidius coordinated the doctrines of the Church developed in the previous centuries and provided what was thought a perfect and permanent system by identifying natural law with the will of God and by supporting monarchic government and the supremacy of ecclesiastical authority. Aquinas' theories also helped to lay the foundations of the Jesuit system and influenced their political activities.

On Kingship*

The Function of a Ruler

[2] THE FIRST STEP in our understanding must be set forth what is to be understood by the term *king*.

---

* This excerpt taken from *On Kingship,* trans. by Gerald B. Pheland, revised, with an introduction and notes by I. T. Eschmann, the Pontifical Institute of Medieval Studies, Toronto, 1949.

[3] In all things that are ordered towards an end wherein this or that course may be adopted, some directive principle is needed through which the due end may be reached by the most direct action. A ship, for example, which moves in different directions according to the impulse of the changing winds, would never reach its destination were it not brought to port by the skill of the pilot. Now, man has an end to which his whole life and all his actions are ordered; for man is an intelligent agent, and it is clearly the part of an intelligent agent to act in view of an end. Men also adopt different methods in proceeding towards their proposed end, as the diversity of men's pursuits and actions clearly indicates. Consequently man needs some directive principle to guide him towards his end.

[4] To be sure, the light of reason is placed by nature in every man, to guide him in his acts towards his end. Wherefore, if man were intended to live alone as many animals do, he would require no other guide to his end. Each man would be a king unto himself, under God, the highest King, inasmuch as he would direct himself in his acts by the light of reason given him from on high. Yet it is natural for man, more than for any other animal, to be a social and political animal, to live in a group.

[5] This is clearly a necessity of man's nature. For all other animals, nature has prepared food, hair as a covering, teeth, horns, claws as means of defense or at least speed in flight, while man alone was made without any natural provisions for these things. Instead of all these, man was endowed with reason, by the use of which he could procure all these things for himself by the work of his hands. Now, one man alone is not able to procure them all for himself, for one man could not sufficiently provide for life unassisted. It is therefore natural that man should live in the society of many. . . .

[6] If, then, it is natural for man to live in the society of many, it is necessary that there exist among men some means

by which the group may be governed. For where there are many man together and each one is looking after his own interest, the multitude would be broken up and scattered unless there were also an agency to take care of what appertains to the commonweal. In like manner, the body of a man or any other animal would disintegrate unless there were a general ruling force within the body which watches over the common good of all members.—With this in mind, Solomon says: "Where there is no governor, the people shall fall." . . .

[10] Now it happens in certain things which are ordained towards an end that one may proceed in a right way and also in a wrong way. So, too, in the government of a multitude there is a distinction between right and wrong. A thing is rightly directed when it is led towards a befitting end; wrongly when it is led toward an unbefitting end. Now the end which befits a multitude of free men is different from that which befits a multitude of slaves, for the free man is he who exists for his own sake, while the slave, as such, exists for the sake of another. If, therefore, a multitude of free men is ordered by the ruler towards the common good of the multitude, that rulership will be right and just, as is suitable to free men. If, on the other hand, a rulership aims, not at the common good of the multitude, but at the private good of the ruler, it will be an unjust and perverted rulership. The Lord, therefore, threatens such rulers, saying by the mouth of Ezechiel: "Woe to the shepherds that feed themselves [seeking, that is, their own interest]: should not the flocks be fed by the shepherd?" Shepherds indeed should seek the good of their flocks, and every ruler, the good of the multitude subject to him. . . .

[14] Now since man must live in a group, because he is not sufficient unto himself to procure the necessities of life were he to remain solitary, it follows that a society will be the more perfect the more it is sufficient unto itself to procure the necessities of life. There is, to some extent, suf-

fiency for life in one *family of one household,* namely, insofar as pertains to the natural acts of nourishment and the begetting of offspring and other things of this kind. Self-sufficiency exists, furthermore, in one *street* with regard to those things which belong to the trade of one guild. In a *city,* which is the perfect community, it exists with regard to all the necessities of life. Still more self-sufficiency is found in a *province* because of the need of fighting together and of mutual help against enemies. Hence the man ruling a perfect community, *i.e.* a city of a province, is antonomastically called *the* king. The ruler of a household is called father, not king, although he bears a certain resemblance to the king, for which reason kings are sometimes called the fathers of their peoples.

[15] It is plain, therefore, from what has been said, that a king is one who rules the people of one city or province, and rules them for the common good. Wherefore Solomon says: "The king ruleth over all the land subject to him."

One Man is Preferable as Chief of State

[36] When a choice is to be made between two things, from both of which danger impends, surely that one should be chosen from which the lesser evil follows. Now, lesser evil follows from the corruption of a monarchy (which is tyranny) than from the corruption of an aristocracy.

[37] Group government [polyarchy] most frequently breeds dissension. This dissension runs counter to the good of peace which is the principal social good. A tyrant, on the other hand, does not destroy this good, rather he obstructs one or the other individual interests of his subjects—unless, of course there be an excess of tyranny and the tyrant rages against the whole community. Monarchy is therefore to be preferred to polyarchy, although either form of government might become dangerous. . . .

[40] The strongest objection why monarchy, although it is "the best form of government," is not agreeable to the

people is that, in fact, it may deviate into tyranny. Yet tyranny is wont to occur not less but more frequently on the basis of a polyarchy than on the basis of a monarchy. It follows that it is, in any case, more expedient to live under one king than under the rule of several men.

[41] Therefore, since the rule of one man, which is the best, is to be preferred, and since it may happen that it be changed into a tyranny, which is the worst (all this is clear from what has been said), a scheme should be carefully worked out which would prevent the multitude ruled by a king from falling into the hands of a tyrant.

[42] First, it is necessary that the man who is raised up to be king by those whom it concerns should be of such condition that it is improbable that he should become a tyrant. Wherefore Daniel, commending the providence of God with respect to the institution of the king says: "The Lord hath sought him a man according to his own heart, and the Lord hath appointed him to be prince over his people." Then, once the king is established, the government of the kingdom must be so arranged that opportunity to tyrannize is removed. At the same time his power should be so tempered that he cannot easily fall into tyranny. . . .

[49] If to provide itself with a king belongs to the right of a given multitude, it is not unjust that the king be deposed or have his power restricted by that same multitude if, becoming a tyrant, he abuses the royal power. It must not be thought that such a multitude is acting unfaithfully in deposing the tyrant, even though it had previously subjected itself to him in perpetuity, because he himself has deserved that the covenant with his subjects should not be kept, since in ruling the multitude, he did not act faithfully as the office of a king demands. . . .

The Reward of a Good Ruler

[63] It is implanted in the minds of all who have the use of reason that the reward of virtue is happiness. The virtue of

anything whatsoever is explained to be that which makes its possessor good and renders his deed good. Moreover, everyone strives by working well to attain that which is most deeply implanted in desire, namely, to be happy. This, no one is able not to wish. It is therefore fitting to expect as a reward for virtue that which makes man happy. Now, if to work well is a virtuous deed, and the king's work is to rule his people well, then that which makes him happy will be the king's reward. What this is has now to be considered. Happiness, we say, is the ultimate end of our desires. Now the movement of desire does not go on to infinity else natural desire would be vain, for infinity cannot be traversed. Since then, the desire of an intellectual nature is for universal good, that good alone can make it truly happy which, when attained, leaves no further good to be desired. Whence happiness is called the perfect good inasmuch as it comprises in itself all things desirable. But no earthly good is such a good. They who have riches desire to have more, they who enjoy pleasure desire to enjoy more, and the like is clear for the rest: and if they do not seek more, they at least desire that those they have should abide or that others should follow in their stead. For nothing permanent is found in earthly things. Consequently there is nothing earthly which can calm desire. Thus, nothing earthly can make man happy, so that it may be a fitting reward for a king.

[64] Again, the last perfection and perfect good of anything one chooses depends upon something higher, for even bodily things are made better by the addition of better things and worse by being mixed with baser things. If gold is mingled with silver, the silver is made better, while by an admixture of lead it is rendered impure. Now it is manifest that all earthly things are beneath the human mind. But happiness is the last perfection and the perfect good of man, which all men desire to reach. Therefore there is no earthly thing which could make man happy, nor is any earthly thing a sufficient reward for a king. For, as Augustine says, "We do not

call Christian princes happy merely because they have reigned a long time, or because after a peaceful death they have left their sons to rule, or because they subdued the enemies of the state, or because they were able to guard against or to suppress citizens who rose up against them. Rather do we call them happy if they rule justly, if they prefer to rule their passions rather than nations, and if they do all things not for the love of vainglory but for the love of eternal happiness. Such Christian emperors we say are happy, now in hope, afterwards in very fact when that which we await shall come to pass." But neither is there any other created thing which would make a man happy and which would be set up as the reward for a king. For the desire of each thing tends towards its source, whence is the cause of its being. But the cause of the human soul is none other than God Who made it to His own image. Therefore it is God alone Who can still the desires of man and make him happy and be the fitting reward for a king.

Dictatorship Is Usually Short-lived

[80] The government of tyrants, on the other hand, cannot last long because it is hateful to the multitude, and what is against the wishes of the multitude cannot be long preserved. For a man can hardly pass through this present life without suffering some adversities, and in the time of his adversity occasion cannot be lacking to rise against the tyrant; and when there is an opportunity there will not be lacking at least one of the multitude to use it. Then the people will fervently favor the insurgent, and what is attempted with the sympathy of the multitude will not easily fail of its effects. It can thus scarcely come to pass that the government of a tyrant will endure for a long time.

[81] This is very clear, too, if we consider the means by which a tyrannical government is upheld. It is not upheld by love, since there is little or no bond of friendship between the subject multitude and the tyrant, as is evident from what

we have said. On the other hand, tyrants cannot rely on the loyalty of their subjects, for such a degree of virtue is not found among the generality of men, that they should be restrained by the virtue of fidelity from throwing off the yoke of unmerited servitude, if they are able to do so. Nor would it perhaps be a violation of fidelity at all, according to the opinion of many, to frustrate the wickedness of tyrants by any means whatsoever. It remains, then, that the government of a tyrant is maintained by fear alone and consequently they strive with all their might to be feared by their subjects. Fear, however, is a weak support. Those who are kept down by fear will rise against their rulers if the opportunity ever occurs when they can hope to do it with impunity, and they will rebel against their rulers all the more furiously the more they have been kept in subjection against their will by fear alone, just as water confined under pressure flows with greater impetus when it finds an outlet. That very fear itself is not without danger, because many become desperate from excessive fear, and despair of safety impels a man boldly to dare anything. Therefore the government of a tyrant cannot be of long duration.

The Characteristics of a Good Ruler

[93] The next point to be considered is what the kingly office is and what qualities the king should have. Since things which are in accordance with art are an imitation of the things which are in accordance with nature (from which we accept the rules to act according to reason), it seems best that we learn about the kingly office from the pattern of the regime of nature.

[94] In things of nature there is both a universal and a particular government. The former is God's government Whose rule embraces all things and Whose providence governs them all. The latter is found in man and it is much like the divine government. Hence man is called a microcosmos. Indeed there is a similitude between both governments in

regard to their form; for just as the universe of corporeal creatures and all spiritual powers comes under the divine government, in like manner the members of the human body and all the powers of the soul are governed by reason. Thus, in a proportionate manner, reason is to man what God is to the world. Since, however, man is by nature a social animal living in a multitude, as we have pointed out above, the analogy with the divine government is found in him not only in this way that one man governs himself by reason, but also in that the multitude of men is governed by the reason of one man. This is what first of all constitutes the office of a king. True, among certain animals that live socially there is a likeness to the king's rulership; so we say that there are kings among bees. Yet animals exercise rulership not through reason but through their natural instinct which is implanted in them by the Great Ruler, the Author of nature.

[95] Therefore let the king recognize that such is the office which he undertakes, namely, that he is to be in the kingdom what the soul is in the body, and what God is in the world. If he reflect seriously upon this, a zeal for justice will be enkindled in him when he contemplates that he has been appointed to this position in place of God, to exercise judgment in his kingdom; further, he will acquire the gentleness of clemency and mildness when he considers as his own members those individuals who are subject to his rule. . . .

[116] Thus the king, taught the law of God, should have for his principal concern the means by which the multitude subject to him may live well.

[117] This concern is threefold: first of all, to establish a virtuous life in the multitude subject to him; second, to preserve it once established; and third, having preserved it, to promote its greater perfection.

[118] For an individual man to lead a good life two things are required. The first and most important is to act in a virtuous manner (for virtue is that by which one lives well);

the second, which is secondary and instrumental, is a sufficiency of those bodily goods whose use is necessary for virtuous life. Yet the unity of man is brought about by nature, while the unity of multitude, which we call peace, must be procured through the efforts of the ruler. Therefore, to establish virtuous living to a multitude three things are necessary. First of all, that the multitude be established in the unity of peace. Second, that the multitude thus united in the bond of peace, be directed to acting well. For just as a man can do nothing well unless unity within his members be presupposed, so a multitude of men lacking the unity of peace will be hindered from virtuous action by the fact that it is fighting against itself. In the third place, it is necessary that there be at hand a sufficient supply of the things required for proper living, procured by the ruler's efforts.

[119] When virtuous living is set up in the multitude by the efforts of the king, it then remains for him to look to its conservation. Now there are three things which prevent the permanence of the public good. One of these arises from nature. The good of the multitude should not be established for one time only; it should be in a sense perpetual. Men, on the other hand, cannot abide forever, because they are mortal. Even while they are alive they do not always preserve the same vigor, for the life of man is subject to many changes, and thus a man is not equally suited to the performance of the same duties throughout the whole span of his life. A second impediment to the preservation of the public good, which comes from within, consists in the perversity of the wills of men, inasmuch as they are either too lazy to perform what the commonweal demands, or, still further, they are harmful to the peace of the multitude because, by transgressing justice, they disturb the peace of others. The third hindrance to the preservation of the commonweal comes from without, namely, when peace is destroyed through the attacks of enemies and, as it sometimes happens, the kingdom or city is completely blotted out.

[120] In regard to these three dangers, a triple charge is laid upon the king. First of all, he must take care of the appointment of men to succeed or replace others in charge of the various offices. Just as in regard to corruptible things (which cannot remain the same forever) the government of God made provision that through generation one would take the place of another in order that, in this way, the integrity of the universe might be maintained, so too the good of the multitude subject to the king will be preserved through his care when he sets himself to attend to the appointment of new men to fill the place of those who drop out. In the second place, by his laws and orders, punishments and rewards, he should restrain the men subject to him from wickedness and induce them to virtuous deeds, following the example of God, Who gave His law to man and requites those who observe it with rewards, and those who transgress it with punishments. The king's third charge is to keep the multitude entrusted to him safe from the enemy, for it would be useless to prevent internal dangers if the multitude could not be defended against external dangers.

[121] Finally, for the proper direction of the multitude there remains the third duty of the kingly office, namely, that he be solicitous for its improvement. He performs this duty when, in each of the things we have mentioned, he corrects what is out of order and supplies what is lacking, and if any of them can be done better he tries to do so. This is why the Apostle exhorts the faithful to be "zealous for the better gifts."

[122] These then are the duties of the kingly office, each of which must now be treated in greater detail.

How a Ruler Should Govern

[102] Just as the founding of a city or kingdom may suitably be learned from the way in which the world was created, so too the way to govern may be learned from the divine government of the world.

[103] Before going into that, however, we should consider that to govern is to lead the thing governed in a suitable way towards its proper end. Thus a ship is said to be governed when, through the skill of the pilot, it is brought unharmed and by a direct route to harbor. Consequently, if a thing be directed to an end outside itself (as a ship to the harbor), it is the governor's duty, not only to preserve the thing unharmed, but further to guide it towards this end. If, on the contrary, there be a thing whose end is not outside itself, then the governor's endeavors will merely tend to preserve the thing undamaged in its proper perfection.

[104] Nothing of this kind is to be found in reality, except God Himself, Who is the end of all. However, as concerns the thing which is directed to an end outside itself, care is exercised by different providers in different ways. One might have the task of preserving a thing in its being, another of bringing it to a further perfection. Such is clearly the case in the example of the ship (the first meaning of the word *gubernator* [governor] is *pilot*). It is the carpenter's business to repair anything which might be broken, while the pilot bears the responsibility of bringing the ship to port. It is the same with man. The doctor sees to it that a man's life is preserved; the tradesman supplies the necessities of life; the teacher takes care that man may learn the truth; and the tutor sees that he lives according to reason.

[105] Now if man were not ordained to another end outside himself, the above-mentioned cares would be sufficient for him. But as long as man's mortal life endures there is an extrinsic good for him, namely, final beatitude which is looked for after death in the enjoyment of God, for as the Apostle says: "As long as we are in the body we are far from the Lord." Consequently the Christian man, for whom that beatitude has been purchased by the blood of Christ, and who, in order to attain it, has received the earnest of the Holy Ghost, needs another and spiritual care to direct him

to the harbor of eternal salvation, and this care is provided for the faithful by the ministers of the church of Christ.

[106] Now the same judgment is to be formed about the end of society as a whole as about the end of one man. If, therefore, the ultimate end of man were some good that existed in himself, then the ultimate end of the multitude to be governed would likewise be for the multitude to acquire such good, and perservere in its possession. If such an ultimate end either of an individual man or a multitude were a corporeal one, namely, life and health of body, to govern would then be a physician's charge. If that ultimate end were an abundance of wealth, then knowledge of economics would have the last word in the community's government. If the good of the knowledge of truth were of such a kind that the multitude might attain to it the king would have to be a teacher. It is, however, clear that the end of a multitude gathered together is to live virtuously. For men form a group for the purpose of *living well* together, a thing which the individual man living alone could not attain, and *good life* is virtuous life. Therefore, virtuous life is the end for which men gather together. The evidence for this lies in the fact that only those who render mutual assistance to one another in living well form a genuine part of an assembled multitude. If men assembled merely to live, then animals and slaves would form a part of the civil community. Or, if men assembled only to accrue wealth, then all those who traded together would belong to one city. Yet we see that only such are regarded as forming one multitude as are directed by the same laws and the same government to live well.

[107] Yet through virtuous living man is further ordained to a higher end, which consists in the enjoyment of God, as we have said above. Consequently, since society must have the same end as the individual man, it is not the ultimate end of an assembled multitude to live virtuously, but through virtuous living to attain to the possession of God.

[108] If this end could be attained by the power of human nature, then the duty of a king would have to include the direction of men to it. We are supposing, of course, that he is called king to whom the supreme power of governing in human affairs is entrusted. Now the higher the end to which a government is ordained, the loftier that government is. Indeed, we always find that the one to whom it pertains to achieve the final end commands those who execute the things that are ordained to that end. For example, the captain, whose business it is to regulate navigation, tells the shipbuilder what kind of ship he must construct to be suitable for navigation, and the ruler of a city, who makes use of arms, tells the blacksmith what kind of arms to make. But because a man does not attain his end, which is the possession of God, by human power but by divine—according to the words of the Apostle: "By the grace of God life everlasting"—therefore the task of leading him to that last end does not pertain to human but to divine government.

ARISTOTLE
(384-322 B.C.)

Greek philosopher and pupil of Plato, is usually judged the first political scientist, since his concept of a science of politics is (contrasted to Plato's political philosophy) based on the observation and classification of political institutions and behavior (found mainly in his *Politics,* an unfinished work, and in the fragments of the *Nicomachean Ethics*). He considered politics the all-comprehensive science, since the highest life of the individual is possible only in the state; ethics, the science of individual good, and economics, the science of domestic good, are thus subdivisions of politics, which aim at the welfare of mankind. The best state is that in which all the citizens are able to lead as complete a political life as possible. Aware of the complexity of the forces which influence public life, Aristotle analyzed the devices of government, their actual workings, and the way in which they might be adjusted to changing conditions and to conflicting interests. He based his *Politics* upon his study of several governments of his time (especially those of Crete, Carthage, Sparta and Athens) and upon the ideas of such philosophers as Phaleas, Hippodamus, and especially Plato. He created a new science—logic (the art and method of correct thinking), although he is also noted for his writings on physics, biology, psychology, metaphysics, ethics, and literature.

The activities of man are of three kinds: theoretical (seeking knowledge), practical (regulating conduct), and productive (making things); the second, the practical, type of activity lies in the field of ethics. As the realm of Nature seems to be drawn toward some ideal, human beings are also drawn toward higher ideals for man; this has a double aspect, since man has both an individual and social character and what he is drawn toward in both roles is his highest well-being, the perfection of his nature or realization of his possibilities (*"eudaemonia,"* happiness).

This is the *summum bonum,* which is the aim of all virtuous living; it is attained by the rule of reason, which counsels moderation in all things. In politics, man by nature cannot be a pure individualist, and reaches his highest good only in his relations with his fellow men. Hence he must understand the structure of the state in which he is a part. The state is an association aimed at helping man to realize his highest good—happiness— which consists in the life of contemplative leisure. Aristotle discussed the ideal commonwealth and the uses of property, favoring moderation by way of education and law. The qualification for citizenship is the ability to perform its functions. The acceptable forms of the state are kingship, aristocracy and polity; the corruptions of these are tyranny, oligarchy and extreme democracy. Which form is best depends upon the character of the people. The ideal state is the one which performs its functions to the maximum degree of effectiveness.

Aristotle's influence on our thinking has been felt through the ages. He established a logical method of political inquiry and made possible a distinct science of the state. His generalizations are applicable to political life in all times and places.

---

*The State**

As the State was formed to make life possible, so it exists to make life good. Consequently if it be allowed that the simple associations, i.e. the household and the village, have a natural existence, so has the State in all cases; for in the State they attain complete development, and Nature implies complete development, as the nature of anything, e.g., of a man, a house or a horse, may be defined to be its condition when the process of production is complete. Or the naturalness of the State may be proved in another way: the object proposed or the complete development of a thing is its highest Good; but independence which is first attained in the

* Excerpt taken from Book I, Ch. 2, and Book III, Chs. 9, 11 of J. E. C. Welldon's translation (1881) of the *Politics.*

State is a complete development or the highest Good and is therefore natural.

Thus we see that the State is a natural institution, that Man is naturally a political animal and that one who is not a citizen of any State, if the cause of his isolation be natural and not accidental, is either a superhuman being or low in the scale of civilization, as he stands alone like a "blot" on the backgammon board. The "clanless, lawless, hearthless" man so bitterly described by Homer is a case in point; for he is naturally a citizen of no state and a lover of war. Also that Man is a political animal in a higher sense than a bee or any other gregarious creature is evident from the fact that Nature as we are fond of asserting, creates nothing without a purpose and Man is the only animal endowed with speech. Now mere senses serve to indicate sensations of pain and pleasure and are therefore assigned to other animals as well as to Man; for their nature does not advance beyond the point of perceiving pain and pleasure and signifying these perceptions to one another. The object of speech on the other hand is to indicate advantage and disadvantage and therefore also justice and injustice. For it is a special characteristic which distinguishes Man from all other animals that he alone enjoys perception of good and evil, justice and injustice and the like. But these are the principles of that association which constitutes a household or a State.

Again, in the order of Nature the State is prior to the household or the individual. For the whole must needs be prior to its parts. For instance, if you take away the body which is the whole, there will not remain any such thing as a foot or a hand, unless we use the same word in a different sense as when we speak of a stone hand as a hand. For a hand separated from the body will be a disabled hand; whereas it is the function or faculty of a thing which makes it what it is, and therefore when things lose their function or faculty it is not correct to call them the same things but rather homonymous, i.e. different things having the same name.

We see then that the State is a natural institution, and also that it is prior to the individual. For if the individual as a separate unit is not independent, he must be a part and must bear the same relation to the State as other parts to their wholes; and one who is incapable of association with others or is independent and has no need of such association is no member of a State, in other words he is either a brute or a God. Now the impulse to political association is innate in all men. Nevertheless the author of the first combination whoever he was was a great benefactor of human kind. For man, as in his condition of complete development, i.e. in the State, he is the noblest of all animals, so apart from law and justice he is the vilest of all. For injustice is always most formidable when it is armed; and Nature has endowed Man with arms which are intended to subserve the purposes of prudence and virtue but are capable of being wholly turned to contrary ends. Hence if Man be devoid of virtue, no animal is so unscrupulous or savage, none so sensual, none so gluttonous. Just action on the other hand is bound up with the existence of a State; for the administration of justice is an ordinance of the political association and the administration of justice is nothing else than the decision of what is just.

. . . Oligarchs and Democrats agree in this, that they both adhere to a certain principle of justice; but they do not advance beyond a certain point or put forward a full statement of justice in the proper sense of the word. Thus the one party, i.e. the Democrats, hold that justice is equality; and so it is, but not for all the world but only for equals. The others, i.e. the Oligarchs, hold that inequality is just, as indeed it is, but not for all the world but only for unequals. Both put out of sight one side of the relation, viz., the persons who are to enjoy the equality or inequality, and consequently form a wrong judgment. The reason is that they are judging of matters which affect themselves, and we are all sorry judges when our personal interests are at stake.

And thus whereas justice is a relative term and, as has been already stated in the Ethics, implies that the ratio of distribution is constant in respect of the things distributed and the persons who receive them, the two parties, while they are of one mind about the equality of the thing, differ as to what constitutes equality in the recipients, principally for the reason just alleged, viz. that they are bad judges where their own interests are concerned, but secondly also because the fact that each maintains a certain principle of justice up to a certain point is one which itself leads them to suppose that they are maintaining a principle of justice in the absolute sense. For the Oligarchs, if they are superior in a particular point, viz. in money, assume themselves to be superior altogether; while the Democrats, if they are equal in a particular point, viz. in personal liberty, assume themselves to be equal altogether. But they omit the point of capital importance. If a multitude of possessions was the sole object of their association or union, then their share in the State is proportionate to their share in the property, and in this case there would seem to be no resisting the argument of the oligarchical party that, where there is, e.g., a capital of one hundred *minae,* the contributor of a single *mina* ought not in justice to enjoy the same share either of the principal or of the profits accruing as a person who has given the remaining ninety-nine. But the truth is that the object of their association is to live well—not merely to live: otherwise slaves and the lower animals might form a State, whereas this is in fact impossible, as they are incapable of happiness or of a life regulated by a definite moral purpose, i.e. of the conditions necessary to a State. Nor is the object military alliance and security against injury from any quarter. Nor again is the end proposed barter and intercommunion; for, if it were, the Tyrrhenians and Carthaginians and all such nations as are connected by commercial treaties might be regarded as citizens of a single State. Among them there certainly exist contracts in regard to Customs, covenants against mutual injury and formal articles of alliance. But there are no magistracies common to all the contracting parties instituted to secure these objects, but different magistracies exist in each of the States; nor do the members of one feel any concern about the right character of members of the other or about the means of preserving all who come under the treaties from being unjust and harboring any kind of wickedness or indeed about any point whatever, except the prevention of mutually injurious actions. Virtue and vice on the other hand are matters of earnest consideration to all whose hearts are set upon good and orderly government. And from this fact it is evident that a State which is not merely nominally but in the true sense of the word a State should devote its attention to virtue. To neglect virtue is to convert the political association into an alliance differing in nothing except in the local contiguity of its members from the alliances formed between distant States, to convert the law into a mere covenant, or, as the sophist Lycophron said, a mere surety for the mutual respect of rights, without any qualification for producing goodness or justice in the citizens. But it is clear that this is the true view of the State, *i.e. that it promotes the virtue of its citizens.* For if one were to combine different localities in one, so that e.g. the walls of Megara and Corinth were contiguous, yet the result would not be a single State. Nor again does the practice of intermarriage necessarily imply a single State, although intermarriage is one of the forms of association which are especially characteristic of States. So too if we suppose the case of certain persons living separately, although not so far apart as to prevent association, but under laws prohibitive of mutual injury in the exchange of goods, if we suppose e.g. *A* to be a carpenter, *B* a husbandman, *C* a cobbler, *D* something else, and the total to amount to ten thousand, but their association to be absolutely confined to such things as barter and military alliance, here again there would certainly not be a State.

What then is the reason? It is assuredly not the absence of

local contiguity in the association. For suppose the members were actually to form a union upon such terms of association as we have described, suppose at the same time that each individual were to use his own household as a separate State, and their intercourse were limited as under the conditions of a defensive alliance to rendering mutual assistance against aggression, still the conception of a State in the strict view would not even then be realized, if their manner of social dealings after the union were to be precisely the same as when they lived apart.

It is clear then that the State is not merely a local association or an association existing to prevent mutual injury and to promote commercial exchange. So far is this from being the case that, although these are indispensable conditions, if a State is to exist, yet all these conditions do not necessarily imply a State. A State on the contrary is first realized when there is an association of households and families.

ST. AUGUSTINE
(Aurelius Augustinus)
(354-430)

Bishop of Hippo, is, along with St. Ambrose, Jerome and Gregory the Great, one of the four great Fathers of the Church. Born in Tagaste (Algeria), of a Christian mother and a pagan father, he first sought his salvation in Manichaeism and led a life of promiscuous pleasure-seeking. By the time he was thirty-three, he had embraced Christianity; he was ordained shortly after his conversion; from 395 until his death he served as Bishop of Hippo, North Africa, and died when the Vandals besieged his episcopal town. Living in the period of the disintegration of the Roman Empire, he contributed much, through his writings (*Expositio Fideis Christianae, 397; De Trinitate,* c. 416; *Confessiones;* and *De Civitate Dei* (*The City of God*), 410-427), to the strengthening of the position of the Christian Church. He defended its established doctrines against heretical attacks and gave it a philosophy of ethics, metaphysics and a lasting philosophy of history. His works deal with the problems of divine omnipotence, predestination, God, the Trinity and creation. They consistently affirm that the Catholic Church, founded by Christ, is the only reliable guide to human reason. Especially in *The City of God* he enunciated the famous doctrine of the four epochs of human history, a doctrine that was accepted in Western civilization until the time of Hegel and Comte. He has been called the "Christian Aristotle," for he was the first to succeed in organizing the truths of religion into a system.

His theology propounded that the world would be most happily governed in a society of small states (thus imitating Plato in his ideal city); but his conception of the church was imperialistic, since it supported a world-wide organization under a single leader. Pointing to Roman history, which the old gods had not saved, he argued that Christianity, if adopted by people and rulers, would save the state. For him, the City of God was not only Heaven, but also its counterpart on earth composed of the body of true believers. Integrating the ideas of Plato, Cicero and the theology of the Christian religion, he justified slavery as a remedy and a divine punishment for sin. He criticized, however, Cicero's idea of the state as the embodiment of justice, propounding that justice could not exist in non-Christian states, and that ecclesiastical authority was independent of the state. The state is partly a punitive and partly a remedial institution. Men were originally equal, but as a consequence of sin some had to be subjected to the authority of others. For St. Augustine, the state was of divine origin; its ruler was the representative of God on earth and had to be obeyed, but the earthly kingdom was inferior to the eternal state of the spirit and of the hereafter. His influence, though immeasurable, is especially notable in Thomas Aquinas, Dante, Wycliffe, Grotius, Luther, Pascal, Descartes and Leibniz. *The City of God* was a favorite book of Charlemagne, and Lord Bryce claimed that the concept of the Holy Roman Empire was built upon it. Augustine's doctrine provided the props for the claims of papal power during the Middle Ages and thereafter. His autobiographical *Confessions* has been regarded for centuries as a manual of self-analysis.

---

*The City of God**

Preface Explaining His Design in Undertaking This Work

THE GLORIOUS CITY OF GOD is my theme in this work, which you, my dearest son Marcellinus, suggested, and which is due to you by my promise. I have undertaken its defense against those who prefer their own gods to the Founder of this city, —a city surpassingly glorious, whether we view it as it still

* This excerpt taken from *Select Library of the Nicene and Post Nicene Fathers,* as translated by Marcus Dodds and edited by Philip Schaff, New York: Charles Scribners, 1899, II, I; 21-22, 82, 93; 205, 245; 249; 262, 282-283; 401, 406-407, 412-413, 509-511.

lives by faith in this fleeting course of time, and sojourns as a stranger in the midst of the ungodly, or as it shall dwell in the fixed stability of its eternal seat, which it now with patience waits for, expecting until "righteousness shall return unto judgment," and it obtain, by virtue of its excellence, final victory and perfect peace. A great work this, and an arduous, but God is my helper. . . .

What Subjects Are To Be Handled in the Following Discourse

But I have still some things to say in confutation of those who refer the disasters of the Roman republic to our religion, because it prohibits the offering of sacrifices to the gods. For this end I must recount all, or as many as may seem sufficient, of the disasters which befell that city and its subject provinces, before these sacrifices were prohibited; for all these disasters they would doubtless have attributed to us, if at that time our religion had shed its light upon them, and had prohibited their sacrifices. I must then go on to show what social well-being the true God, in whose hand are all kingdoms, vouchsafed to grant to them that their empire might increase. I must show why He did so, and how their false gods, instead of at all aiding them, greatly injured them by guile and deceit. And, lastly, I must meet those who, when on this point convinced and confuted by irrefragable proofs, endeavor to maintain that they worship the gods, not hoping for the present advantages of this life, but for those which are to be enjoyed after death. And this, if I am not mistaken, will be the most difficult part of my task, and will be worthy of the loftiest argument; for we must then enter the lists with the philosophers, not the mere common herd of philosophers, but the most renowned, who in many points agree with ourselves, as regarding the immortality of the soul, and that the true God created the world, and by His providence rules all He has created. But as they differ from us on other points, we must not shrink from the task of exposing their errors, that, having refuted the gainsaying of the wicked with such ability as God may vouchsafe, we may assert the city of God, and true piety, and the worship of God, to which alone the promise of true and everlasting felicity is attached. Here, then, let us conclude, that we may enter on these subjects in a fresh book. . . .

That the Times of all Kings and Kingdoms Are Ordained By the Judgment and Power of the True God

Therefore that God, the author and giver of felicity, because He alone is the true God, Himself gives earthly kingdoms both to good and bad. Neither does He do this rashly, and, as it were, fortuitously,—because He is God, not fortune, —but according to the order of things and times, which is hidden from us, but thoroughly known to Himself; which same order of times, however, He does not serve as subject to it, but Himself rules as lord and appoints as governor. Felicity He gives only to the good. Whether a man be a subject or a king makes no difference; he may equally either possess or not possess it. And it shall be full in that life where kings and subjects exist no longer. And therefore earthly kingdoms are given by Him both to the good and the bad lest His worshippers, still under the conduct of a very weak mind, should covet these gifts from Him as some great things. And this is the mystery of the Old Testament, in which the New was hidden, that there even earthly gifts are promised: those who were spiritual, understanding even then, although not yet openly declaring, both the eternity which was symbolized by these earthly things, and in what gifts of God true felicity could be found. . . .

Concerning the Universal Providence of God in the Laws of Which All Things Are Comprehended

Therefore God supreme and true, with His Word and

Holy Spirit (which three are one), one God omnipotent, creator and maker of every soul and of every body; by whose gift all are happy who are happy through verity and not through vanity; who made man a rational animal consisting of soul and body, who, when he sinned, neither permitted him to go unpunished, nor left him without mercy; who has given, to the good and to the evil, being (in common with stones), vegetable life (in common with trees), sensuous life (in common with brutes), intellectual life (in common with angels alone); from whom is every mode, every species, every order; from whom are measure, number, weight; from whom is everything which has an existence in nature, of whatever kind it be, and of whatever value; from whom are the seeds of forms and the forms of seeds, and the motion of seeds and of forms; who gave also to flesh its origin, beauty, health, reproductive fecundity, disposition of members, and the salutary concord of its parts; who also to the irrational soul has given memory, sense, appetite, but to the rational soul, in addition to these, has given intelligence and will; who has not left, not to speak of heaven and earth, angels and men, but not even the entrails of the smallest and most contemptible animal, or the feather of a bird, or the little flower of a plant, or the leaf of a tree, without an harmony, and, as it were, a mutual peace among all its parts;—that God can never be believed to have left the kingdoms of men, their dominations and servitudes outside of the laws of His providence. . . .

Of the Fall of the First Man, Through Which Mortality Has Been Contracted

Having disposed of the very difficult questions concerning the origin of our world and the beginning of the human race, the natural order requires that we now discuss the fall of the first man (we may say of the first men), and of the origin and propagation of human death. For God had not made man like the angels, in such a condition that, even though they had sinned, they could none the more die. He had so made them, that if they discharged the obligations of obedience, an angelic immortality and a blessed eternity might ensue, without the intervention of death, but if they disobeyed, death should be visited on them with just sentence—which, too, has been spoken to in the preceding book. . . .

JEREMY BENTHAM
(1748-1832)

Noted English social thinker, was a sympathizer of the American and French revolutions, whose ideas paralleled those of the Founding Fathers more closely than those of the French Jacobins. His most comprehensive political work was *The Introduction to Morals and Legislation* (1789); but the clearest and simplest presentation of his ideas can be found in *The Fragment on Government* (1776). His other fields of interests were handled in *Defense of Usury* (1787), *Emancipate Your Colonies* (1793), *Discourse on Civil and Penal Legislation* (1802), *Theory of Punishments and Rewards* (1811), *Treatise on Judicial Evidence* (1813) and *Constitutional Code* (1830, 1841). While his early writings took for granted a traditional social structure rooted in landed property, established status and hereditary monarchy, later, observing the impact of industrialization, Bentham favored the passing of rational legislation adapted to the changing conditions of the time. Politics, therefore, should not be guided by an uncritical appreciation for traditions but by the deliberate will of reasonable men; thus he called for an efficient government, and favored penal reform and the use of civil servants to handle municipal sanitation and factory regulations. His notion that law and administration can be instruments for improving human conditions formed a link between political theory and political institutions.

He defined the function of good government as the effort to promote the greatest happiness of the greatest number of citizens and to effect harmony between public and private interests, and declared that the American government was the only good government because it upheld these principles. According to him, happiness is identical with pleasure and serves as the underlying motivation of human behavior; thus happiness can be the only criterion of morals and legislation. He is known as the "father of the Utilitarian school"; his criterion of utility was revived by his disciple, James Mill. His writings on legislation were translated into French for Mirabeau and the procedure of the French Assembly was based largely on a sketch by Bentham. His doctrines were widespread in Russia, Portugal, Spain and parts of South America, and were used by the spokesmen of the national movements that defeated the Holy Alliance and built up new nations on the remnants of the Spanish and Turkish Empires. He also contributed, sometimes on request, to the revision of the legal codes of many countries; for instance, in 1811 he made an offer to President Madison to draw up a scientific code of law for the U.S.; later he made the same offer to the Czar of Russia and to the governor of Pennsylvania. Some of his words—"international," "utilitarian," "codification" and "minimize"—are now part and parcel of the English language.

---

*Of the Limits Which Separate Morals from Legislation**

MORALITY in general is the act of directing the actions of men, so as to produce the greatest possible amount of happiness.

Legislation ought to have precisely the same object in view.

But although these two arts, or these two sciences have the same end in view, they differ much in their extent. All actions, whether public or private, are the springs of morals. It is a guide which may conduct an individual, as it were by the hand, through all the details of life, through all the relationships of society. Legislation cannot do this, and if it could, it ought not to exercise a continual and direct interference with the conduct of men. Morality prescribes to each individual to do whatever is advantageous to himself and to the community. But as there are many acts useful to the community which the legislator ought never to com-

* This excerpt taken from Jeremy Bentham, *Principles of Legislation,* 1802, in an edition of Bentham's work by Stephen Dumont.

mand: So are there many hurtful acts, which he ought not to forbid, although morality may. Legislation in a word has much the same center as morality, though not the same circumference.

There are two reasons for the difference: 1. Legislation cannot secretly influence the conduct of men but by punishment: these punishments are so many evils, which are no further justifiable, than as they produce a greater sum of good. But in many cases where we might wish to strengthen a moral precept by a penalty, the evil of the fault would be less than the evil of the penalty; the means necessary for securing the execution of the law would be of a nature to spread a degree of alarm more hurtful than the evil that we might wish to prevent.

2. Legislation is often stopped by the fear of including the innocent while striving to reach the guilty. Whence comes the danger? From the difficulty of defining the offense, of giving a clear and precise idea of it. For example, severity, ingratitude, perfidy, and other vices which the popular sanction punishes, cannot come within the supervision of the law, for we cannot give an exact definition of them, as of robbery, homicide, perjury, etc. . . .

General Rule. Leave to individuals the greatest possible latitude, in every case where they can only injure themselves, for they are the best judges of their own interests. If they deceive themselves, the moment they perceive their error, it is to be presumed they will not persist. Do not suffer the power of the law to interfere, unless to prevent their injuring each other. It is there that law is necessary; it is there that the application of punishment is truly useful, since the rigor shown toward one may ensure the safety of all. . . .

Conclusion

I shall finish with a general observation. The language of error is always obscure, feeble, and changeable. A great abundance of words only serves to hide the poverty and falsity of ideas. The more the terms are varied, the more easy it is to lead people astray. The language of truth is uniform and simple: the same ideas, the same terms. All these refer to pleasures and to pains. We avoid all that may hide or intercept that familiar notion.—*From such or such an act, results such or such an impression of pain or pleasure.* Do not trust to me; trust to experience; and above all, to your own. *Between two opposite modes of action, would you know to which the preference is due? Calculate the effects, in good and ill, and decide for that which promises the greatest amount of happiness.*

EDMUND BURKE
(1729-1797)

A famed British philosopher, in his *Vindication of Natural Society* (1756), *Causes of our Present Discontent* (1770), *Reflections on the Revolution in France* (1790), *Appeal from the New to the Old Whigs* (1791), and *Thoughts on French Affairs* (1791), attacked practical men because they are guided by theoretical considerations. He favored politicians not encumbered by ideas, since they should be men of action, not dreamers of abstract thought. In his political pamphlets, parliamentary speeches and essays he elucidated the philosophical issues inherent in practical matters. Some of his essays show the influence of Kant, Hegel and many aestheticians of the eighteenth century. At the same time, he was an ardent partisan, for he blended his partisan spirit and his realism with romanticism, and demanded a rigorous honesty and cautious regard for actual circumstances, traditions and expediences. He was always ready to combat imminent dangers and evils, and is now considered the greatest prophet of the English conservative tradition. Like Rousseau, he was a phrase-maker of the first order. Yet by origin and temperament, he was profoundly un-English, an Irishman by birth, though master of the English language and one of the greatest orators in the history of the British Parliament. Basically, he believed that the human individual is incapable of creating anything new; that all useful and legitimate innovations must grow out of the collective mind in accordance with tradition. He strongly opposed changes in the British Constitution, whose form was dogma to him, fought for the removal of administrative abuses and opposed corruption, particularly the efforts of King George III to enslave both houses of Parliament. He denounced the French Revolution as a crime because it made a break with the past, served as a challenge to true wisdom and experience and was a threat to liberty and prosperity. With his derision of the theory of the "Rights of Man," Burke became the vanguard of the European counterrevolution. His main contribution to political science was his stress upon the value of studying actual institutions and on the evolutionary nature of successful reform. He was thus the exponent of a new evolutionary historical sense, and his influence on English politics has been compared with the influence of Wesley on English religion. His views on the American question are expressed in the Speech on American Taxation (1774) and the Speech on Conciliation with America (March 22, 1775). Both are performances of the first order, and the latter, in which he attacked the pedantic methods which lost the American colonies, contains some of the most famous of his phrases.

---

*On Conciliation with America**

IN THE CHARACTER of the Americans a love of freedom is the predominating feature which marks and distinguishes the whole; and as an ardent is always a jealous affection, your colonies become suspicious, restive, and untractable whenever they see the least attempt to wrest from them by force, or shuffle from them by chicane, what they think the only advantage worth living for. This fierce spirit of liberty is stronger in the English colonies probably than in any other people of the earth, and this from a great variety of powerful causes; which, to understand the true temper of their minds, and the direction which this spirit takes, it will not be amiss to lay open somewhat more largely.

First, the people of the colonies are descendants of Englishmen. England, Sir, is a nation, which still I hope respects, and formerly adored, her freedom. The colonists emigrated from you when this part of your character was most predominant, and they took this bias and direction the moment

* This excerpt taken from Edmund Burke, *Speech on Conciliation with America,* edited by C. H. Ward, Chicago: Scott, Foresman & Co., 1919, pp. 60-68.

they parted from your hands. They are therefore not only devoted to liberty, but to liberty according to English ideas and on English principles. Abstract liberty, like other mere abstractions, is not to be found. Liberty inheres in some sensible object; and every nation has formed to itself some favorite point which, by way of eminence, becomes the criterion of their happiness. It happened, you know, Sir, that the great contests for freedom in this country were from the earliest times chiefly upon the question of taxing. Most of the contests in the ancient commonwealths turned primarily on the right of election of magistrates, or on the balance among the several orders of the state. The question of money was not with them so immediate. But in England it was otherwise. On this point of taxes the ablest pens and most eloquent tongues have been exercised; the greatest spirits have acted and suffered. In order to give the fullest satisfaction concerning the importance of this point, it was not only necessary for those who in argument defended the excellence of the English Constitution to insist on this privilege of granting money as a dry point of fact, and to prove that the right had been acknowledged in ancient parchments and blind usages to reside in a certain body called a House of Commons. They went much further; they attempted to prove—and they succeeded—that in theory it ought to be so, from the particular nature of a House of Commons as an immediate representative of the people, whether the old records had delivered this oracle or not. They took infinite pains to inculcate, as a fundamental principle, that in all monarchies the people must in effect themselves mediately or immediately, possess the power of granting their own money, or no shadow of liberty could subsist. The colonies draw from you, as with their lifeblood, these ideas and principles. Their love of liberty, as with you, fixed and attached on this specific point of taxing. Liberty might be safe, or might be endangered, in twenty other particulars, without their being much pleased or alarmed. Here they felt its pulse;

and as they found that beat, they thought themselves sick or sound. I do not say whether they were right or wrong in applying your general arguments to their own case. It is not easy, indeed, to make a monopoly of theorems and corollaries. The fact is that they did thus apply those general arguments; and your mode of governing them—whether through lenity or indolence, through wisdom or mistake—confirmed them in the imagination that they, as well as you, had an interest in these common principles.

They were further confirmed in this pleasing error by the form of their provincial legislative assemblies. Their governments are popular in a high degree; some are merely popular; in all, the popular representative is the most weighty, and this share of the people in their ordinary government never fails to inspire them with lofty sentiments, and with a strong aversion from whatever tends to deprive them of their chief importance.

If anything were wanting to this necessary operation of the form of government, religion would have given it a complete effect. Religion, always a principle of energy, in this new people is no way worn out or impaired; and their mode of professing it is also one main cause of this free spirit. The people are Protestants, and of that kind which is the most adverse to all implicit submission of mind and opinion. This is a persuasion not only favorable to liberty, but built upon it. I do not think, Sir, that the reason of this averseness in the dissenting churches from all that looks like absolute government is so much to be sought in their religious tenets as in their history. Every one knows that the Roman Catholic religion is at least coeval with most of the governments where it prevails, that it has generally gone hand in hand with them, and received great favor and every kind of support from authority. The Church of England, too, was formed from her cradle under the nursing care of regular government. But the dissenting interests have sprung up in direct opposition to all the ordinary powers of the world, and could justify that opposition only on a strong claim for natural liberty. Their very existence depended on the powerful and unremitted assertion of that claim. All Protestantism, even the most cold and passive, is a sort of dissent. But the religion most prevalent in our northern colonies is a refinement on the principle of resistance; it is the dissidence of dissent, and the protestantism of the Protestant religion. This religion, under a variety of denominations agreeing in nothing but in the communion of the spirit of liberty, is predominant in most of the northern provinces, where the Church of England, notwithstanding its legal rights, is in reality no more than a sort of private sect, not composing, most probably, the tenth of the people. The colonists left England when this spirit was high, and in the emigrants was the highest of all; and even that stream of foreigners which has been constantly flowing into these colonies has, for the greatest part, been composed of dissenters from the establishments of their several countries, who have brought with them a temper and character far from alien to that of the people with whom they mixed.

Sir, I can perceive by their manner that some gentlemen object to the latitude of this description, because in the southern colonies the Church of England forms a large body, and has a regular establishment. It is certainly true. There is, however, a circumstance attending these colonies, which in my opinion fully counterbalances this difference, and makes the spirit of liberty still more high and haughty than in those to the northward. It is that in Virginia and the Carolinas they have a vast multitude of slaves. Where this is the case in any part of the world, those who are free are by far the most proud and jealous of their freedom. Freedom is to them not only an enjoyment, but a kind of rank and privilege. Not seeing there that freedom, as in countries where it is a common blessing and as broad and general as the air, may be united with much abject toil, with great misery, with all the exterior of servitude, liberty looks amongst them like something that is more noble and liberal. I do not mean, Sir, to commend the superior morality of this sentiment, which has at least as much pride as virtue in it; but I cannot alter the nature of man. The fact is so: and these people of the southern colonies are much more strongly, and with a higher and more stubborn spirit, attached to liberty, than those to the northward. Such were all the ancient commonwealths, such were our Gothic ancestors; such in our days were the Poles; and such will be all masters of slaves. . . . In such a people, the haughtiness of domination combines with the spirit of freedom, fortifies it, and renders it invincible.

Permit me, Sir, to add another circumstance in our colonies which contributes no mean part towards the growth and effect of this untractable spirit. I mean their education. In no country perhaps in the world is the law so general a study. The profession itself is numerous and powerful, and in most provinces it takes the lead. The greater number of the deputies sent to the Congress were lawyers. But all who read—and most do read—endeavor to obtain some smattering in that science. I have been told by an eminent book-seller that in no branch of his business, after tracts of popular devotion, were so many books as those on the law exported to the plantations. The colonists have now fallen into the way of printing them for their own use. I hear that they have sold nearly as many of Blackstone's Commentaries in America as in England. General Gage marks out this disposition very particularly in a letter on your table. He states that all the people in his government are lawyers, or smatterers in law; and that in Boston they have been enabled, by successful chicane, wholly to evade many parts of one of your capital penal constitutions. The smartness of debate will say that this knowledge ought to teach them more clearly the rights of legislature, their obligations to obedience, and the penalties of rebellion. All this is mighty well. But my honorable and learned friend on the floor, who condescends to mark what I say for animadversion, will disdain that ground. He has heard, as well as I, that when great honors and great emoluments do not win over this knowledge to the service of the state, it is a formidable adversary to government. If the spirit be not tamed and broken by these happy methods, it is stubborn and litigious. *Abeunt studia in mores* [studies pass over into character.] This study renders men acute, inquisitive, dextrous, prompt in attack, ready in defense, full of resources. In other countries the people, more simple and of a less mercurial cast, judge of an ill principle in government only by an actual grievance; here they anticipate the evil, and judge of the pressure of the grievance by the badness of the principle. They augur misgovernment at a distance, and snuff the approach of tyranny in every tainted breeze.

SIR WINSTON LEONARD SPENCER CHURCHILL

(1874-   )

English author and statesman, Conservative in political affiliation and holder of numerous British governmental offices, including those of First Lord of the Admiralty (1911-1915, 1939-1940), Chancellor of the Exchequer (1924-1929), and Prime Minister (1940-1945). Was unpopular during World War I because of his handling of naval affairs in his position as First Lord of the Admiralty, and in the period preceding World War II because of his criticism of Prime Minister Chamberlain's appeasement policies toward Hitler. But during World War II, as Prime Minister he became extremely popular in England and the United States, because of his personality and the confidence and encouragement of his speeches. Books by him include: *The World Crisis* (1923-1929), covering World War I; *Marlborough* (1933-1938), a biography of an earlier English statesman, the author's ancestor; *Blood, Sweat, and Tears* (1940); *War Memoirs* (1948); *The Second World War,* 10 vols. (1960); *Memoirs of the Second World War* (1959); and *The Great Democracies: A History of the English Speaking Peoples,* 4 vols. (1958). But none of these works bring out the dual characteristics that Churchill derives in equal measure from his British and American sides; he is not a strictly British phenomenon and the American in him is very strong. If he gets his aristocratic sense of the well-being of the state, his specifically political being from the Churchills, he gets the zest for life, the boyishness, the unconquerable optimism and high spirits and all the fabulous charm from his mother's family, the Jeromes. He adheres to the old-fashioned view that national destiny is most often marred or furthered by the action upon the contemporary environment of men of will power and genius. "The fortunes of mankind are largely the result of the impact upon events of superior beings." He is one of those rare men who have not only studied and written history but have also made it. Few historians have been gifted with a style of equal subtlety and vigor, a style at once classical and romantic, precise and imaginative, tolerant yet gently ironical, deeply sensitive to the tragedy of human failure and scornful only of those men who are faithless to the virtue within them.

Speech, June 4, 1940

WE SHALL GO on to the end, we shall fight in France, we shall fight on the seas and oceans, we shall fight with growing confidence and growing strength in the air, we shall defend our Island whatever the cost may be, we shall fight on the landing grounds, we shall fight in the fields and in the streets, we shall fight in the hills; we shall never surrender, and even if, which I do not for a moment believe, this Island or a large part of it were subjugated and starving, then our Empire beyond the seas, armed and guarded by the British Fleet, would carry on the struggle, until, in God's good time, the New World, with all its power and might steps forth to the rescue and the liberation of the old.

The "Iron Curtain" Speech
(March 5, 1946, Westminster College, Fulton, Missouri) *

A SHADOW has fallen upon the scenes so lately lighted by the Allied victory. Nobody knows what Soviet Russia and its Communist international organization intends to do in the immediate future, or what are the limits, if any, to their expansive and proselytizing tendencies. I have a strong admiration and regard for the valiant Russian people and for my wartime comrade, Marshal Stalin. There is deep sympathy and goodwill in Britain—and I doubt not here also—towards the peoples of all the Russias and a resolve to perse-

* Text: Winston S. Churchill, *The Sinews of Peace: Post-War Speeches*, edited by Randolph S. Churchill, Boston: Houghton Mifflin Co. and Curtis Brown, pp. 100-105.

vere through many differences and rebuffs in establishing lasting friendships. We understand the Russian need to be secure on her western frontiers by the removal of all possibility of German aggression. We welcome Russia to her rightful place among the leading nations of the world. We welcome her flag upon the seas. Above all, we welcome constant, frequent and growing contacts between the Russian people and our own people on both sides of the Atlantic. It is my duty however, for I am sure you would wish me to state the facts as I see them to you, to place before you certain facts about the present position in Europe.

From Stettin in the Baltic to Trieste in the Adriatic, an iron curtain has descended across the Continent. Behind that line lie all the capitals of the ancient states of Central and Eastern Europe. Warsaw, Berlin, Prague, Vienna, Budapest, Belgrade, Bucharest and Sofia, all these famous cities and the populations around them lie in what I must call the Soviet sphere and all are subject in one form or another, not only to Soviet influence but to a very high and, in many cases, increasing measure of control from Moscow. Athens alone—Greece with its immortal glories—is free to decide its future at an election under British, American and French observation. The Russian-dominated Polish Government has been encouraged to make enormous and wrongful inroads upon Germany, and mass expulsions of millions of Germans on a scale grievous and undreamed-of are now taking place. The Communist parties, which were very small in all these Eastern States of Europe, have been raised to pre-eminence and power far beyond their numbers and are seeking everywhere to obtain totalitarian control. Police governments are prevailing in nearly every case, and so far, except in Czechoslovakia, there is no true democracy.

Turkey and Persia are both profoundly alarmed and disturbed at the claims which are being made upon them and at the pressure being exerted by the Moscow Government. An attempt is being made by the Russians in Berlin to build up a quasi-Communist party in their zones of Occupied Germany by showing special favors to groups of left-wing German leaders. At the end of the fighting last June, the American and British Armies withdrew westwards, in accordance with an earlier agreement, to a depth at some points of 150 miles upon a front of nearly four hundred miles, in order to allow our Russian allies to occupy this vast expanse of territory which the Western Democracies had conquered.

If now the Soviet Government tries by separate action, to build up a pro-Communist Germany in their areas, this will cause new serious difficulties in the British and American zones, and will give the defeated Germans the power of putting themselves up to auction between the Soviets and the Western Democracies. Whatever conclusions may be drawn from these facts—and facts they are—this is certainly not the Liberated Europe we fought to build up. Nor is it one which contains the essentials of permanent peace.

The safety of the world requires a new unity in Europe, from which no nation should be permanently outcast. It is from the quarrels of the strong parent races in Europe that the world wars we have witnessed, or which occurred in former times, have sprung. Twice in our own lifetime we have seen the United States, against their wishes and their traditions, against arguments, the force of which it is impossible not to comprehend, drawn by irresistible forces, into these wars in time to secure the victory of the good cause, but only after frightful slaughter and devastation had occurred. Twice the United States has had to send several millions of its young men across the Atlantic to find the war; but now war can find any nation, wherever it may dwell between dusk and dawn. Surely we should work with conscious purpose for a grand pacification of Europe, within the structure of the United Nations and in accordance with its Charter. That I feel is an open cause of policy of very great importance.

In front of the iron curtain which lies across Europe are other causes for anxiety. In Italy the Communist Party is seriously hampered by having to support the Communist-trained Marshal Tito's claims to former Italian territory at the head of the Adriatic. Nevertheless the future of Italy hangs in the balance. Again one cannot imagine a regenerated Europe without a strong France. All my public life I have worked for a strong France and I never lost faith in her destiny, even in the darkest hours. I will not lose faith now. However, in a great number of countries, far from the Russian frontiers and throughout the world, Communist fifth columns are established and work in complete unity and absolute obedience to the directions they receive from the Communist centre. Except in the British Commonwealth and in the United States where Communism is in its infancy, the Communist parties or fifth columns constitute a growing challenge and peril to Christian civilization. These are sombre facts for anyone to have to recite on the morrow of a victory gained by so much splendid comradeship in arms and in the cause of freedom and democracy; but we should be most unwise not to face them squarely while time remains. . . .

On the other hand I repulse the idea that a new war is inevitable; still more that it is imminent. It is because I am sure that our fortunes are still in our own hands and that we hold the power to save the future, that I feel the duty to speak out now that I have the occasion and the opportunity to do so. I do not believe that Soviet Russia desires war. What they desire is the fruits of war and the indefinite expansion of their power and doctrines. But what we have to consider here to-day while time remains, is the permanent prevention of war and the establishment of conditions of freedom and democracy as rapidly as possible in all countries. Our difficulties and dangers will not be removed by closing our eyes to them. They will not be removed by mere waiting to see what happens; nor will they be removed by a policy of appeasement. What is needed is a settlement, and the longer this is delayed, the more difficult it will be and the greater our dangers will become.

From what I have seen of our Russian friends and Allies during the war, I am convinced that there is nothing they admire so much as strength, and there is nothing for which they have less respect than for weakness, especially military weakness. For that reason the old doctrine of a balance of power is unsound. We cannot afford, if we can help it, to work on narrow margins, offering temptations to a trial of strength. If the Western Democracies stand together in strict adherence to the principles of the United Nations Charter, their influence for furthering those principles will be immense and no one is likely to molest them. If however they become divided or falter in their duty and if these all-important years are allowed to slip away then indeed catastrophe may overwhelm us all.

Last time I saw it all coming and cried aloud to my own fellow-countrymen and to the world, but no one paid any attention. Up till the year 1933 or even 1935, Germany might have been saved from the awful fate which has overtaken her and we might all have been spared the miseries Hitler let loose upon mankind. There never was a war in all history easier to prevent by timely action than the one which has just desolated such great areas of the globe. It could have been prevented in my belief without the firing of a single shot, and Germany might be powerful, prosperous and honored to-day; but no one would listen and one by one we were all sucked into the awful whirlpool. We surely must not let that happen again. This can only be achieved by reaching now, in 1946, a good understanding on all points with Russia under the general authority of the United Nations Organization and by the maintenance of that good understanding through many peaceful years, by the world instrument, supported by the whole strength of the English-speaking world and all its connections. . . .

Let no man underrate the abiding power of the British Empire and Commonwealth. Because you see the 46 millions in our island harassed about their food supply, of which they only grow one half, even in war-time, or because we have difficulty in restarting our industries and export trade after six years of passionate war effort, do not suppose that we shall not come through these dark years of privation as we have come through the glorious years of agony, or that half a century from now, you will not see 70 or 80 millions of Britons spread about the world and united in defense of our traditions, our way of life, and of the world causes which you and we espouse. If the population of the English-speaking Commonwealths be added to that of the United States with all that such co-operation implies in the air, on the sea, all over the globe and in science and in industry, and in moral force, there will be no quivering, precarious balance of power to offer its temptation to ambition or adventure. On the contrary, there will be an overwhelming assurance of security. If we adhere faithfully to the Charter of the United Nations and walk forward in sedate and sober strength seeking no one's land or treasure, seeking to lay no arbitrary control upon the thoughts of men; if all British moral and material forces and convictions are joined with your own in fraternal association, the highroads of the future will be clear, not only for us but for all, not only for our time, but for a century to come.

MARCUS TULLIUS CICERO

(106-43 B.C.)

The outstanding political theorist of the Roman period, was not especially original in his political ideas; but his concepts of justice and natural law influenced Roman legal thought, and especially the later imperial jurists and early Christian writers. Even Voltaire praised two of Cicero's books as "of the noblest works that were ever written," and the Founding Fathers of the United States were especially enthusiastic about him. Thomas Jefferson read *De Senectute* (On Old Age) every year; John Adams, the second President of the United States, declared that "all the epochs of world history combined were unable to produce a statesman or philosopher as great as Cicero. His authority should have considerable weight." John Quincy Adams, his son, while lecturing at Harvard University, supported Cicero's doctrine that eloquence was the mainstay of liberty. Cicero's ideas of world unity and of universal law and authority held the center of political thinking throughout the whole Middle Ages (and are still mirrored in the modern experiments of the League of Nations, United Nations and the various proposals for world government).

Cicero's ideas can be found mainly in *De Republica* (which imitated Plato's *Republic,* even to the dialogue form), which tried to define the abstract ethical principles of justice and to outline the form of an ideal state. He believed that the state is the natural result of the social instincts of man (thus following, in general, the Stoic idea of the state as a rational and desirable institution), but differed from the Stoics in conceiving the state as a political institution, distinct from society in general, and in making a further distinction between state and government, assigning ultimate political authority to the people as a whole, with the government acting as their agent. He considered monarchy the best form of government, aristocracy next, with democracy least desirable, but preferred a mixed form of government and viewed the republican system of Rome as a good example of the checks and balances necessary for stability and good government. But Cicero's most influential contribution was in the idea of natural law. Following the ideas of Plato that the principles of right and justice are eternal, and of the Stoics that a supreme universal law exists in nature, Cicero stated that any law enacted by man, or any custom practiced by the people, which does not conform to natural law is illegitimate and invalid—and though man may be compelled by the superior physical force of his rulers to obey decrees which contravene nature, he is under no moral obligation to do so. He differed radically with Aristotle in stressing the ability of individual human reason to ascertain the natural law. Basically, Cicero was an aristocrat, both in temperament and in practice, and continually stressed the need for giving eminent citizens a place of influence in the political structure. (In addition to the *De Republica,* his political ideas were presented also in the *De Legibus,* and the *De Officiis*).

---

*On Justice**

THE great foundation of justice is faithfulness, which consists in being constantly firm to your word, and a conscientious performance of all compacts and bargains. The vice that is opposite to justice is injustice, of which there are two sorts: the first consists in the actual doing an injury to another; the second, in tamely looking on while he is injured, and not helping and defending him though we are able. He that injuriously falls on another, whether prompted by rage or other violent passion, does, as it were, leap at the throat of his companion; and he that refuses to help him

* Reprinted from "Cicero," pp. 237-238, in Dagobert D. Runes, ed., *Treasury of Philosophy,* New York: Philosophical Library, 1955.

when injured, and to ward off the wrong if it lies in his power, is as guilty of injustice as though he had deserted his father, his friends or native country.

It is observable that the limits of justice are not fixed. Respect must be had to general rules as the ground and foundation of all justice—first, that no injury be done to another; and, secondly, that we make it our earnest endeavor to promote the good of all mankind: so that our duty is not always the same, but various, according to circumstances.

* * *

There are certain duties to be strictly observed, even towards those who have injured us; for we ought not to go beyond certain bounds in exacting revenge and punishment of another; in which particular it may, perhaps, be enough to make him that has wronged us repent of the wrong done, so that both he himself may abstain from the like, and others may be discouraged from injuring us in the future.

There are certain peculiar laws of war, also, which are of all things most strictly to be observed in the commonwealth; for there being two sorts of disputing in the world, the one by reason, and the other by open force; and the former of these being that which is agreeable to the nature of man, and the latter to that of brutes. When we cannot obtain what is our right by the one, we must of necessity have recourse to the other. It is allowable, therefore, to undertake wars, but it must always be with the design of obtaining a secure peace; and when we have got the better of our enemies, we should rest content with the victory alone unless they are such as have been very cruel and committed inhuman barbarities in the war. In my opinion, it is always our duty to do what we can for a fair and safe peace.

Unless a man be governed by the rules of justice, and fight for the safety and good of the public, his is a sort of courage that is altogether blamable.

CONFUCIUS

(556-479 B.C.)

Kung Fu Tse, the Grand Master, was officially worshiped in China from 195 B.C. to 1912, and this traditional cult still persists in almost every district of China. His writings (*Lus Yu,* analects, aphorisms recorded by his followers) show considerable social maturity, and suggest that many centuries of experience must have lain behind them; nevertheless, they are still essentially religious in their outlook. Confucius takes for granted the worship of ancestors and reverence for the political ruler. Practically everything in his teachings rests upon filial piety and reverence for the established social and political order. He promulgated an ideal conduct of life, the basis of which was learning, wisdom, moral perfection and decency in behavior. His doctrine of reciprocity in man's relations with his fellow man paralleled, in almost the same words, the concept of the Golden Rule. He demanded that his followers practice the virtues of sincerity, justice, benevolence, courtesy, respect for older people and ancestor reverence, and urged them to live in harmony among themselves because that was a condition requisite for harmony between the individual and the universe. He constantly exhorted that all intellectual and moral energies be channeled toward self-perfection, the common good, and social and universal peace. He held high office for a short time, using his power to initiate reforms and punish evildoers, even when they were mandarins; but his services were not adequately appreciated by the ruler.

---

*The Laws of Heaven and the Earthly Order**

WHAT is meant by 'In order rightly to govern the State, it is

* This excerpt taken from Alfred O. Mendel, ed., presented by Alfred Doeblin, *The Living Thoughts of Confucius,* Philadelphia: David McKay Co., 1950, pp. 48-50 (copyright by Longmans, Green & Co.).

necessary first to regulate the family,' is this:—it is not possible for one to teach others, while he cannot teach his own family. Therefore, the ruler, without going beyond his family, completes the lessons for the State. There is filial piety:—therewith the sovereign should be served. There is fraternal submission:—therewith elders and superiors should be served. There is kindness:—therewith the multitude should be treated.

In the Announcement to K'ang, it is said, '*Act* as if you were watching over an infant.' If (a *mother*) is really anxious about it, though she may not hit *exactly the wants of her infant,* she will not be far from doing so. There never has been a *girl* who learned to bring up a child, that she might afterwards marry.

From the loving *example* of one family a whole state becomes loving, and from its courtesies the whole State becomes courteous, while, from the ambition, and perverseness of the One man, the whole state may be led to rebellious disorder;—such is the nature of the influence. This verifies the saying, 'affairs may be ruined by a single sentence; a kingdom may be settled by its One man.'

Yâo and Shun led on the kingdom with benevolence, and the people followed them. Chieh and Chu led on the kingdom with violence, and the people followed them. The orders which these issued were contrary to the practices which they loved, and so the people did not follow them. On this account, the ruler must himself be possessed of the *good* qualities, and then he may require them in the people. He must not have *the bad qualities* in himself, and then he may require that they shall not be in the people. Never has there been a man, who, not having reference to his own character and wishes in dealing with others, was able effectually to instruct them.

Thus we see how the government of the State depends on the regulation of the family.

In the Book of Poetry, it is said, 'That peach tree, so

delicate and elegant! How luxuriant is its foliage! This girl is going to her husband's house. She will rightly order her household.' Let the household be rightly ordered, and then the people of the State may be taught.

In the Book of Poetry, it is said, 'They can discharge their duties to their elder brothers. They can discharge their duties to their younger brothers.' Let the ruler discharge his duties to his elder and younger brothers, and then he may teach the people of the State.

In the Book of Poetry, it is said, 'In his deportment there is nothing wrong; he rectifies all the people of the State.' *Yes;* when the ruler, as a father, a son, and a brother, is a model, then the people imitate him.

This is what is meant by saying, 'The government of his kingdom depends on his regulation of the family.'

BENEDETTO CROCE
(1866-1952)

The dominating figure of Italian culture during the first two decades of the present century, helped to spread moral contempt for the democracies (*Estetica,* 1902; *Terze Pagine Sparse,* 1955; *Indagini su Hegel,* 1952; *Logica come Scienza del Concetto Puro,* 1928; *Cultura e Unita Morale,* 1926; *Nuovi Saggi di Estetica,* 1926; *Saggio sullo Hegel,* 1948; *Ultimi Saggi,* 1935; *Discorsi di Varia Filosofia,* 1945; *Filosofia Della Pratica,* 1923; *Teoria e Storia della Storiografia,* 1927; see: De Gennaro, Angelo A., *The Philosophy of Benedetto Croce,* (Philosophical Library, 1961). He fought what he termed the "masonic mentality," or a naïve faith in the rationalistic and optimistic principles of the eighteenth century and a fatuous belief in social remedies that were to end men's conflicts and wars. He leaned favorably toward imperial Germany, republished the writings of conservatives and even reactionaries (such as Vittorio Imbriania), but later his bent toward opposition led him stoutly to resist Fascism.

---

*Croce on Machiavelli**

THE name of Machiavelli has become almost the symbol of pure politics and it certainly marks a sharp crisis in the development of science. Not that antiquity did not have some inkling of the distinction and contrast between politics and ethics: this is shown in the very fact that their subject matter was attributed to two different disciplines; and debates like

* From Croce, Benedetto, *Politics and Morals,* translated by Salvatore J. Castiglione, Philosophical Library, 1946.

those on just and unjust law, on natural and conventional law, on force and justice, etc., show how the contrast was sometimes felt and how the correlative problem appeared in outline. But the contrast never came to the forefront and never became the focus of deep study and meditation. This did not even happen in the long centuries of the domination of Christian thought, because the contrast between the *civitas Dei* and the *civitas terrena,* and later between Church and Empire, had its solution in the doctrine of the double rule instituted by God, or possibly in the doctrine of the supremacy of Church over Empire or of Empire over Church; and it was not sharpened by philosophical dissension. But there is no doubt that Christian thought, in which the examination of the moral consciousness plays so great a part, was preparing, by making this consciousness more keen, the dissension that was to break out. Niccolò Machiavelli is considered a pure expression of the Italian Renaissance; but he should also be connected in some way with the movement of the Reformation, with that general need, which asserted itself in his time, in Italy and elsewhere, to know man and to study the problem of the soul.

It is known that Machiavelli discovered the necessity and autonomy of politics, of politics which is beyond or, rather, below moral good and evil, which has its own laws against which it is useless to rebel, politics that cannot be exorcized and driven from the world with holy water. This is the concept which pervades all his works. Although this concept is not formulated with that didactic and scholastic exactness which is usually mistaken for philosophy, and although it is sometimes disturbed by fantastic idols, by figures that waver between political virtue and wicked lust of power, it must nevertheless be termed a profoundly philosophical concept, and it represents the true foundation of a philosophy of politics.

But what usually passes unobserved is the decided bitterness with which Machiavelli accompanies this assertion of politics as an intrinsic necessity. "If all men were good," he says, these precepts "would not be good." But men are "ungrateful and fickle; they flee from dangers and are eager for gains." Therefore it is well to see to it that you are feared rather than loved, to provide first for fear and then, if possible, for love. You must learn "to be not good." You must fail to keep your word when it is to your advantage to do so, because otherwise others would fail to keep their word to you; you must defeat those who are waiting for the opportunity to defeat you. Machiavelli yearns for an unattainable society of good and pure men; and he fancies it to be found in the distant past. In the meantime he prefers the less civilized peoples to the more civilized, the people of Germany and the mountaineers of Switzerland to the Italians, the French and the Spanish (then at the height of their glory), who are the "corruption of the world." It is his feeling, and he expresses it with a shudder, that whoever reads of the horrors which history relates to us "will undoubtedly, if he is born of man, be frightened by every imitation of the evil times and will be kindled by the great desire to follow the good times." In the face of such evident signs of a stern and sorrowful moral conscience, it is amazing that there has been so much idle talk about Machiavelli's immorality; but the common people term as moral only moralistic unctuosity and bigoted hypocrisy. The lack of this bitter pessimism distinguishes Guicciardini from Machiavelli. The former feels only a sort of contempt toward men in whom he finds so "little goodness," and he settles down peacefully in this discredited world, aiming only at the advantage of his own "personal being." If he had not had to serve the Medici popes because of this "personal being" of his, he would have loved "Martin Luther more than himself," because he would have hoped that the rebel friar might undo the ecclesiastic state and destroy the "wicked tyranny of the priests." Guicciardini's man is different in temperament from Machiavelli's man.

It is still more important to observe that Machiavelli is as though divided in spirit and mind with respect to the politics whose autonomy he has discovered. At times it seems to him a sad necessity to have to soil his hands by dealing with ugly people, and at times it seems to him a sublime art to found and support that great institution which is the State. Quite often he speaks of the State in a religious tone, as when he recalls the saying that one must be prepared for the sake of the State to lose not only one's reputation, but also the salvation of one's own soul; or as when he looks back, with ill-concealed envy, at the pagan religion, which exalted, as the highest good, honor in this world, extolling human glory, and praising greatness of spirit, strength of body, and all the virtues which make man powerful; whereas the Christian religion, by showing the truth and the real way to the world beyond, despises this world, and praises abjection, setting contemplative men above the others, and endurance above action. Is politics diabolical or divine? Machiavelli imagines it in the guise of the Centaur, described by poets as a very beautiful creature, part man part beast, and he describes his prince as half man and half beast. In order that there may be no doubt as to the integrity of the human self of this creature, he assigns even the subtleties of the mind, such as craftiness, to the animal self, recommending that, it be part fox and part lion, because the lion does not defend himself against traps and the fox does not defend himself against wolves. One would be acting as a novice in the art of ruling if one wished "always to carry on as a lion." The art and science of politics, of pure politics, brought to maturity by the Italians, were to him a source of pride. For this reason he answered Cardinal de Rohan, who used to tell him that the Italians knew nothing about war, by saying that "the French knew nothing about the State."

The continuation of Machiavelli's thoughts must not be sought among the Machiavellians, who continue his political casuistry and body of maxims and write about the *"raison d'état,"* frequently mixing moralizing trivialities with these maxims: nor among the anti-Machiavellians, who proclaim the fusion and identification of politics with morality and conceive States founded on pure dictates of goodness and justice: nor among the eclectics, who place in juxtaposition theories of morality and theories of politics, and take the edge off antinomies and make them empirical, instead of solving them, and change them to misfortunes and inconveniences which happen in life but have the character of accidental things. It must be sought in those who made an effort to classify the concept of "prudence," of "shrewdness" and, in short, of "political virtue," without confusing it with the concept of "moral virtue" and, also, without in the least denying the latter. (One of these was Zuccolo, a seventeenth century writer.) And it must be sought in some powerful spirits who, beyond the shrewdness and sagacity of the individual, as analyzed by Machiavelli asserted the divine work of Providence. Such a person was Tommaso Campanella. But Machiavelli's true and worthy successor, the powerful intellect who gathered together and strengthened both these scattered suggestions of criticisms and the immortal thought of the Florentine secretary, was another Italian, Vico. In truth, the whole philosophy of politics in its central idea is symbolized in two Italians. Vico is not kind to Machiavelli, yet is full of his spirit which he tries to clarify and purify by integrating Machiavelli's concept of politics and of history, by settling his theoretical difficulties and by brightening his pessimism.

OLIVER CROMWELL

(1599-1658)

England's first Lord Protector, was a dictator hailed by the democratically inclined for his steadfast antiroyalist stand, yet denounced by the autocratically inclined as an illegal usurper and rabble-rouser. Though his life spans a rare revolutionary interlude in normally staid British politics, the chief firebrand of the pyrotechnic period was seldom fiery, despite his rather quick temper. More often he was vacillating and introspective, frequently mired in melancholia. His father was a gentleman farmer. Young Oliver received his early education at the hands of a puritanical Dr. Beard, who taught that God intervened directly in mundane matters to punish the wicked. Elected to Parliament in 1628, he stood firmly with the Puritans from the very first. In the Long Parliament he was active in the Puritan cause, though not an outstanding leader. During the First Civil War he rose rapidly in the Parliamentary Army because of his military skill (which is believed to have come from assiduous reading of Sweden's King Gustavus Adolphus). He and his men distinguished themselves at the battles of Edgehill (1642), Marston Moor (1644) and many minor engagements and often got credit for turning the tide when the Parliamentary cause looked hopeless. When dissension between the army, in which all forms of Puritanism flourished, and the Presbyterian-controlled Parliament erupted, Cromwell became commander (with Sir Thomas Fairfax) of the New Model Army which defeated King Charles (1645); thereafter Cromwell repelled a Scottish royalist invasion and gained in power and influence. After giving up hope that King Charles would come to terms, at his trial (1649) Cromwell was among the most adamant in demanding his execution. (When the young Algernon Sidney suggested that such a move might amount to *lèse-majesté*, Cromwell replied:

"I tell you we will cut off his head with the crown upon it.") During the Commonwealth, Cromwell led a punitive expedition against Ireland, where royalists and Catholics had joined forces and is remembered for his massacres at Drogheda and Wexford (where his men put to the sword the defenders of both places and all the Catholic priests they could find). In 1653 he dissolved the Rump Parliament and tried to work with a Parliament appointed by himself from lists supplied by the congregations. When that body dissolved itself, he accepted the Instrument of Government drawn up by certain army officers and became Lord Protector. The Parliament offered him the crown, but he declined; in 1657, a new constitution strengthened his powers and he assumed more of the pomp and ceremony of royalty. Politically, he tried to steer a course between the Presbyterians (who had been pusillanimous with the monarchy) and various Puritan sects (which called for such radical reforms that they were not revived until more than a century later in the American and French revolutions). When compromise failed, he imposed solutions that sometimes satisfied only himself, complaining, "I am as much for government by consent as any man, but where shall we find that consent?" At a time when religious toleration was as unthinkable as beheading monarchs, Cromwell was more tolerant than most; but fear of royalist resurgence and "Popish plots" permitted toleration only to non-Anglican Protestants and Jews (expelled during the reign of Edward I and permitted to return by Cromwell). In foreign affairs, he tried to build up a league of Protestant nations, but cooperated with Catholic powers when he thought it to England's advantage. The English re-embraced monarchy shortly after his death (1658), but firmly established was the principle that henceforth the King would be subordinate to Parliament. Hobbes' theory of politics probably influenced Cromwell in deciding to assume dictatorial powers; as the successor to Sir Thomas More, he brought into being the modern centralized state, and also brought to England the first manuscript copy of Machiavelli's *Prince*. To Cromwell (as to Luther, Knox and Bunyan), Protestant Christianity represented truth, without which all mankind was doomed to perish. He was re-evaluated, historically, as a strong leader by Carlyle, for whom he was more important than England and for whom he represented (with Napoleon) the concept of "the Hero as King."

---

*The Puritan Commonwealth**

For order sake, it's very natural for us to consider, what our condition was in civils, in spirituals [at the beginning of the Commonwealth]. What was our condition? Every man's hand (almost) was against his brother, at least his heart, little regarding anything that should cement and might have a tendency in it to cause us to grow into one. All the dispensations of God, his terrible ones, he having met us in the way of his judgment in a ten years' civil war, a very sharp one, his merciful dispensations, they did not, they did not work upon us, but we had our humours and interests; and indeed I fear our humours were more than our interests. And certainly as it fell out, in such cases, our passions were more than our judgments.

Was not everything (almost) grown arbitrary? Who knew where, or how to have right, without some obstruction or other intervening? Indeed, we were almost grown arbitrary in everything.

What was the face that was upon our affairs as to the interest of the nation? to the authority of the nation? to the magistracy? to the ranks and orders of men, whereby England hath been known for hundreds of years? A nobleman, a gentleman, a yeoman? (That is a good interest of the nation and a great one.) The magistracy of the nation, was it not almost trampled under foot, under despite and contempt by men of Levelling principles?

I beseech you, for the orders of men and ranks of men, did not that Levelling principle tend to the reducing all to

---

* This excerpt taken from Wilbur Cortez Abbott, ed., *The Writings and Speeches of Oliver Cromwell*, Cambridge: Harvard University Press, 1945, Vol. III, pp. 435-43, *passim*.

an equality? Did it think to do so, or did it practise towards it for propriety [property] and interest? What was the design, but to make the tenant as liberal a fortune as the landlord? Which I think, if obtained, would not have lasted long! The men of that principle, after they had served their own turns, would have cried up interest and property then fast enough.

This instance is instead of many, and that it may appear that this thing did extend far, is manifest, because it was a pleasing voice to all poor men, and truly not unwelcome to all bad men. To my thinking, it is a consideration that, in your endeavours after settlement, you will be so well minded of, that I might well have spared this; but let that pass. . . .

I wish it may not too justly be said that there was severity and sharpness, yea, too much of an imposing spirit in matter of conscience, a spirit unchristian enough in any times, most unfit for these,—denying liberty to those who have earned it with their blood, who have gained civil liberty, and religious also, for those who would thus impose upon them.

We may reckon among these, our spiritual evils, an evil that hath more refinedness in it, and more colour for it, and hath deceived more people of integrity than the rest have done. For few have been catched with the former mistakes, but such as have apostatized from their holy profession, such as being corrupt in their consciences, have been forsaken by God and left to such noisome opinions. But, I say, there are others more refined, many honest people, whose hearts are sincere, many of them belonging to God, and that is the mistaken notion of the Fifth Monarchy. A thing pretending more spirituality than anything else. A notion I hope we all honour, wait, and hope for, that Jesus Christ will have a time to set up his reign in our hearts, by subduing those corruptions and lusts and evils that are there, which reign now more in the world than, I hope, in due time they shall do. And when more fullness of the Spirit is poured forth to subdue iniquity and bring in everlasting righteousness, then will the approach of that glory be. The carnal divisions and contentions amongst Christians, so common, are not the symptoms of that kingdom.

But for men to entitle themselves, upon this principle, that they are the only men to rule kingdoms, govern nations, and give laws to people; to determine of property and liberty and everything else, upon such a pretence as this is: truly, they had need give clear manifestations of God's presence with them, before wise men will receive or submit to their conclusions. . . .

If men do but pretend for justice and righteousness, and be of peaceable spirits and will manifest this, let them be the subjects of the magistrate's encouragement. And if the magistrate [*i.e.*, Cromwell] by punishing visible miscarriages save them by that discipline, (God having ordained him for that end,) I hope it will evidence love, and no hatred, to punish where there is cause. . . .

In the meantime all endeavours possible were used to hinder the work in Ireland, and the progress of the work of God in Scotland, by continual intelligences and correspondences both at home and abroad, from hence into Ireland, and from hence into Scotland. Persons were stirred up and encouraged from these divisions and discomposure of affairs, to do all they could to encourage and foment the war in both those places.

To add yet to our misery, whilst we were in this condition, we were in war, deeply engaged in a war with the Portugal [Portuguese], whereby our trade ceased; and the evil consequences by that war were manifest and very considerable.

And not only this, but we had a war with Holland, consuming our treasure, occasioning a vast burden upon the people; a war that cost this nation full as much as the taxes came unto. The navy being one hundred and sixty ships, which cost this nation above one hundred thousand pounds a month, besides the contingencies which would make it six score thousand pounds a month. That very one war did engage us to so great a charge.

At the same time also we were in a war with France. The advantages that were taken at the discontents and divisions, among ourselves, did almost foment that war, and at least hinder us of an honourable peace, every man being confident that we could not hold out long. And surely they did not calculate amiss, if the Lord had not been exceeding gracious to us.

I say at the same time we had a war with France. And besides the sufferings in respect of the trade of the nation, it's most evident, that the purse of the nation had not been possibly able longer to bear it, by reason of the advantages taken by other States to improve their own and spoil our manufacture of cloth and hinder the vent thereof, which is the great staple commodity of this nation.

This was our condition; spoiled in our trade, and we at this vast expense, thus dissettled at home, and having these engagements abroad.

These things being thus, (as I am persuaded it is not hard to convince every person here, they were thus,) what a heap of confusions were upon these poor nations! And either things must have been left to have sunk into the miseries these premises would suppose, or a remedy must be applied.

A remedy hath been applied; that hath been this government. . . .

It hath had some things in desire, and it hath done some things actually. It hath desired to reform the laws, to reform them; and for that end, it hath called together persons (without reflection) of as great ability and as great integrity as are in these nations, to consider how the laws might be made plain and short, and less chargeable to the people, how to lessen expense for the good of the nation. And those things are in preparation and bills prepared, which in due time, I make no question, will be tendered to you. There hath been care taken to put the administration of the laws into the hands of just men, men of the most known integrity and ability.

The Chancery hath been reformed,—and I hope to the

just satisfaction of all good men,—and the things depending there, which made the burden and work of the honourable persons intrusted in those services beyond their ability; it hath referred many of them to those places where Englishmen love to have their rights tried, the Courts of Law at Westminster.

It hath endeavoured to put a stop to that heady way (touched of likewise this day) of every man making himself a Minister and a preacher. It hath endeavoured to settle a way for the approbation of men of piety and ability for the discharge of that work. And I think I may say, it hath committed that work to the trust of persons, both of the Presbyterian and Independent judgments, men of as known ability, piety, and integrity, as I believe any this nation hath. And I believe also that in that care they have taken, they have laboured to approve themselves to Christ, the nation, and their own consciences. And indeed I think if there be anything of quarrel, against them, it is, (though I am not here to justify the proceedings of any) I say it is that they go upon such a character as the Scripture warrants to put men into that great employment; and to approve men for it, who are men that have received gifts from Him that ascended up on high, and gave gifts for the work of the Ministry and for the edifying of the body of Christ.

It hath taken care, we hope, for the expulsion of all those who may be judged any way unfit for this work, who are scandalous, and who are the common scorn and contempt of that administration.

One thing more this government hath done. It hath been instrumental to call a free Parliament, which, blessed be God, we see here this day. I say a free Parliament; and that it may continue so, I hope is in the heart and spirit of every good man in England, save such discontented persons as I have formerly mentioned. It is that which, as I have desired above my life, I shall desire to keep it so above my life.

DEMOSTHENES

(385?-322 B.C.)

Athenian statesman, is commonly judged the greatest of the Greek orators. Tradition has it that he would walk by the seashore with pebbles in his mouth, trying to make himself heard about the roar of the sea to strengthen his voice. The name of his three *Philippics,* scathing orations attacking Philip of Macedon, has become proverbial. He died after taking poison to escape capture by his enemies. There is a portrait-statue of him in the Vatican.

---

*The First Philippic**

. . . HAD THE QUESTION for debate been any thing new, Athenians, I should have waited till most of the usual speakers had been heard; if any of their counsels had been to my liking, I had remained silent, else proceeded to impart my own. But as the subject of discussion is one upon which they have spoken oft before, I imagine, though I rise the first, I am entitled to indulgence. For if these men had advised properly in time past, there would be no necessity for deliberating now.

First I say you must not despond, Athenians, under your present circumstances, wretched as they are; for that which is worst in them as regards the past, is best for the future. What do I mean? That your affairs are amiss, men of Athens, because you do nothing which is needful; if notwith-

* This excerpt taken from Charles Rann Kennedy, ed., *The Olynthia and other Public Orations of Demosthenes,* New York: Harper, 1857, pp. 61-65.

standing you performed your duties, it were the same, there would be no hope of amendment.

Consider next, what you know by report, and men of experience remember, how vast a power the Lacedaemonians had not long ago, yet how nobly and becomingly you consulted the dignity of Athens, and undertook the war against them for the rights of Greece. Why do I mention this? To show and convince you, Athenians, that nothing, if you take precaution, is to be feared, nothing if you are negligent, goes as you desire. Take for examples the strength of the Lacedaemonians then, which you overcame by attention to your duties, and the insolence of this man now, by which through neglect of our interests we are confounded. But if any among you, Athenians, deem Philip hard to be conquered, looking at the magnitude of his existing power, and the loss by us of all our strongholds, they reason rightly, but should reflect, that once we held Pydna and Potidaea and Methone and all the region round about as our own, and many of the nations now leagued with him were independent and free, and preferred our friendship to his. Had Philip then taken it into his head, that it was difficult to contend with Athens, when she had so many fortresses to infest his country, and he was destitute of allies, nothing that he has accomplished would he have undertaken, and never would he have acquired so large a dominion. But he saw well, Athenians, that all these places are the open prizes of war, that the possessions of the absent naturally belong to the present, those of the remiss to them that will venture and toil. Acting on such principle, he has won every thing and keeps it, either by way of conquest, or by friendly attachment and alliance; for all men will side with and respect those, whom they see prepared and willing to make proper exertion. If you, Athenians, will adopt this principle now, though you did not before, and every man, where he can and ought to give his service to the state, be ready to give it without excuse, the wealthy to contribute, the able-bodied to enlist;

in a word, plainly, if you will become your own masters; and cease each expecting to do nothing himself, while his neighbor does every thing for him, you shall then with heaven's permission recover your own, and get back what has been frittered away, and chastise Philip. Do not imagine, that his empire is everlastingly secured to him as a god. There are some who hate and fear and envy him, Athenians, even among those that seem most friendly; and all feelings that are in other men belong, we may assume, to his confederates. But now they are all cowed, having no refuge through your tardiness and indolence, which I say you must abandon forthwith. For you see, Athenians, the case, to what pitch of arrogance the man has advanced, who leaves you not even the choice of action or inaction, but threatens and uses (they say) outrageous language, and, unable to rest in possession of his conquests, continually widens their circle, and, while we dally and delay, throws his net all around us. When then, Athenians, when will ye act as becomes you? In what event? In that of necessity, I suppose. And how should we regard the events happening now? Methinks, to freemen the strongest necessity is the disgrace of their condition. Or tell me, do ye like walking about and asking one another:—is there any news? Why, could there be greater news than a man of Macedonia subduing Athenians, and directing the affairs of Greece? Is Philip dead? No, but he is sick. And what matters it to you? Should any thing befall this man, you will soon create another Philip, if you attended to business thus. For even he has been exalted not so much by his own strength, as by our negligence. And again; should any thing happen to him; should fortune, which still takes better care of us than we of ourselves, be good enough to accomplish this; observe that, being on the spot, you would step in while things were in confusion, and manage them as you pleased; but as you now are, though occasion offered Amphipolis, you would not be in a position to accept it, with neither forces nor counsels at hand.

However, as to the importance of a general zeal in the discharge of duty, believing you are convinced and satisfied, I say no more.

As to the kind of force which I think may extricate you from your difficulties, the amount, the supplies of money, the best and speediest method (in my judgment) of providing all the necessaries, I shall endeavor to inform you forthwith, making only one request, men of Athens. When you have heard all, determine; prejudge not before. And let none think I delay our operations, because I recommend an entirely new force. Not those that cry, quickly! to-day! speak most to the purpose; (for what has already happened we shall not be able to prevent by our present armament;) but he that shows what and how great and whence procured must be the force capable of enduring, till either we have advisedly terminated the war, or overcome our enemies: for so shall we escape annoyance in future. This I think I am able to show without offense to any other man who has a plan to offer. My promise indeed is large; it shall be tested by the performance; and you shall be my judges.

First, then, Athenians, I say we must provide fifty warships, and hold ourselves prepared, in case of emergency, to embark and sail. I require also an equipment of transports for half the cavalry and sufficient boats. This we must have ready against his sudden marches from his own country to Thermopylae, the Chersonese, Olynthus, and any where he likes. For he should entertain the belief, that possibly you may rouse from this over-carelessness, and start off, as you did to Euboea, and formerly (they say) to Haliartus, and very lately to Thermopylae. And although you should not pursue just the course I would advise, it is no slight matter, that Philip, knowing you to be in readiness—know it he will for certain; there are too many among our own people who report every thing to him—may either keep quiet from apprehension, or, not heeding your arrangements, be taken off his guard, there being nothing to prevent your sailing, if he give you a chance, to attack his territories. Such an armament, I say, ought instantly to be agreed upon and provided. But besides, men of Athens, you should keep in hand some force, that will incessantly make war and annoy him: none of your ten or twenty thousand mercenaries, not your forces on paper, but one that shall belong to the state, and, whether you appoint one or more generals, or this or that man or any other, shall obey and follow him. Subsistence too I require for it. What the force shall be, how large, from what source maintained, how rendered efficient, I will show you, stating every particular. Mercenaries I recommend—and beware of doing what has often been injurious—thinking all measures below the occasion, adopting the strongest in your decrees, you fail to accomplish the least—rather, I say, perform and procure a little, add to it afterward, if it prove insufficient. I advise then two thousand soldiers in all, five hundred to be Athenians, of whatever age you think right, serving a limited time, not long, but such time as you think right, so as to relieve one another; the rest should be mercenaries. And with them two hundred horse, fifty at least Athenians, like the foot, on the same terms of service; and transports for them. Well; what besides? Ten swift galleys: for, as Philip has a navy, we must have swift galleys also, to convoy our power. How shall subsistence for these troops be provided? I will state and explain; but first let me tell you why I consider a force of this amount sufficient, and why I wish the men to be citizens . . .

BENJAMIN DISRAELI
(First Earl of Beaconsfield)
(1804-1881)

Prime Minister of England (1874-1880), and a novelist, nicknamed "Dizzy," hoped that by granting the workers the franchise he would win them over permanently to the Conservative party. He lived in the historical period when the issue between idealism and realism posed by the French Revolution continuously presented itself to European statesmen. The terms of that issue were made clear in the great debate between Disraeli, as Prime Minister, and William Gladstone, his successor, on the occasion of the atrocities perpetrated by Turkey against the Bulgarians (1876). As the supporter of British imperialism (formulated in his famed speech at the Crystal Palace in London, in 1872, "For the Great Britain") Disraeli purchased the Khedive of Egypt's shares in the Suez Canal Company for four million pounds. The idea of British imperialism was, in fact, promulgated for the first time by the Conservatives under Disraeli in the campaign for the elections of 1874 (and was later developed by Joseph Chamberlain and Winston Churchill). Its program was essentially one of consolidation, not of expansion; it sought to secure and exploit what had already been appropriated; it endeavored to stabilize the distribution of power which had been accumulated by the creation of the British Empire. When Kipling justified British imperialism as "the white man's burden," the burden had already been shouldered, and from the 1870's on, Britain's "imperialism" was in the main a policy of maintaining the *status quo*. Yet anti-imperialists in Great Britain and elsewhere, accepting the imperialistic slogans of Disraeli (and Chamberlain) at face value and mistaking the effects of imperialism for imperialism itself, opposed the British policy of exploitation and consolidation, especially in Africa and India, as "imperialistic."

(In fact, in 1942 Churchill refused "to preside over the liquidation of the British Empire.")

---

*To Viscount Palmerston**

MY LORD: The Minister who maintains himself in power in spite of the contempt of a whole nation must be gifted with no ordinary capacity. Your Lordship's talents have never had justice done to them. Permit me to approach you in the spirit of eulogy; if novelty have charms, this encomium must gratify you. Our language commands no expression of scorn which has not been exhausted in the celebration of your character; there is no conceivable idea of degradation which has not been, at some period or another, associated with your career. Yet the seven Prime Ministers, all of whom have served with equal fidelity, might suffice, one would think, with their united certificates, to vamp up the fruit; and, as for your conduct, so distinguished an orator as your Lordship was recently turned out can never want a medium for its triumphant vindication, even if it were denied the columns of that favoured journal where we occasionally trace the finished flippancy of your Lordship's airy pen.

The bigoted Tories under whose auspices your Lordship entered public life had always, if I mistake not, some narrow-minded misgiving of your honesty as well as your talents, and with characteristic illiberality doomed you to official insignificance. It was generally understood that under no circumstances was your Lordship ever to be permitted to enter the Cabinet. Had you been an anticipated Aislabie, you could not have been more rigidly excluded from that select society; you were rapidly advanced to a position which, though eminent, was also impassable; and having attained this acme of second-rate statesmanship, you remained fixed on your pedes-

* This excerpt taken from Benjamin Disraeli, *Venetia,* New York & London: M. Walter Dunne, 1904, pp. 115-116.

tal for years, the Great Apollo of aspiring understrappers.

When the ambition of Mr. Canning deprived him of the ablest of his colleagues, your Lordship, with that dexterity which has never deserted you, and which seems a happy compound of the smartness of an attorney's clerk and the intrigue of a Greek of the Lower Empire, wriggled yourself into the vacant Cabinet. The Minister who was forced to solicit the co-operation of a Lansdowne might be pardoned for accepting the proffer of a Palmerston; but even in his extreme distress, Mr. Canning was careful not to promote you from your subordinate office. . . .

FRIEDRICH ENGELS

(1820-1895)

Was the intimate friend, collaborator and supporter of Karl Marx, through whose generosity and charity Marx was able, so to speak, to "survive." Several of their writings were the collaboration of both (and it is not fully known which writings signed by Marx were the products of Engels). But Engels was always ready to recognize Marx as his superior. After Marx's death, Engels edited the second and third volumes of his *Capital.* When socialists disagreed about the meaning of the work, or adversaries distorted it, Engels untiringly interpreted his late friend's meaning. Engels was the descendant of a dynasty of German industrialists who adhered to religious orthodoxy and political conservatism. In his youth he planned to become a poet, for he was an enthusiast of German romanticism, the historical past and beauty and nature in art. When a new Oriental crisis threatened to cause war between France and Germany in 1848, as an excited nationalist he dreamed of German military victories. A sojourn in London and military service in the Prussian Army made him revise his beliefs; he abandoned German nationalism, and all prospects of succeeding his father in his successful business, and devoted his life to the fight for the working class and the realization of Marx's plan. In 1845 he published his pamphlet, *On the Situation of The Working Class,* in England (under the influence of Constantin Pecqueur, who also wrote a pamphlet on the same subject). In his later years Engels blended dialectial materialism (as Marx had conceived it) with philosophic materialism, and tried to expand the meaning of Marx's terminology. In his *The Origin of the Family, Private Property, and the State* (1894) he developed a great interest in ethnology in order to attack social conventions with arguments that demonstrated the relativity of social values. Until his death, he remained the executor of Marx's will.

---

*The Origin of the State**

THE STATE is by no means a power forced on society from without; just as little is it "the reality of the ethical idea," "the image and reality of reason," as Hegel maintains. Rather, it is a product of society at a certain stage of development; it is the admission that this society has become entangled in an insoluble contradiction with itself, that it is cleft into irreconcilable antagonisms which it is powerless to dispel. But in order that these antagonisms, classes with conflicting economic interests, might not consume themselves and society in sterile struggle, a power seemingly standing above society became necessary for the purpose of moderating the conflict, of keeping it within the bounds of "order"; and this power, arisen out of society, but placing itself above it, and increasingly alienating itself from it, is the state.

In contradistinction to the old gentile organization, the state, first, divides its subjects *according to territory.* As we have seen, the old gentile associations, built upon and held together by ties of blood, became inadequate, largely because they presupposed that the members were bound to a given territory, a bond which had long ceased to exist. The territory remained, but the people had become mobile. Hence, division according to territory was taken as the point of departure, and citizens were allowed to exercise their public rights and duties wherever they settled, irrespective of gens and tribe. This organization of citizens according to locality is a feature common to all states. That is why it seems natural to

* **Excerpts from Friedrich Engels, *The Origin of the Family, Private Property, and the State, Selected Works,* Moscow: Foreign Language Publishing House, 1955, Vol. II, pp. 317-321.**

us; but we have seen what long and arduous struggles were needed before it could replace, in Athens and Rome, the old organization according to *gentes.*

The second is the establishment of a *public power* which no longer directly coincided with the population organizing itself as an armed force. This special public power is necessary, because a self-acting armed organization of the population has become impossible since the cleavage into classes. The slaves also belonged to the population; the 90,000 citizens of Athens formed only a privileged class as against the 365,000 slaves. The people's army of the Athenian democracy was an aristocratic public power against the slaves, whom it kept in check; however, a gendarmerie also became necessary to keep the citizens in check, as we related above. This public power exists in every state; it consists not merely of armed people but also of coercion of all kinds, of which gentile society knew nothing. It may be very insignificant, almost infinitesimal, in societies where class antagonisms are still undeveloped and in out-of-the-way places as was the case at certain times and in certain regions in the United States of America. It grows stronger, however, in proportion as class antagonisms within the state become more acute, and as adjacent states become larger and more populated. We have only to look at our present-day Europe, where class struggle and rivalry in conquest have screwed up the public power to such a pitch that it threatens to devour the whole of society and even the state.

In order to maintain this public power, contributions from the citizens become necessary—*taxes.* These were absolutely unknown in gentile society; but we know enough about them today. As civilization advances, these taxes become inadequate; the state makes drafts on the future, contracts loans, *public debts.* Old Europe can tell a tale about these, too.

In possession of the public power and of the right to levy taxes, the officials, as organs of society, now stand *above* society. The free, voluntary respect that was accorded to the organs of the gentile constitution does not satisfy them, even if they could gain it; being the vehicles of a power that is becoming alien to society, respect for them must be enforced by means of exceptional laws by virtue of which they enjoy special sanctity and inviolability. The shabbiest police servant in the civilized state has more "authority" than all the organs of gentile society put together; but the most powerful prince and the greatest statesman, or general, of civilization may well envy the humblest gentile chief for the uncoerced and undisputed respect that is paid to him. The one stands in the midst of society, the other is forced to attempt to represent something outside and above it.

As the state arose from the need to hold class antagonisms in check, but as it arose, at the same time, in the midst of the conflict of these classes, it is, as a rule, the state of the most powerful, economically dominant class, which, through the medium of the state, becomes also the politically dominant class, and thus acquires new means of holding down and exploiting the oppressed class. Thus, the state of antiquity was above all the state of the slave owners for the purpose of holding down the slaves, as the feudal state was the organ of the nobility for holding down the peasant serfs and bondsmen, and the modern representative state is an instrument of exploitation of wage labour by capital. By way of exception, however, periods occur in which the warring classes balance each other so nearly that the state power, as ostensible mediator, acquires, for the moment, a certain degree of independence of both. Such was the absolute monarchy of the seventeenth and eighteenth centuries, which held the balance between the nobility and the class of burghers; such was the Bonapartism of the First, and still more of the Second, French Empire, which played off the proletariat against the bourgeoisie and the bourgeoisie against the proletariat. . . .

In most of the historical states, the rights of citizens are, besides, apportioned according to their wealth, thus directly expressing the fact that the state is an organization of the possessing class for its protection against the nonpossessing class. It was so already in the Athenian and Roman classification according to property. It was so in the medieval feudal state, in which the alignment of political power was in conformity with the amount of land owned. It is seen in the electoral qualifications of the modern representative states. Yet this political recognition of property distinctions is by no means essential. On the contrary, it marks a low state of state development. The highest form of the state, the democratic republic, which under our modern conditions of society is more and more becoming an inevitable necessity, and is the form of state in which alone the last decisive struggle between proletariat and bourgeoisie can be fought out—the democratic republic officially knows nothing any more of property distinctions. In it wealth exercises its power indirectly, but all the more surely. On the one hand, in the form of the direct corruption of officials, of which America provides the classical example; on the other hand, in the form of an alliance between government and Stock Exchange, which becomes easier to achieve the more the public debt increases and the more joint stock companies concentrate in their hands not only transport but also production itself, using the Stock Exchange as their centre. . . . And lastly, the possessing class rules directly through the medium of universal suffrage. As long as the oppressed class, in our case, therefore, the proletariat, is not yet ripe to emancipate itself, it will in its majority regard the existing order of society as the only one possible and, politically, will form the tail of the capitalist class, its extreme Left wing. To the extent, however, that this class matures for its self-emancipation, it constitutes itself as its own party and elects its own representatives, and not those of the capitalists. Thus, universal suffrage is the gauge of the maturity of the working class. It cannot and never will be anything more in the present-day state; but that is sufficient. On the day the thermometer of universal suffrage registers boiling point among the workers, both they and the capitalists will know what to do.

The state, then, has not existed from all eternity. There have been societies that did without it, that had no conception of the state and state power. At a certain stage of economic development, which was necessarily bound up with the cleavage of society into classes. the state became a necessity owing to this cleavage. We are now rapidly approaching a stage in the development of production at which the existence of these classes not only will have ceased to be a necessity, but will become a positive hindrance to production. They will fall as inevitably as they arose at an earlier stage. Along with them the state will inevitably fall. The society that will organize production on the basis of a free and equal association of the producers will put the whole machinery of state where it will then belong; into the Museum of Antiquities, by the side of the spinning wheel and the bronze axe . . .

MOHANDAS KARAMCHAND GANDHI
(1869-1948)

Called *MAHATMA* (great-souled) *GANDHI;* Hindu nationalist leader, studied law in London and practiced in India and in South Africa, where he championed the cause of Indians living there. During the Boer War and the Zulu uprising in Natal, Gandhi led an Indian ambulance corps; in World War I, he again organized an ambulance corps and conducted a recruiting campaign in the Kaira district. In 1918 he assumed the leadership of the Indian nationalist movement, introducing new methods; he rejected armed rebellion and recommended the overthrow of British rule through the peaceful methods of noncooperation and nonviolent civil disobedience (*"satyagraha"*), a conception which transferred ideas of Tolstoy from the field of social revolution to that of national emancipation. (It has been also claimed that this was a typical expression of the unwarlike and somewhat passive southern Hindu mentality, although history will remember one of his most prominent pupils, Nehru, for his armed seizure of Goa in 1961.) The Gandhi movement spread and in 1922 he was sentenced to six years' imprisonment, but was released in 1924 and became President of the Indian National Congress. His behavior, his suffering and his ascetic life won great prestige for him among the Hindus. From 1925 to 1929, he kept in the background, but came to the fore again in April, 1930, when he started the salt "*satyagraha,*" violating the unpopular salt monopoly of the government by publicly distilling salt from sea water on the shore. He was interned again but released in January, 1931, to go to the round-table conference in London. On March 31, 1931, he signed a truce with Lord Irwin, the Viceroy. Following further unrest, he was once more arrested in January, 1933, and again released in May, 1933. In 1934 he left the National Congress, stating he wished to retire from politics but, living in the village of Wardha, C.P., he remained the most influential figure in the Indian nationalist movement. He showed some inclination toward the right-wing group in the Congress and used his secret influence in a way not always welcome to the Socialist Congress leader Nehru. After the outbreak of World War II, he condemned Hitler's methods of force and thereafter his attitude was not essentially anti-British. He was assassinated by a Hindu Nationalist at New Delhi on January 30, 1948. His ideas were expressed in such books as *An Autobiography, or the Story of my Experiments with Truth* (1940); *Delhi Diary* (1948); *Indian Home Rule* (1922); *Young India* (1923); *Sermon on the Sea* (1924). He had no equal in modern times in his ability to use spiritual weapons for political aims, in his power to make the resistance of the powerless irresistible. He restored the self-reliance of Hinduism after he had been imbued with the spirit of Western civilization and had rejected it. Nonviolence was conceived by him as "conscious suffering," not as meek submission to the will of the evildoer, but "the putting of one's whole soul against the will of the tyrant." This meant the restitution of the ancient Indian law of self-sacrifice. He repeatedly protested against being regarded as a visionary; instead, he described himself as a "practical idealist" and rightly claimed "to know my millions" and to "recognize no God except the God that is to be found in the hearts of the dumb millions."

---

*Ahiṃsā or the Way of Non-Violence**

NON-VIOLENCE is the greatest force at the disposal of mankind. It is mightier than the mightiest weapon of destruction devised by the ingenuity of man. Destruction is not the law of the humans. Man lives freely by his readiness to die, if need be, at the hands of his brother, never by killing him. Every murder or other injury, no matter for what cause, committed or inflicted on another is a crime against humanity.

---

* Excerpt taken from Mahatma Gandhi, *All Men Are Brothers,* New York: UNESCO and Columbia University Press, 1958, pp. 85-87.

The first condition of non-violence is justice all round in every department of life. Perhaps, it is too much to expect of human nature. I do not, however, think so. No one should dogmatize about the capacity of human nature for degradation or exaltation.

Just as one must learn the art of killing in the training for violence, so one must learn the art of dying in the training for non-violence. Violence does not mean emancipation from fear. Non-violence, on the other hand, has no cause for fear. The votary of non-violence has to cultivate the capacity for sacrifice of the highest type in order to be free from fear. He recks not if he should lose his land, his wealth, his life. He who has not overcome all fear cannot practise *ahiṃsã* to perfection. The votary of *ahiṃsã* has only one fear, that is of God. He who seeks refuge in God ought to have a glimpse of the *Atma* that transcends the body; and the moment one has a glimpse of the imperishable *Atma* one sheds the love of the perishable body. Training in non-violence is thus diametrically opposed to training in violence. Violence is needed for the protection of things external, non-violence is needed for the protection of the *Atma,* for the protection of one's honor.

It is no non-violence if we merely love those that love us. It is non-violence only when we love those that hate us. I know how difficult it is to follow this grand law of love. But are not all great and good things difficult to do? Love of the hater is the most difficult of all. But by the grace of God even this most difficult thing becomes easy to accomplish if we want to do it.

I have found that life persists in the midst of destruction and therefore there must be a higher law than that of destruction. Only under that law would a well-ordered society be intelligible and life worth living. And if that is the law of life, we have to work it out in daily life. Whenever there are jars, wherever you are confronted with an opponent conquer him with love. In this crude manner I have worked it out in my life. That does not mean that all my difficulties are solved. Only I have found that this law of love has answered as the law of destruction has never done.

It is not that I am incapable of anger, for instance, but I succeed on almost all occasions to keep my feelings under control. Whatever may be the result, there is always in me conscious struggle for following the law of non-violence deliberately and ceaselessly. Such a struggle leaves one stronger for it. The more I work at this law, the more I feel the delight in my life, the delight in the scheme of the universe. It gives me a peace and a meaning of the mysteries of nature that I have no power to describe.

I saw that nations like individuals could only be made through the agony of the Cross and in no other way. Joy comes not out of infliction of pain on others but out of pain voluntarily borne by oneself.

If we turn our eyes to the time of which history has any record down to our own time, we shall find that man has been steadily progressing towards *ahiṃsā.* Our remote ancestors were cannibals. Then came a time when they were fed up with cannibalism and they began to live on chase. Next came a stage when man was ashamed of leading the life of a wandering hunter. He therefore took to agriculture and depended principally on mother earth for his food. Thus from being a nomad he settled down to civilized stable life, founded villages and towns, and from member of a family he became member of a community and a nation. All these are signs of progressive *ahiṃsā* and diminishing *hiṃsā.* Had it been otherwise, the human species should have been extinct by now, even as many of the lower species have disappeared.

Prophets and *avatārs* have also taught the lesson of *ahiṃsā* more or less. Not one of them has professed to teach *hiṃsā.* And how should it be otherwise? *Hiṃsā* does not need to be taught. Man as animal is violent, but as Spirit is non-violent. The moment he awakes to the Spirit within, he cannot remain violent. Either he progresses towards *ahiṃsā* or rushes to his doom. That is why the prophets and *avatārs* have taught the lesson of truth, harmony, brotherhood, justice, etc.—all attributes of *ahiṃsā*.

I claim that even now, though the social structure is not based on a conscious acceptance of non-violence, all the world over mankind lives and men retain their possessions on the sufferance of one another. If they had not done so, only the fewest and the most ferocious would have survived. But such is not the case. Families are bound together by ties of love, and so are groups in the so-called civilized society called nations. Only they do not recognize the supremacy of the law of non-violence. It follows, therefore, that they have not investigated its vast possibilities. Hitherto, out of sheer inertia, shall I say, we have taken it for granted that complete non-violence is possible only for the few who take the vow of non-possession and the allied abstinences. Whilst it is true that the votaries alone can carry on research work and declare from time to time the new possibilities of the great eternal law governing man, if it is a law, it must hold good for all. The many failures we see are not of the law but of the followers, many of whom do not even know that they are under that law willy-nilly. When a mother dies for her child she unknowingly obeys the law. I have been pleading for the past fifty years for a conscious acceptance of the law and its zealous practice even in the face of failures. Fifty years' work has shown marvelous results and strengthened my faith. I do claim that by constant practice we shall come to a state of things when lawful possession will commend universal and voluntary respect. No doubt such possession will not be tainted. It will not be an insolent demonstration of the inequalities that surround us everywhere.

HUGO GROTIUS
(Hugues de Groot)
(1583-1654)

Was a Dutch jurist and statesman, whose *De Jure Delli et Pacis* (1625), written after his escape to France as leader of the Remonstrants, is considered the real beginning of international law. Grotius was internationally recognized as a scholar while living in exile, and later was recognized by his own country as one of the greatest Dutchmen of all times. He was not the first to expound natural law, but he was the first to construct a system of international jurisprudence in which the distinction between natural and historical law was essential. According to him, the principle of natural morality is written by God in the hearts and minds of mankind; it is to be ascertained by reason. On the other hand, the existing institutions and laws of the nations are products of human will. The ultimate end of legal development must be the establishment of the supreme command of natural law. For the time being, some minimum demands must be formulated in order to eliminate license in making and conducting war. Grotius' significant work, *On the Law of Peace and War,* was directed against arbitrary power policy and radical pacifists, although "just wars" were admitted; previously, Grotius, in his *Mare Liberum* (*Free Sea,* 1609), had tried to secure the rights of neutral ships against ruthless force on the part of Portugal, Spain and England. His main argument was that sovereign states could not live in isolation any more than individuals could; forced to associate for self-preservation, they made contracts, in the same way as individuals, based on natural law, a product of reason. This law among states was obligatory for them, and could be executed by appropriate agents and derived its force from the will of nations. It had to be observed, or the social order could not be maintained. Law among nations held in war as in peace. War ought not be started except "for the enforcement of rights," and should be waged "only within the bounds of law and good faith." War happened because there was no superior organization which stood in the same relation to individual states as the state does to its citizens—able to impose its will on all. Until such an organization was formed, there were three methods of avoiding war: conferences, arbitration and lot. The hope that international law can govern international relations has been propounded since then by many theoreticians, and promoted by such organizations as the Carnegie Endowment for International Peace, the *American Journal of International Law* and various international organizations. The Library of the Permanent Court of Justice at The Hague has a special section devoted to Grotius' works.

---

*The Rational Basis of International Law**

THE civil law, both that of Rome and that of each nation in particular, has been treated of by many, with a view either to elucidate it, through commentaries, or to present it in a compendious form. But that law which regards the relations between peoples, or between rulers of peoples, whether it proceed from nature or be instituted by divine commands or introduced by custom and tacit agreement, has been touched on by few, and has by no one been treated as a whole and in an orderly manner. And yet that this be done is of concern to the human race.

And such a work is the more necessary because of the fact that persons in our time, as well as in former ages, have held in contempt what has been done in this province of jurisprudence, as if no such thing existed, as a mere name. Every one is familiar with the saying of Euphemius in Thucydides, that for a king or city who has authority to maintain, nothing is unjust which is useful; and to the same

* Excerpts taken from *The Encyclopedia of Philosophy,* by Grotius, translated by Gustav Emil Miller, New York: Philosophical Library, 1955.

effect is the saying that with good fortune equity is where strength is, and that the commonwealth cannot be administered without doing some wrong. To this we add that the controversies which arise between peoples and between kings commonly have war as their arbiter. But that war has nothing to do with laws is not the opinion of the ignorant; even wise and learned men often let fall expressions which support such an opinion. For nothing is more common than to place laws and arms in opposition to each other. . . .

Since our discussion of law is undertaken in vain if there is no law, it will serve both to commend and fortify our work if we refute briefly this very grave error. And that we may not have to deal with a mob of opponents, let us appoint an advocate to speak for them. And whom can we select fitter than Carneades, who had arrived at the point—the supreme aim of his academic philosophy—where he could use the strength of his eloquence for falsehood as easily as for truth? When he undertook to argue against justice—especially, the justice of which we here treat, he found no argument stronger than this: that men had, as utility prompted, established laws, differing among different peoples as manners differed, and, among the same people, often changing with the change of times; but that there is no natural law, since all men, as well as other animals, are impelled by nature to seek their own advantage; and that either there is no justice, or if it exist, it is the highest folly since through it one harms oneself in consulting the interests of others.

But what this philosopher says, and, following him, the poet—"Nature cannot distinguish the just from the unjust," must by no means be admitted. For though man is indeed an animal, he is an uncommon animal, differing much more from all other animals than they differ from one another; this is evidenced in many actions peculiar to the human species. Among the attributes peculiar to man is the desire for society—that is for communion with his fellow-men, and not for communion simply, but for a tranquil association and one suited to the quality of his intellect; this the Stoics called *Oykeiosin*. Therefore, the statement that by nature every animal is impelled to seek only its own advantage cannot be conceded in this general form.

Even in other animals their desires for their own good are tempered by regard for their offspring and for others of their species; this we believe to proceed from some intelligence outside of themselves; for with regard to other acts not at all more difficult than these an equal degree of intelligence does not appear. The same is to be said of infants, in whom, previous to all teaching, there is manifested a certain disposition to do good to others, as is sagaciously remarked by Plutarch; for example, at that age compassion breaks forth spontaneously. A man of full age knows how to act similarly in similar cases, and he has exceptional craving for society, whose peculiar instrument, language, he alone among all animals possesses; accordingly he has the faculty of knowing and acting according to general principles; the tendencies which agree with this faculty do not belong to all animals, but are the peculiar properties of human nature.

This concern for society, which we have now stated in a rude manner, and which is in agreement with the nature of the human intellect, is the source of law, properly so called, of which we are speaking. It is law that determines the abstention from another's property; the restitution of another's goods which we have in our possession and of any gain we have derived from such possession; the obligation to fulfill promises; the reparation for damage wrongfully done; and the retribution of punishments.

From this signification of law there has flowed another larger meaning. For man is superior to other animals not only in the social impulse of which we have spoken, but also in his judgment in estimating what is pleasant and what is injurious—not only for the present but for the future also, and the things which may lead to good or to ill. We know, therefore, that, in accordance with the quality of the human intellect, it is congruous to human nature to follow, in such matters, a judgment rightly formed and not to be misled by fear or by the enticement of present pleasure, or to be carried away by heedless impulse; and that what is plainly repugnant to such judgment is likewise contrary to natural law, that is, to natural human law.

And here comes the question of a wise assignment in bestowing upon each individual and each body of men the things which peculiarly belong to them; this disposition will sometimes prefer the wiser man to the less wise, the neighbor to a stranger, the poor man to the rich man, according as the nature of each act and each matter requires. This question some have made a part of law, strictly and properly so called; though law, properly speaking, has a very different nature; for it consists in this—that each should leave to another what is his and give to him what is his due.

What we have said would still be in point even if we should grant, what we cannot without great wickedness, that there is no God, or that He bestows no regard upon human affairs. Since we are assured of the contrary, partly by our reason and partly by constant tradition, confirmed by many arguments and by miracles attested by all ages, it follows that God, as our creator to whom we owe our being and all that we have, is to be obeyed by us without exception, especially since He has in many ways shown himself to be supremely good and supremely powerful. Wherefore, He is able to bestow upon those who obey Him the highest rewards, even eternal rewards, since He himself is eternal; and He must be believed to be willing to do this, particularly if He has promised to do so in plain words; and this we as Christians believe, convinced by the indubitable faith of testimonies.

And here we find another origin of law, besides that natural source of which we have spoken; it is the free will of God, to which our reason indisputably tells us we must submit ourselves. But even natural law—whether it be the natural social law, or law in the looser meaning of which we have spoken—may yet be rightfully ascribed to God, though it proceed from the principles of man's inner nature; for it was in accordance with His will that such principles came to exist within us. In this sense Chrysippus and the Stoics said that the origin of law was not to be sought in any other source than Jove himself; and it may be conjectured that the Latins took the word *jus* from the name *Jove*.

It may be added that God has made these principles more manifest by the commandments which He has given in order that they might be understood by those whose minds have weaker powers of reasoning. And He has controlled the aberrations of our impulses, which drive us this way and that, to the injury of ourselves and of others; bridling our more vehement passions, and restraining them within due limits.

In the next place, since it is conformable to natural law to observe compacts (for some mode of obliging themselves was necessary among men, and no other natural mode can be imagined) civil rights were derived from that very source. For those who joined any community, or put themselves in subjection to any man or men, either expressly promised or from the nature of the case must have been understood to promise tacitly, that they would conform to that which either the majority of the community, or those whom power was assigned, should determine.

And therefore what Carneades said, and what has been said by others—that utility is the mother of justice and right—is, if we are to speak accurately, not true. For the mother of natural law is human nature itself, which would lead us to desire mutual society even though we were driven thereto by other wants. The mother of civil law is obligation by compact; and since compacts derive their force from natural law, nature may be said to be the great-grandmother of civil law. But utility supplements (*accedit*) natural law. For the Author of nature ordained that we, as individuals, should be weak and in need of many things for living well, in order that we might be the more impelled to cherish society. But utility furnished the occasion for civil law; for that association or subjection of which we have spoken, was at the first instituted for the sake of some utility. Accordingly, those who prescribe for others ordinarily design, or should design, some utility in their laws.

But just as the laws of each state regard the utility of that state, so also between all states, or, at least, between most of them, certain laws could be established by consent—and it appears that laws have been established—which regard the utility, not of particular communities but of the great aggregate of communities. And this is what is called the law of nations (*jus gentium*), in so far as we distinguish it from natural law. This part of law is omitted by Carneades, who divides all law into natural law and the civil law of particular peoples; although as he was about to treat of that law which obtains between one people and another (for he subjoins a discussion upon war and acquisitions by war), he was especially called upon to make mention of law of this kind.

Moreover, Carneades improperly traduces justice when he calls it folly. For since, as he himself acknowledges, the citizen is not foolish who in a state obeys the civil law, although in consequence of such respect for the law he may lose some things which are useful to him, so too a people is not to be deemed foolish which does not estimate its interests so highly as to disregard the common laws between peoples for the sake of its own advantage. The reason is the same in both cases. For as a citizen who disobeys the civil law for the sake of present utility destroys that in which the perpetual utility of himself and his posterity is bound up, so too a people which violates the laws of nature and of nations breaks down the bulwark of its own tranquillity for future time. Even though no utility were to be looked on from the observation of law, such a course would be one not of folly but of wisdom, to which we feel ourselves drawn by nature.

Wherefore, that saying that we were compelled to establish laws from fear of wrong, is not universally true; this opinion is explained by a speaker in Plato's dialogues, who says that laws were introduced because of the fear of receiving wrong, and that men are driven to respect justice by a certain compulsion. But this applies only to those institutions and statutes which were devised for the more easy enforcement of law; as when many, individually weak, fearing oppression by those who were stronger, combined to establish judicial authorities and to protect them by their common strength, so that those whom they could not resist singly, they might, united, control. Only in this sense may we properly accept the statement that law is that which pleases the stronger party: namely, that we are to understand that law does not attain its external end unless it has force as its servant. Thus Solon accomplished great things, as he himself said, *by linking together force and law.*

But even law that is unsupported by force is not destitute of all effect; for justice brings serenity to the conscience, while injustice brings torments and remorse such as Plato describes as afflicting the hearts of tyrants. The common feeling of upright men approves justice and condemns injustice. The important point is that justice has for its friend, God, while injustice has Him as an enemy; He reserves his judgments for another life, yet in such manner that He often exhibits their power in this life; we have many examples of this in history.

The error which many commit who, while they require justice in citizens, hold it to be superfluous in a people or the ruler of a people, is caused primarily by this fact: they are regarding only the utility which arises from the law. This utility is evident in the case of citizens, who individually are too weak to secure their own protection. Great states, on the other hand, which seem to embrace within themselves all that is necessary to support life, do not appear to have need of that virtue which regards extraneous parties and is called justice.

But—not to repeat what I have already said, that law is not established for the sake of utility alone—there is no state so strong that it may not at some time need the aid of others external to itself, either in the way of commerce or in order to repel the force of many nations combined against it. Hence we see that alliances are sought even by the most powerful peoples and kings; the force of such alliances is entirely destroyed by those who confine law within the boundaries of a state. It is most true that everything becomes uncertain if we withdraw from law.

Since, for the reasons which I have stated, I hold it to be completely proved that there is between nations a common law which is of force with respect to war and in war, I have had many and grave reasons why I should write a work on that subject. For I saw prevailing throughout the Christian world a license in making war of which even barbarous nations would have been ashamed, recourse being had to arms for slight reasons or for no reason; and when arms were once taken up, all reverence for divine and human law was lost, just as men were henceforth authorized to commit all crimes without restraint.

It remains now that I briefly explain with what aids and with what care I have undertaken this work. In the first place, it was my object to refer to the truth of the things which belong to natural law to certain notions so certain that no one can deny them without doing violence to his own nature. For the principles of that law, if you attend to them rightly, are of themselves patent and evident almost in the same way as things which we perceive by our external senses; for these do not deceive us, if the organs are rightly disposed and other necessary things are not wanting.

For the demonstration of natural law I have used the testimonies of philosophers, historians, poets, and finally orators. Not that these are to be trusted indiscriminately; for they are ordinarily writing to serve their sect, their argument, or their cause. But when many, writing in different times and places, affirm the same thing as true, their unanimity must be referred to some universal cause, which, in the questions with which we are concerned, can be no other than either a right deduction proceeding from principles of nature, or some common agreement. The former cause points to the law of nature, the latter to the law of nations; the difference between these two is to be discerned not in the testimonies themselves (for writers everywhere confound the law of nature and the law of nations), but in the quality of the matter. For what can not be deduced from certain principles by unerring reasoning, and yet is seen to be observed everywhere, must have its origin in free consent.

Passages of history have a two-fold use in our argument: they supply both examples and judgments. In proportion as examples belong to better times and better nations, they have greater authority; we have therefore preferred the examples from ancient Greece and Rome. Nor are judgments to be despised, especially when many of them agree; for natural law is, as we have said, to be proved by such concord; and the law of nations can be proved in no other manner.

The opinions of poets and orators have not so much weight; and these we often use not so much to gain confirmation from them as to give to what we are trying to say some ornamentation from their modes of expression.

The books written by men inspired by God, or approved by them, I often use as authority, with a distinction between the Old and the New Testament. . . .

ALEXANDER HAMILTON
(1757-1804)

One of the Founding Fathers of the United States was born in the West Indies (Nevis); he was always—perhaps deliberately —vague about the year, and 1757 has long been thought the year of his birth, since he described himself in 1773 as "about sixteen." His mother (of French Huguenot stock) had been married at the age of sixteen to a middle-aged merchant of the Danish island of St. Croix. A year before the American Revolution started, he registered at King's College (now Columbia University); during the war he became a captain in the New York Artillery and a military secretary to George Washington; passed over (1781) for the post of adjutant-general, he quarreled with Washington and resigned as his aide. In December, 1780, he married General Philip Schuyler's daughter, Elizabeth, and united his fortunes with those of the rich patron of the Hudson Valley. After Yorktown he practiced as a lawyer, was receiver of Continental taxes for New York, represented New York at the Annapolis and Philadelphia conventions and was appointed Secretary of the Treasury (September, 1789-January, 1795). As a joint author (*Work,* edited by J. C. Hamilton, 1851) with Madison of the Constitution and of the *Federalist* (Hamilton, James Madison and John Jay), these 85 essays which, more perhaps than anything else, secured the passing of the Constitution in New York, he was one of the architects of the American political system. This man of effervescent charm, short in stature, but fair and "uncommonly handsome," this West Indian immigrant then became "Prime Minister" to the First President of the United States. As Secretary of the Treasury, his report on credit and his banking policies established the solvency of the new nation and set the course of the new state; he was also a major contributor to George Washington's Farewell Address.

When Jefferson objected that the Constitution did not permit the establishment of a bank in which the government owned stock, he answered with the famous doctrine of "implied powers" —that the power to charter private corporations or a bank was a natural outcome of the power of the federal government to coin money, raise taxes and incur debts. He provided a national revenue by imposing indirect taxes on imported goods and an excise tax on home-produced liquor—two measures of profound significance; the first created a high volume of imports from Britain and so linked the United States with her economically and diplomatically, and the second produced the Whiskey Rebellion of the Pennsylvania farmers (1794). The vehement suppression of the latter produced a display of the strength of the national government. He advocated republicanism but not democracy. ("The voice of the people has been said to be the voice of God; and however as generally this maxim has been quoted and believed, it is not true in fact. The people are turbulent and changing; they seldom judge or determine right.") The power of the Supreme Court to declare laws unconstitutional was an important aspect of his theory, influenced by Locke, Montesquieu and Hume. He died in a duel with Aaron Burr.

The Constitutionality of the Bank (February 23, 1791) *

THE SECRETARY of the Treasury having perused with attention the papers containing the opinions of the Secretary of State and the Attorney-General, concerning the constitutionality of the bill for establishing a National Bank, proceeds, according to the order of the President, to submit the reasons which have induced him to entertain a different opinion. . . .

. . . In entering upon the argument, it ought to be premised that the objections of the Secretary of State and the Attorney-General are founded on a general denial of the authority of the United States to erect corporations. . . .

* This excerpt taken from *The Work of Alexander Hamilton*, J. C. Hamilton, ed., New York: 1851, IV, pp. 104 ff.

Now it appears to the Secretary of the Treasury that this *general principle* is *inherent* in the very *definition* of government, and *essential* to every step of the progress to be made by that of the United States, namely: That every power vested in a government is in its nature *sovereign,* and includes, by *force* of the *term* a right to employ all the *means* requisite and fairly applicable to the attainment of the *ends* of such power, and which are not precluded by restrictions and exceptions specified in the Constitution, or not immoral, or not contrary to the *essential ends* of political society. . . .

If it would be necessary to bring proof to a proposition so clear, as that which affirms that the powers of the federal government, as to *its objects,* were sovereign, there is a clause of the Constitution which would be decisive. It is that which declares that the Constitution, and the laws of the United States made in pursuance of it, and all treaties made . . . under their authority shall be the *supreme law of the land.* The power which can create *a supreme law of the land,* in any case, is doubtless *sovereign* as to such case.

This general and indisputable principle puts at once an end to the *abstract* question, whether the United States have power to erect a corporation; that is to say, to give a *legal* or *artificial capacity* to one or more persons, distinct from the *natural.* For it is unquestionably incident to *sovereign power* to erect corporations, and consequently to that of the United States, in *relation* to the *objects* intrusted to the management of the government. The difference is this: where the authority of the government is general, it can create corporations in *all cases;* where it is confined to certain branches of legislation, it can create corporations *only* in those cases. . . .

It is not denied that there are *implied* as well as *express powers,* and that the *former* are as effectually delegated as the *latter.* And for the sake of accuracy it shall be mentioned, that there is another class of powers, which may be properly denominated *resulting powers.* It will not be doubted, that if the United States should make a conquest of any of the territories of its neighbors they would possess sovereign jurisdiction over the conquered territory. This would be rather a result, from the whole mass of the powers of the government, and from the nature of political society, than a consequence of either of the powers specially enumerated. . . .

To return:—It is conceded that *implied powers* are to be considered equally with *express ones*. Then it follows, that as a power of erecting a corporation may as well be *implied* as any other thing, it may as well be employed as an *instrument* or *means* of carrying into execution any of the specified powers, as any other *instrument* or *mean* whatever. The only question must be, in this as in every other case, whether the mean to be employed, or in this instance, the corporation to be erected, has a natural relation to any of the acknowledged objects or lawful ends of the government. Thus a corporation may not be erected by Congress for superintending the police of the city of Philadelphia, because they are not authorized to *regulate* the *police* of that city. But one may be erected in the relation to the collection of taxes, or to the trade with foreign countries, or to the trade between the States, or with the Indian tribes; because it is the province of the federal government to *regulate* those objects and because it is incident to a general *sovereign* or *legislative* power to *regulate* a thing, to employ all the means which relate to its regulation to the best and greatest advantage. . . .

Through this mode of reasoning respecting the right of employing all the means requisite to the execution of the specified powers of the government, it is objected, that none but necessary and proper means are to be employed; and the Secretary of State maintains, that no means are to be considered as *necessary* but those without which the grant of the power would be *nugatory*. . . .

It is essential to the being of the national government, that so erroneous a conception of the meaning of the word *necessary* should be exploded.

It is certain, that neither the grammatical nor popular sense of the term requires that construction. According to both, *necessary* often means no more than *needful, requisite, incidental, useful* or *conducive to*. . . . And it is the true one in which it is to be understood as used in the Constitution. The whole turn of the clause containing it indicates, that was the intent of the Convention, by that clause, to give a liberal latitude to the exercise of the specified powers. The expressions have peculiar comprehensiveness. They are "to make all *laws* necessary and proper for *carrying into execution* the *foregoing powers,* and *all other powers* vested by the Constitution in the *government* of the United States, or in any *department* or *officer* thereof."

To understand the word as the Secretary of State does, would be to depart from its obvious and popular sense, and to give it a restrictive operation, an idea never before entertained. It would be to give it the same force as if the word *absolutely* or *indispensably* had been prefixed to it.

The *degree* in which a measure is necessary, can never be a *test* of the legal right to adopt it; that must be a matter of opinion, and can only be a *test* of expediency. The *relation* between the *measure* and the *end;* between the *nature* of the *mean* employed towards the execution of a power, and the object of that power, must be the criterion of constitutionality, not the more or less of *necessity* or *utility*. . . .

This restrictive interpretation of the word *necessary* is also contrary to this sound maxim of construction; namely, that the powers contained in a constitution of government, especially those which concern the general administration of the affairs of a country, its finances, trade, defence, &c., ought to be construed liberally in advancement of the public good. . . . The means by which national exigencies are to be provided for, national inconveniences obviated, national prosperity promoted, are of such infinite variety, extent, and complexity, that there must of necessity be great latitude of discretion in the selection and application of those means.

Hence, consequently, the necessity and propriety of exercising the authorities intrusted to a government on principles of liberal construction . . .

GEORG WILHELM FRIEDRICH HEGEL

(1770-1831)

One of the most influential philosophers of modern times, represents the climax of German idealistic political thought rooted in the writings of Plato and Aristotle. This thought held, among other principles, that political philosophy is basically an ethical study, that the state is a natural society, that man is a member of the political community by his very nature, that the end of the state is partnership in a life of virtue, that law is the expression of pure reason, and that each individual must discharge his proper duties in the life of the community. In his writings, Hegel regarded the human mind as one of the manifestations of the Absolute, which he defined as spirit. The world is penetrable to thought, which is another term for the Absolute. Cosmic reason operates within the soul of man, whose consciousness is the area of the subjective spirit; the objective spirit is manifest in cultural and social institutions such as law and morality; and the absolute spirit can be grasped in the arts, religion and philosophy. Human history and social life, culminating in the state, represent the highest level of a gradation that rises from inorganic nature to human genius, from "mere existence" to consciousness, knowledge of truth and action in accordance with recognized duties. The history of the world is the progressive realization of freedom, which can be demonstrated by purely logical development. The cause of historical change is the movement of thought, which integrates a thesis and its antithesis into a synthesis, which, in turn, evokes a new antithesis with which it becomes integrated into a new synthesis. These succeeding syntheses will eventually bring the world to reason; in this way, evolution was conceived by Hegel as a purely logical procedure for which he claimed the acknowledgment of real necessity.

The state is the medium whereby the ultimate goal of the world and society is to be achieved; it is the highest embodiment of the divine idea on earth and the chief instrumentality used by the Absolute in manifesting itself as it proceeds toward perfect fulfillment. It is an organic whole composed of individuals grouped into classes, voluntary associations and local communities, and these parts have no meaning except in relation to and as part of the whole. It is only as a member of the body politic that the individual has objectivity, genuine individuality and an ethical life. As the embodiment of the Absolute, the state is not a means for securing the welfare of the individual; it is an end in itself. Since it has a higher end than its parts, it can demand that these be sacrificed to its interests. Right, as the thesis, represents the objective demands of the individual on society. Morality, as the antithesis, represents the subjective duty of the individual in his relations with others. The synthesis is found in concrete ethical life with the state as the supreme actuality of the ethical idea. The freedom of the individual is thus directly related to the actualization of the universal, and does not consist of satisfying his individual desires without reference to the universal will. True liberty consists of acting in harmony with universal reason as it progressively develops. Since the state expresses the universal will, the individual is really obeying the laws of his own true rational self and will find genuine freedom by serving and obeying the state. Reason dictates that the government be entrusted to a trained and professional bureaucracy; this elite corps should participate in law-making as well as administration. Conflict between states is as healthy as it is inevitable. Hegel's intellectual formulas have influenced many philosophers of England, America, Italy, France and Germany (especially Karl Marx, T. H. Green, Edward and John Caird, J. H. Bradley, Bernard Bosanquet, W. T. Harris, Royce, Creighton and John Dewey), and can be found in Fascism, Nazism, Marxism and neo-Marxism, Leninism and contemporary interpreters of Sovietism.

Georg Wilhelm Friedrich Hegel

*The Nature of Freedom**

NOW THIS IS FREEDOM, exactly. For if I am dependent, my being is referred to something else which I am not; I cannot exist independently of something external. I am free, on the contrary, when my existence depends upon myself. This self-contained existence of Spirit is none other than self-consciousness—consciousness of one's own being. Two things must be distinguished in consciousness; first, the fact *that I know*; secondly, *what I know*. In *self* consciousness these are merged in one; for Spirit *knows itself*. It involves an appreciation of its own nature, as also an energy enabling it to realize itself; to make itself *actually* that which it is *potentially*. According to this abstract definition it may be said of Universal History, that it is the exhibition of Spirit in the process of working out the knowledge of that which it is potentially. And as the germ bears in itself the whole nature of the tree, and the taste and form of its fruits, so do the first traces of Spirit virtually contain the whole of that History. . . . The history of the world is none other than the progress of the consciousness of Freedom; a progress whose development according to the necessity of its nature, it is our business to investigate.

The general statement given above, of the various grades in the consciousness of Freedom—and which we applied in the first instance to the fact that the Eastern nations knew only that *one* is free; the Greek and Roman world only that *some* are free; whilst *we* know that all men absolutely (man *as man*) are free—supplies us with the natural division of Universal History, and suggests the mode of its discussion. This is remarked, however, only incidentally and anticipatively; some other ideas must be first explained.

---

* Excerpt taken from G. W. F. Hegel, *Lectures on the Philosophy of History*, London: George Bell and Sons, 1881, pp. 18, 19-21, and 467-468.

The destiny of the spiritual World, and—since this is the *substantial World,* while the physical remains subordinate to it, or, in the language of speculation, has no truth as *against* the spiritual—the *final cause of the World at large,* we allege to be the *consciousness* of its own freedom on the part of Spirit, and *ipso facto,* the *reality* of that freedom. But that this term "Freedom," without further qualification, is an indefinite, and incalculable ambiguous term; and that while that which it represents is the *ne plus ultra* of attainment, it is liable to an infinity of misunderstandings, confusions and errors, and to become the occasion for all imaginable excesses—has never been more clearly known and felt than in modern times. Yet, for the present, we must content ourselves with the term itself without further definition. Attention was also directed to the importance of the infinite difference between a principle in the abstract, and its realization in the concrete. In the process before us, the essential nature of freedom—which involves in it absolute necessity—is to be displayed as coming to a consciousness of itself (for it is in its very nature, self-consciousness) and thereby realizing its existence. Itself is its own object of attainment, and the sole aim of Spirit. This result it is, at which the process of the World's History has been continually aiming; and to which the sacrifices that have ever and anon been laid on the vast altar of the earth, through the long lapse of ages, have been offered. This is the only aim that sees itself realized and fulfilled; the only pole of repose amid the ceaseless change of events and conditions, and the sole efficient principle that pervades them. This final aim is God's purpose with the world; but God is the absolutely perfect Being, and can, therefore, will nothing other than himself—his own Will. The Nature of His Will—that is, His Nature itself—is what we here call the Idea of Freedom; translating the language of Religion into that of Thought.

Freedom presents two aspects: the one concerns its substance and purport, its objectivity—the thing itself—(that which is performed as a free act); the other relates to the Form of Freedom, involving the consciousness of his activity on the part of the individual; for Freedom demands that the individual recognize himself in such acts, that they should be veritably his, it being his interest that the result in question should be attained. The three elements and powers of the State in actual working must be contemplated according to the above analysis.

Laws of Rationality—of intrinsic Right—Objective or Real Freedom: to this category belong Freedom of Property and Freedom of Person. Those relics of that condition of servitude which the feudal relation had introduced are hereby swept away, and all those fiscal ordinances which were the bequest of the feudal law—its tithes and dues, are abrogated. Real (practical) Liberty requires moreover freedom in regard to trades and professions—the permission to everyone to use his abilities without restriction—and the free admission to all offices of State. This is a summary of the elements of real Freedom, and which are not based on feeling—for feeling allows of the continuance even of serfdom and slavery—but on the thought and self-consciousness of man recognizing the spiritual character of his existence.

But the agency which gives the laws practical effect is the *Government* generally. Government is primarily the formal execution of the laws and the maintenance of their authority: in respect to foreign relations it prosecutes the interest of the State; that is, it assists the independence of the nation as an individuality against other nations; lastly, it has to provide for the internal weal of the State and all its classes—what is called administration: for it is not enough that the citizen is allowed to pursue a trade or calling, it must also be a source of gain to him; it is not enough that men are permitted to use their powers, they must also find an opportunity of applying them to purpose. Thus the state involves a body of abstract principles and a practical application of them. This application must be the work of a subjective will, a will which resolves and decides. Legislation itself—the invention and positive enactment of these statutory arrangements—is an application of such general principles. The next step, then, consists in (specific) determination and execution. Here then the question presents itself: what is the decisive will to be? The ultimate decision is the prerogative of the monarch: but if the State is based on Liberty, the many wills of individuals also desire to have a share in the political decisions. But the *Many* are *All*; and it seems but a poor expedient, rather a monstrous inconsistency, to allow only a few to take part in those decisions since each wishes that his volition should have a share in determining what is to be law for him. The Few assume to be the *deputies,* but they are often only the *despoilers* of the Many. Nor is the sway of the Majority over the Minority a less palpable inconsistency.

This collision of subjective wills leads therefore to the consideration of a third point, that of *Disposition*—an *ex animo acquiesence* in the laws; not the mere customary observance of them, but the cordial recognition of laws and the Constitution as in principle fixed and immutable, and of the supreme obligation of individuals to subject their particular wills to them. There may be various opinions and views respecting laws, constitution and government, but there must be a disposition on the part of the citizens to regard all these opinions as subordinate to the substantial interest of the State, and to insist upon them no farther than that interest will allow; moreover nothing must be considered higher and more sacred than good will towards the State; or, if Religion be looked upon as higher and more sacred, it must involve nothing really alien or opposed to the Constitution. It is, indeed, regarded as a maxim of the profoundest wisdom entirely to separate the laws and constitution of the State from Religion, since bigotry and hypocrisy are to be feared as the results of a State Religion. But although the aspects of Religion and the State are different, they are radically *one*; and the laws find their highest confirmation in Religion.

ADOLF HITLER

(1889-1945)

German Chancellor and *Führer* (1933-1945), was born at Braunau, Austria, son of a customs officer and attended the four lower classes of a secondary school at Linz, at that time a center of Pan-Germanism, a fact which strongly influenced his subsequent thought and career. When he went to Vienna with the intention of becoming a painter, he failed the entrance examination of the Viennese Academy of Arts, then worked as a bricklayer for some time, and later lived in a casual way, earning a small income by painting colored postcards which he used to sell visitors in public bars. He liked to talk politics, voicing pan-German, anti-Hapsburg, anti-socialist and anti-Jewish opinions. In 1911 he went to Munich, where he lived on the occasional sale of paintings. At the outbreak of World War I, he enrolled as a volunteer in the German Army, refusing to join his native Austrian Army because of his hatred of the non-German Hapsburg monarchy. Serving on the Western front throughout the war, he reached no higher rank than that of private first class. After the war, he was employed by the *Reichswehr* (the German postwar army) as a secret agent for the supervision of political meetings and thus came into contact with a dining club calling itself the German Labor party and consisting of six members who held conferences in the back room of a Munich inn. The founder and leader was a worker named Drexler. Hitler became the party's seventh member and started agitation for its enlargement. The party grew and Hitler ousted Drexler and the name was changed to the National Social (Nazi) German Labor party. In 1923 the Party attempted a *coup* in Munich which proved abortive and Hitler was sentenced to five years' imprisonment (actually, confinement) at the Landsberg fortress in Bavaria. There he wrote *Mein Kampf* (*My Struggle*), setting forth his political program. Released prematurely after eight months with the help of nationalistic authorities, he reconstructed his party and wrote the second volume of *Mein Kampf* (1925-1927).

In essence, Hitler saw the core of all life in race and blood. There is a superior race in the world, the Aryan race (sometimes also referred to as the Nordic race), which has subdued peoples of inferior races and erected our present civilization on the basis of their labor. But the Aryans committed the sin of crossbreeding with their inferior subjects, thus spoiling their blood and bringing about gradual physical decline and spiritual decadence. There is a sinister power desirous of the destruction of the Aryan peoples: the Jews, with their world-wide organization. Their principal object is the disintegration of the racial basis of the Aryan peoples by the systematic mixing of blood, so that the resulting decadent race of mongrels will easily succumb to Jewish domination. The most outspoken Aryan power in the world is Germany, and therefore the chief object of Jewish hostility. The Jews are also behind Bolshevism; and Marxist socialism, in general, is nothing but a trick of the Jews for obtaining world domination. Communists, Socialists, Democrats and Freemasons work for Jewish-Bolshevik aims in all countries. Thus Hitler called upon Germany to save Aryan mankind. His program called for a strong nationalist state under Nazi leadership to suppress all other parties, to combat the Jews and to concentrate on racial improvement; all Germans (or their descendants) must be united within the Reich, and Germany must conquer new soil for her people. "Germany will be either a World Power or she will not be at all."

This potpourri of ideas, called the "propagandist masterpiece of the age," and by Hendrik Willem Van Loon "one of the most extraordinary historical documents of all time," combining "the naïveté of Jean Jacques Rousseau with the frenzied wrath of an Old Testament prophet," and by Norman Cousins as "by far the most effective book of the twentieth century," became the political bible of the German people and guided the policies of the Third Reich from 1933 until 1945. Hitler's eulogy of the "Big Lie" in *Mein Kampf* is one of the effective passages in the book. Hitler transmuted Hegel's mystical deification of the state into an abstruse emulation of the *Volk* (Nation); he also gave a special twist to the leadership principle derived from the Fascists (charisma); enlisted the so-called science of geopolitics (Haushofer, Ratzel and others) in the service of Nazi political theory; and agreed with the dictum of Kant and Fichte that the individual possesses no rights, only duties. Nazism also agreed with Herbert Spencer that the struggle for existence, natural selection and the survival of the fittest constitute the fundamental law of life (but did not follow Spencer's belief that the social struggle is between individuals). It was impressed with Walter Bagehot's idea that the social struggle is essentially among groups. Gobineau and Chamberlain provided its race theories; race also provided the Nazis with a principle which enabled them to outdo Machiavelli in subordinating ethics to political expediency. The Nazis also elaborated Social Darwinism and the anti-intellectualism (or irrationalism) which had received a great impetus from the naturalism of Rousseau, Schopenhauer, Nietzsche, James, Bergson, Sorel, Mosca and Pareto. Irrationalism led the Nazis to attach great importance to Sorel's idea of the social myth. The defeat of Nazi Germany has not destroyed Nazism, and much of Hitler's (Nazi) ideology has survived in Germany and elsewhere.

---

*The Racial State**

Role of the leader. The individual has as little right to question the action of the political leaders as the soldier to question the orders of his military superiors. And just as the Party demands the subjection of the people to its will, so within the Party itself this same subjection must be an immutable law. There is no possibility of release from obedience to this principle. He who will not render this complete obedience cannot look for obedience from others. And if from the bourgeoisie we often hear the objections: "Ah, yes,

* Excerpt taken from *The Speeches of Adolf Hitler, April 1922-August 1939,* edited by Norman H. Baynes, New York: Oxford University Press, 1942, pp. 447-448, 464-471.

the Leader, but the Party—that is another matter!" I answer: "No! Gentlemen, the Leader is the Party and the Party is the Leader." As I feel myself to be only a part of this Party, so the Party feels itself to be only a part of me. When I shall close my eyes in death I do not know. But that the Party will live on—that I know, and that over all persons, over weakness and strength it will triumph and will successfully fashion the future of the German nation—that I believe, that I know! For the Party guarantees the stability of the leadership of the people and of the Reich, and through its own stability it guarantees that this leadership shall exercise the authority which it needs.

From this sure foundation there will grow up the Constitution of the new German Reich. This Party as *weltanschaulich* moulder and as political guide of the destiny of Germany has to give the Leader to the nation and therefore to the Reich. The more this principle is proclaimed and observed as the natural and uncontested basis of government the stronger will Germany be. The army as representative and the organizer of the military forces of our people must ever maintain the organized military force of the Reich entrusted to it and in loyalty and obedience must place it at the disposal of the Leader who has been given to the Nation by the Party. For after the Proclamation of the new Leader from time to time he becomes the lord (*Herr*) of the Party, the supreme Commander of the Army.

Race and Political Leadership. In order to understand the diseases from which a people suffers, it is first necessary to understand how a people is built up. Almost all the peoples of the world are composed today of different racial primary elements (*Grundstoffen*). These original elements are each characterized by different capacities. Only in the primitive functions of life can men be considered as precisely like each other. Beyond these primitive functions they immediately begin to be differentiated in their characters, their dispositions, and capacities. The differences between the individual races, both in part externally and, of course, also in their inset natures, can be quite enormous and in fact are so. The gulf between the lowest creature which can still be styled man and our highest races is greater than that between the lowest type of man and the highest ape.

If on this earth there were not some races which to-day determine its cultural appearance, it would hardly be possible to speak of any such thing as human civilization (*Kultur*). For this neither climate nor education can be regarded as responsible, but only man himself who was endowed by Providence with this capacity.

But if this cultural capacity is fundamentally inherent in certain races, its full effect is realized only under certain favourable circumstances. Man as an individual, whatever powers he may have in himself, will be incapable of higher achievements unless he can place the powers of many in the service of a single idea, a single conception, a single will and can unite them for a single action.

A glance at Nature shows us that creatures belonging to a pure race, not merely corporeally but in character and capacities, are more or less of equal value. This equality is the greatest hindrance in the way of the formation of any community in work (*Arbeitsgemeinschaft*); for since every higher civilization receives its stamp through achievements which are possible only through uniting the forces of human labour, it is thus essential that a number of individuals must sacrifice a part of their individual freedom and must subject themselves to a single will. However much reason may counsel such a course, in reality it would be difficult amongst those who are complete equals to demonstrate the reasons why in the last resort one must be in a position to assert his will as against that of the others.

The two concepts—Command and Obedience—however, exercise quite another and more compelling force when folk of different value come into conflict or association with each other, and then through the action of the stronger section are bound together in pursuit of a common purpose.

The most primitive form of association traced at the moment when man forces his supremacy upon the animals, tears them from the freedom of their former life, and builds them into his own life-process without troubling himself whether his animal-helper consents thereto or not.

But long ago man has proceeded in the same way with his fellowman. The higher race—at first "higher" in the sense of possessing a greater gift for organization—subjects to itself a lower race and thus constitutes a relationship which now embraces races of unequal value. Thus there results the subjection of a number of people under the will often of only a few persons, a subjection based simply on the right of the stronger, a right which, as we see it in Nature, can be regarded as the sole conceivable right because founded on reason. The wild mustang does not take upon itself the yoke imposed by man either voluntarily or joyfully; neither does one people welcome the violence of another.

But, despite this, in the course of a long development this compulsion has very often been converted into a blessing for all parties. Thus were formed those communities which created the essential features of human organization through the welding together of different races. And this organization always demands the subjection of the will and the activity of many under the will and the energy of a single individual. As men come to discover the astonishing results of this concentration of their capacity and labour-force they begin to recognize not merely the expediency but also the necessity of such action. And thus it is that a great and significant Aryan civilization did not arise where Aryans alone were living in racial purity, but always where they formed a vital association with races otherwise constituted, an association founded not on mixture of blood but on the basis of an organic community of purpose. And what was at first undoubtedly felt by the conquered as bitter compulsion later became in spite of this even for them a blessing. Unconsciously in the master-people there grew up ever more clearly and vitally a recognition of the ethical demand that their supremacy must be no arbitrary rule but must be controlled by a noble reasonableness. The capacity to subdue others was not given to them by Providence in order to make the subjects feel that the lordship of their conqueror was a meaningless tyranny, a mere oppression: that capacity was given that through the union of the conqueror's genius with the strength of the conquered they might create for both alike an existence which because it was useful was not degrading to man.

However this process of the formation of a people and a State was begun, its beginning signified the close of humanity's communistic age. For Communism is not a higher stage of development: rather it is the most primitive form of life—the starting-point.

Men of completely similar characteristics, men who are precisely like each other and endowed with the same capacities, will be of necessity also alike in their achievement. This condition is realized in the case of peoples who are throughout of one and the same race. Where these conditions are realized, the individual result of the activity of each will correspond only with the general average of all. . . . In this case it can be a question only of quite primitive values, and the condition for any clear definition of the idea of property is lacking because of the absence of any differentiation in achievement which is essential for the rise of such a concept. Equal achievement carries with it the equal division of the results of that achievement. In such a state Communism is therefore a natural and morally comprehensible ordering of society. But when men of very different values have met together, the result of their achievements will also be different; that is to say that the race which stands higher in the scale of quality will contribute more to the sum total of common work than the race which is lower in the qualitative scale. And in particular men's capacities will lie on different levels. The primitive capacity of the one race will from the first produce values other than those more highly developed or otherwise constituted values produced by the other partner in the common life. As a consequence the administration of the labour-product will necessarily lead to a division which proceeds from a consideration of the character of the achievement; in other words: that which has been created will be administered as property on the same basis as that of its origin. The conception of private property is thus inseparably connected with the conviction that the capacities of men are different alike in character and in value and thus, further, that men themselves are different in character and value.

THOMAS HOBBES
(1588-1679)

Is the first English-speaking political philosopher in the strict sense that he tried to state the abstract principles of social and political life (thus by-passing Sir Thomas More, whose *Utopia* added little to either Plato or St. Augustine). Born the son of a vicar of the Church of England during the descent of the Spanish Armada on the English coast, he was educated at Magdalen College, Oxford (one of the chief schools of the Church). But he was little influenced by the scholasticism of Magdalen or the growing Puritanism of the England of his time. In 1608, he was hired as a tutor in the family of the Earl of Devonshire, a powerful noble family, one of the chief supporters of the Royalist cause, and thus came into contact with the Royalist party. In 1610, he traveled with his pupil to France and Italy, where he came into contact with the scientific and philosophical movements of those countries. He also met Sir Francis Bacon, for whom he had considerable admiration (Bacon was the arch-foe of Aristotle and of scholasticism). But while Bacon interested Hobbes in the physical sciences, he did not succeed in interesting him in the inductive, empirical method. Probably he was more influenced by Galileo (whom he met in 1636 on a second trip to the Continent); he adapted Galileo's views in physics to politics, believing that the mechanistic interpretation could be applied to human relations (anticipating the "social physics" of the nineteenth century in his view that the principle involved in the only reality in the world was that of "motion"). He was one of the first to flee from the Puritan revolution to become the tutor to the Prince of Wales (later Charles II of England). In 1647, he published his first political work, *De Cive.* This was followed by other publications, all gathered in *The Leviathan* (1651), which he presented with much pride to the Royalist court, then in exile in Paris. But the court received it with suspicion, since it was based on the mechanistic principle and denied God's direct hand in human affairs. Unfriendliness at court forced him to return to London, where in turn, he was received coldly by Cromwell's government. After the Restoration, he went into hiding, but Charles II granted him a pension. (In many respects his life and thinking paralleled that of Herbert Spencer in the nineteenth century.)

The Leviathan is filled with definitions and propositions that are carefully reasoned out deductively. Hobbes' general premise was the materialistic one, that there were only motions and particles in motion in the universe. He paid little attention to human history or to actual social life, and believed that a few simple principles, such as self-interest, could adequately explain human behavior. His political thinking was based upon a doctrine of human nature and he is considered one of the founders of psychology. All ideas are the result of impressions on an organ of sense by the motion of some external object. All man's movements are controlled by self-interest, and all aim at happiness, continual success in gratifying desires. Hence all men have a perpetual desire for power, since power is the effective means of gratifying all desires. He deduced from his egoistic theory of human nature that the natural state of man is war, of all and against all. In this state of nature, men live solitary, poor, nasty, brutal and sordid lives. The perpetual strife of war is caused by: (1) competition to gratify desires; (2) the fear of each lest another surpass him in power and so in ability to gratify appetites; (3) the craving in human nature for admiration through being superior to another, or the love of glory. In a state of nature there is natural right, the liberty of every man to do what seems best to him for his own preservation and for his own existence. But there is also natural right which implies the restraint of reason, and reason forbids any act or omission unfavorable to self-preservation. Natural right imposes three fundamental precepts: (1) men must seek peace and observe it and thus must escape from the state of actual or potential war; (2) men must mutually abandon their natural rights to all things; (3) all promises made must be kept, or else men will be back in the state of nature again. This results in men giving up their natural rights and making covenants with their neighbors, leading to mutual agreement for the foundation of some external power to enforce these covenants. Thus is created the state and society, because no society exists until it is organized. Justice is impossible outside the state. Since the sovereign is a third party chosen to enforce promises, he is outside and above the social contract or the law of the state. Hence the sovereign power must be absolute and indivisible and all citizens must submit to it. Every man, by accepting the social order in which he lives, tacitly accepts the social contract and cannot rebel against this order, while the sovereign power is the power that makes the laws, is above the law, above justice and morality, and has no duties toward the people. The state is a mortal god to whom, under the immortal God, we owe our safety and defense. Hobbes favored monarchy because it is the type of sovereignty which best maintains the unity of the state. He subordinated individual opinion, intellectual and religious life, as well as social behavior, to the state.

Basically, Hobbes was unhistorical in his approach and had no theory of social development and none of social progress; he was interested only in certain elements of political life that he regarded as fixed, and had no place for ethics (which he absorbed into politics). His ideas probably influenced Cromwell in assuming dictatorial powers, and were revived in the second half of the eighteenth century by Bentham and Austin. His comparison of the state to a human organism was developed later by Spencer and the sociologists. Spinoza also used some of his ideas. But Hobbes remained the most extreme proponent of the absolute nature of sovereignty (surpassing Machiavelli, Bodin and Grotius). He was in line with Bodin and Richelieu, regarding sovereign power as the only basis for effective government, and reinforced his arguments for absolutism by means of the social contract theory—a leading premise among political thinkers up to the French Revolution. Hobbes has also been accused of providing Communist and Fascist totalitarians with a verbal defense for their aggressions.

Thomas Hobbes

*Of the Natural Condition of Mankind as Concerning Their Felicity And Misery**

NATURE HATH MADE men so equal, in the faculties of the body and mind; as that though there be found one man sometimes manifestly stronger in body, or of quicker mind than another, yet when all is reckoned together, the difference between man and man, is not so considerable, as that one man can thereupon claim to himself any benefit, to which another may not pretend, as well as he. For as to the strength of body, the weakest has strength enough to kill the strongest, either by secret machination, or by confederacy with others, there are in the same danger with himself.

And as to the faculties of the mind, setting aside the arts grounded upon words, and especially that skill proceeding upon general and infallible rules, called science; which very few have, and but in few things; as being not a native faculty, born with us; nor attained, as prudence, while we look after somewhat else, I find yet a greater equality amongst men than that of strength. For prudence is but experience; which equal time, equally bestows on all men, in those things they equally apply themselves unto. That which may perhaps make such equality incredible, is but a vain conceit of one's own wisdom, which almost all men think they have in a greater degree than the vulgar; that is, than all men but themselves, and a few others, whom by fame or for concurring with themselves, they approve. For such is the nature of men, that howsoever they may acknowledge many others to be more witty, or more eloquent, or more learned; yet they will hardly believe there be many so wise as themselves; for they see their own wit at hand,

* This excerpt taken from Thomas Hobbes, *The Leviathan, or the Matter, Form and Power of a Commonwealth, Ecclesiastical and Civil,* London, n.d., pp. 63-65; 82-88.

and other men's at a distance. But this proveth rather that men are in that point equal, than unequal. For there is not ordinarily a greater sign of the equal distribution of anything, than that every man is contented with his share.

From this equality of ability, ariseth equality of hope in the attaining of our ends. And therefore if any two men desire the same thing, which nevertheless they cannot both enjoy, they become enemies; and in the way to their end, which is principally their own conservation, and sometimes their delectation only, endeavour to destroy or subdue one another. And from hence it comes to pass, that where an invader hath no more to fear than another man's single power; if one plant, sow, build, or possess a convenient seat, others may probably be expected to come prepared with forces united, to dispossess and deprive him, not only of the fruit of his labour, but also of his life or liberty. And the invader again is in the like danger of another.

And from this diffidence of one another, there is no way for any man to secure himself, so reasonable, as anticipation; that is, by force, or wiles, to master the persons of all men he can, so long, till he see no other power great enough to endanger him: and this is no more than his own conservation requireth, and is generally allowed. Also because there be some, that taking pleasure in contemplating their own power in the acts of conquest, which they pursue farther than their security requires; if others, that otherwise would be glad to be at ease within modest bounds, should not by invasion increase their power, they would not be able, long time, by standing only on their defence, to subsist. And by consequence, such augmentation of dominion over men being necessary to a man's conservation, it ought to be allowed him.

Again, men have no pleasure, but on the contrary a great deal of grief, in keeping company, where there is no power able to overawe them all. For every man looketh that his companion should value him, at the same rate he sets upon himself: and upon all signs of contempt, or undervaluing, naturally endeavors, as far as he dares (which amongst them that have no common power to keep them in quiet, is far enough to make them destroy each other) to exort a greater value from his contemners, by damage; and from others, by the example.

So that in the nature of man, we find three principal causes of quarrel. First, competition; secondly, diffidence; thirdly, glory.

The first, maketh men invade for gain; the second, for safety; and the third, for reputation. The first use violence, to make themselves masters of other men's persons, wives, children and cattle; the second, to defend them; the third, for trifles, as a word, a smile, a different opinion, and any other sign of undervalue, either direct in their persons, or by reflection in their kindred, their friends, their nation, their profession, or their name.

Hereby it is manifest, that during the time men live without a common power to keep them all in awe, they are in that condition which is called war; and such a war, as is of every man, against every man. For "war" consisteth not in battle only, or the act of fighting but in a tract of time, wherein the will to contend by battle is sufficiently known: and therefore the notion of "time" is to be considered in the nature of war, as it is in the nature of weather. For as the nature of foul weather lieth not in a shower or two of rain, but in an inclination thereto of many days together; so the nature of war consisteth not in actual fighting but in the known disposition thereto during all the time there is no assurance to the contrary. All other time is "peace."

Whatsoever therefore is consequent to time of war, where every man is enemy to every man, the same is consequent to the time wherein men live without other security than what their own strength and their own invention shall furnish them withal. In such condition there is no place for industry, because the fruit thereof is uncertain, and consequently no culture of the earth; no navigation, nor use of the commodities that may be imported by sea, no commodious building; no instruments of moving and removing such things as require much force; no knowledge of the face of the earth; no account of time; no arts, no letters, no society; and, which is worst of all, continual fear and danger of violent death; and the life of man, solitary, poor, nasty, brutish, and short.

It may seem strange to some man, that has not well weighed these things, that Nature should thus dissociate, and render men apt to invade and destroy one another; and he may therefore, not trusting to this inference made from the passions, desire perhaps to have the same confirmed by experience. Let him therefore consider with himself, when taking a journey, he arms himself, and seeks to go well accompanied; when going to sleep, he locks his doors; when even in his house, he locks his chests; and this when he knows there be laws, and public officers, armed, to revenge all injuries shall be done him; what opinion he has of his fellow-subjects, when he rides armed; of his fellow-citizens, when he locks his doors; and of his children and servants, when he locks his chests. Does he not there as much accuse mankind by his actions as I do by my words? But neither of us accuse man's nature in it. The desires and other passions of man are in themselves no sin. No more are the actions that proceed from those passions, till they know a law that forbids them; which till laws be made they cannot know, nor can any law be made till they have agreed upon the person that shall make it.

It may peradventure be thought there was never such a time nor condition of war as this; and I believe it was never generally so, over all the world, but there are many places where they live so now. For the savage people in many places of America, except the government of small families, the concord whereof dependeth on natural lust, have no government at all, and live at this day in that brutish manner, as I said before. Howsoever, it may be perceived what manner of life there would be, where there were no common power to fear, by the manner of life which men that have formerly lived under a peaceful government, use to degenerate into a civil war.

But though there had never been any time, wherein particular men were in a condition of war one against another; yet in all times, kings, and persons of sovereign authority, because of the independency, are in continual jealousies, and in the state and posture of gladiators; having their weapons pointing, and their eyes fixed on one another; that is, their forts, garrisons and guns upon the frontiers of their kingdoms; and continual spies upon their neighbours; which is a posture of war. But because they uphold thereby the industry of their subjects; there does not follow it that misery which accompanies the liberty of particular men.

To this war of every man, against every man, this also is consequent; that nothing can be unjust. The notions of right and wrong, justice and injustice, have there no place. Where there is no common power, there is no law: where no law, no justice. Force and fraud, are in war the two cardinal virtues. Justice and injustice are none of the faculties neither of the body nor mind. If they were, they might be in a man that were alone in the world, as well as his senses, and passions. They are qualities that relate to men in society, not in solitude. It is consequent also to the same condition, that there be no propriety, no dominion, no "mine" and "thine" distinct; but only that to be every man's, that he can get; and for so long, as he can keep it. And thus much for the ill condition, which man by mere nature is actually placed in; though with a possibility to come out of it, consisting partly in the passions, partly in his reason.

The passions that incline men to peace, are fear of death; desire of such things as are necessary to commodious living; and a hope by their industry to obtain them. And reason suggesteth convenient articles of peace, upon which men may be drawn to agreement. These articles are they which otherwise are called the Laws of Nature. . . .

The Right of Nature, which writers commonly call *jus naturale,* is the liberty each man hath, to use his own power, as he will himself, for the preservation of his own nature; that is to say, of his own life: and consequently, of doing anything, which in his own judgement and reason, he shall conceive to be the aptest means thereunto.

By liberty, is understood, according to the proper signification of the word, the absence of external impediments: which impediments, may oft take away part of a man's power to do what he would but cannot hinder him from using the power left him, according as his judgment, and reason shall dictate to him.

A law of nature, *lex naturalis,* is a precept or general rule, found out by reason, by which a man is forbidden to do that, which is destructive of his life, or taketh away the means of preserving the same: and to omit that, by which he thinketh it may be best preserved. For though they that speak of this subject, use to confound *jus,* and *lex, right* and *law*: yet they ought to be distinguished; because right, consisteth in liberty to do, or to forbear; whereas law, determineth, and bindeth to one of them: so that law, and right, differ as much, as obligation, and liberty; which in one and the same matter are inconsistent.

And because the condition of man, as hath been declared in the precedent chapter, is a condition of war of every one against every one; in which case every one is governed by his own reason; and there is nothing he can make use of, that may not be a help unto him, in preserving his life against his enemies; it followeth, that in such a condition, every man has a right to every thing; even to one another's body. And therefore, as long as this natural right of every man to every thing endureth, there can be no security to any man, how strong or wise soever he be, of living out the time, which nature ordinarily alloweth men to live. And consequently it is a precept, or general rule of reason, *that every man, ought to endeavour peace, as far as he has hope of ob-*

taining it; and when he cannot obtain it, that he may seek, and use, all helps, and advantages of war. The first branch of which rule, containeth the first, and fundamental law of nature: which is, *to seek peace, and follow it.* The second, the sum of the right of nature; which is, *by all means we can, to defend ourselves.*

From this fundamental law of nature, by which men are commanded to endeavour peace, is derived this second law; *that a man be willing, when others are so too, as far forth, as for peace, and defence of himself he shall think it necessary, to lay down this right to all things; and be contented with so much liberty against other men, as he would allow other men against himself.* For as long as every man holdeth this right, of doing any thing he liketh; so long are all men in the condition of war. But if other men will not lay down their right, as well as he; then there is no reason for anyone, to divest himself of his: for that were to expose himself to peace. This is that law of the Gospel; *whatsoever you require that others should do to you, that do ye to them. . . .*

If a convenant be made, wherein neither of the parties perform presently, but trust one another; in the condition of mere nature, which is a condition of war of every man against every man, upon any reasonable suspicion, it is void: but if there be a common power set over them both, with right and force sufficient to compel performance, it is not void. For he that performeth first, has no assurance the other will perform after; because the bonds of words are too weak to bridle men's ambition, avarice, anger, and other passions, without the fear of some coercive power; which in the condition of mere nature, where all men are equal, and judges of the justness of their own fears cannot possibly be supposed. . . .

The force of words, being . . . too weak to hold men to the performance of their covenants; there are in man's nature, but two imaginable helps to strengthen it. And those are either a fear of the consequence of breaking their word; or a glory, or pride in appearing not to need to break it. This latter is a generosity too rarely found to be presumed on, especially in the pursuers of wealth, command, or sensual pleasure; which are the greatest part of mankind. The passion to be reckoned upon, is fear; whereof there be two very general objects: one, the power of spirits invisible; the other, the power of those men they shall therein offend. Of these two, though the former be the greater power, yet the fear of the latter is commonly the greater fear. The fear of the former is in every man, his own religion: which hath place in the nature of man before civil society. The latter hath not so; at least not place enough, to keep men to their promises; because in the condition of mere nature, the inequality of power is not discerned, but by the event of battle. So that before the time of civil society, or in the interruption thereof by war, there is nothing can strengthen a covenant of peace agreed on, against the temptations of avarice, ambition, lust, or other strong desire, but the fear of that invisible power, which they every one worship as God; and fear as a revenger of their perfidy. . . .

THOMAS JEFFERSON
(1743-1826)

Third President of the United States (1801-1809), gentleman and a scholar, with diplomatic and legal training, drafted the Declaration of Independence, became Governor of Virginia (1779-1781), was U.S. Minister to France (1785-1789), and founded the Democratic Republican party which won him the Presidential election as the successor to John Adams. As an opponent of the Federal party, he was bitterly attacked by Alexander Hamilton, another great thinker. During Jefferson's administration occurred the war with Tripoli, the Louisiana Purchase and the reduction of the national debt. He retired to Monticello in Virginia and died (as did John Adams) on Independence Day, July 4. On his tombstone, according to his will, is this inscription:

> Here was buried Thomas Jefferson
> Author of the Declaration of American Independence
> Of the Statute of Virginia for Religious Freedom
> and Father of the University of Virginia.

Jefferson did not want mentioned that he had held numerous political offices and often protested that he disliked politics and preferred the peaceful life on his farm and among his books. With his meditative mind, he was not really a man of action, and yet for decades he was involved in political struggles because they concerned not so much his material interests as his philosophy; and it was his philosophy which, in broad outlines, produced a great political upheaval and resulted in his victory over men of action and his election to the Presidency. In religion he was a Deist, but he considered religious belief a purely individual matter.

His *Autobiography* (1821) reveals his fundamental outlook

on life (together with his *Works,* ed. by P. L. Lord, 1892, 10 vols.). His political philosophy was founded upon his idea of human nature; his motto was: "I cannot act as if all men were unfaithful because some are so. . . . I had rather be the victim of occasional infidelities than relinquish my general confidence in the honesty of man." This confidence disregarded differences of education, wealth and social position. The aim of his political activity was a life of freedom in which every individual would be able to develop his moral and intellectual nature and pursue his happiness. He firmly believed that Providence created man for society and endowed him with a sense of right and wrong so that an orderly society could exist. He was opposed to Calvinistic orthodoxy, advocated religious tolerance, emancipation of slaves and public education; as the leader of small farmers, shopkeepers and artisans, he disliked big business and large-scale industrialization. His ideas were rooted in Algernon Sydney and John Locke, liberalized to a certain point by Thomas Paine. While opposing monarchy, he believed in a natural aristocracy of ability and intelligence, that the consent of the people was a necessary basis of government, that an occasional revolution was a medicine needed for the health of the state, and he propounded a regular procedure for the periodic revision of fundamental law at nineteen-year intervals. While he added little to political theory, the political consequences of his ideas identified the United States with the world-wide revolution of today. At the same time, nineteenth-century Southerners saw Jefferson as the "Father of States' Rights," while a century later, extreme nationalists saw the Jeffersonian spirit as the directing force of the New Deal. With the dedication of the Jefferson Memorial by Franklin D. Roosevelt in 1945, during the Jefferson Bicentennial, the "Sage of Monticello" passed into the American pantheon, where, as the first of the great American liberators, he lives on. His case against totalitarianism, though scattered through his numerous papers and correspondence and never summed up in a formal essay, is one of the most definite expositions of history. From the moving prologue to the Declaration of Independence to the vivid epilogue in the letters he wrote in 1826, he asserted the capacity of human nature to achieve both freedom and order without resort to coercion—

and, *per contra,* the impossibility of achieving either by means of coercion. His was the greatest influence among the Founders of the United States; he told Americans in which direction to go, to be generous in practicing liberty, to value all human beings, and to find equality as the solution to the problem of a free society, to cherish solidarity, and to be reasonable and moderate. His liberal theories were developed further by Jackson and Lincoln, and applied in the reforms of Republican and Democratic administrations in the present century.

---

*Jefferson's First Inaugural Address**

Friends and Fellow Citizens:

CALLED UPON to undertake the duties of the first executive office of our country, I avail myself of the presence of that portion of my fellow-citizens which is here assembled to express my grateful thanks for the favor with which they have been pleased to look toward me, to declare a sincere consciousness that the task is above my talents, and that I approach it with those anxious and awful presentiments which the greatness of the charge and the weakness of my powers so justly inspire. A rising nation, spread over a wide and fruitful land, traversing all the seas with the rich productions of their industry, engaged in commerce with nations who feel power and forget right, advancing rapidly to destinies beyond the reach of mortal eye—when I contemplate these transcendent objects, and see the honor, the happiness, and the hopes of this beloved country committed to the issue and the auspices of this day, I shrink from the contemplation, and humble myself before the magnitude of the undertaking. Utterly, indeed, should I despair did not the presence of many whom I here see remind me that in the other high

* This excerpt taken from Harold C. Syrett, ed., *American Historical Documents,* New York: Barnes & Noble, 1960, pp. 150-151.

authorities provided by our Constitution I shall find resources of wisdom, of virtue, and of zeal on which to rely under all difficulties. To you, then, gentlemen, who are charged with the sovereign functions of legislation, and to those associated with you, I look with encouragement for that guidance and support which may enable us to steer with safety the vessel in which we are all embarked amidst the conflicting elements of a troubled world.

During the contest of opinion through which we have passed the animation of discussions and of exertions has sometimes worn an aspect which might impose on strangers unused to think freely and to speak and to write what they think; but this being now decided by the voice of the nation, announced according to the rules of the Constitution, all will, of course, arrange themselves under the will of the law, and unite in common efforts for the common good. All, too, will bear in mind this sacred principle, that though the will of the majority is in all cases to prevail, that will to be rightful must be reasonable; that the minority possess their equal rights, which law must protect, and to violate would be oppression. Let us, then, fellow-citizens, unite with one heart and one mind. Let us restore to social intercourse that harmony and affection without which liberty and even life itself are but dreary things. And let us reflect that, having banished from our land that religious intolerance under which mankind so long bled and suffered, we have yet gained little if we countenance a political intolerance as despotic, as wicked, and capable of as bitter and bloody persecutions. During the throes and convulsions of the ancient world, during the agonizing spasms of infuriated man, seeking through blood and slaughter his long-lost liberty, was it not wonderful that the agitation of the billows should reach even this distant and peaceful shore; that this should be more felt and feared by some and less by others, and should divide opinions as to measures of safety. But every difference of opinion is more difference of principle. We have called different names brethren of the same principle. We are all Republicans, we are all Federalists. If there be any among us who would wish to dissolve this Union or to change its republican form, let them stand undisturbed as monuments of the safety with which error of opinion may be tolerated where reason is left free to combat it. I know, indeed, that some honest men fear that a republican government can not be strong, that this Government is not strong enough; but would the honest patriot, in the full tide of successful experiment abandon a government which has so far kept us free and firm on the theoretic and visionary fear that this Government, the world's best hope, may by possibility want energy to preserve itself? I trust not. I believe this, on the contrary, the strongest Government on earth. . . .

IN CONGRESS, JULY 4, 1776.

A DECLARATION

BY THE REPRESENTATIVES OF THE UNITED STATES OF AMERICA, IN GENERAL CONGRESS ASSEMBLED.

WHEN in the Course of human Events, it becomes necessary for one People to dissolve the Political Bands which have connected them with the Earth, the separate and equal Station to which the Laws of Nature and of Nature's God entitle them, a decent Respect to the Opinions of Mankind requires that they should declare the causes which impel them to the Separation.

WE hold these Truths to be self-evident, that all Men are created equal, that they are endowed by their Creator with [inherent and] *certain* unalienable Rights, that among these are Life, Liberty, and the Pursuit of Happiness—That to secure these Rights, Governments are instituted among Men, deriving their just Powers from the Consent of the Governed, that whenever any Form of Government becomes destructive of these Ends, it is the Right of the People to alter or to abolish it, and to institute new Government, laying its Foundation on such Principles, and organizing its Powers in such Form, as to them shall seem most likely to effect their Safety and Happiness. Prudence, indeed, will dictate that Government long established should not be changed for light and transient Causes; and accordingly all Experience hath shewn, that Mankind are more disposed to suffer, while Evils are sufferable, than to right themselves by abolishing the Forms to which they are accustomed. But when a long Train of Abuses and Usurpations [begun at a distinguished period and], pursuing invariably the same Object, evinces a Design to reduce them under absolute Despotism, it is their Right, it is their Duty, to throw off such Government, and to provide new Guards for their future Security. Such has been the patient Sufferance of these Colonies; and such is now the Necessity which constrains them to [expunge] *alter* their former Systems of Government. The History of the present King of Great-Britain is a History of [unremitting] *repeated* Injuries and Usurpations, [among which appears no solitary fact to contradict the uniform tenor of the rest, but all have] *all having* in direct Object the Establishment of an absolute Tyranny over these States. To prove this, let Facts be submitted to a candid World [for the truth of which we pledge a faith yet unsullied by falsehood].

He has refused his Assent to Laws, the most wholesome and necessary for the public Good.

He has forbidden his Governors to pass Laws of immediate and pressing Importance, unless suspended in their Operation till his Assent should be obtained; and when so suspended, he has utterly neglected to attend to them.

He has refused to pass other Laws for the Accommodation of large Districts of People, unless those People would relinquish the Right of Representation in the Legislature, a Right inestimable to them, and formidable to Tyrants only.

He has called together Legislative Bodies at Places unusual, uncomfortable, and distant from the Depository of their public Records, for the sole Purpose of fatiguing them into Compliance with his Measures.

He has dissolved Representative Houses repeatedly [and continually], for opposing with manly Firmness his Invasions on the Rights of the People.

He has refused for a long Time, after such Dissolutions, to cause others to be elected; whereby the Legislative Powers, incapable of Annihilation, have returned to the People at large for their exercise; the State remaining in the mean time exposed to all the Dangers of Invasion from without, and Convulsions within.

He has endeavoured to prevent the Population of these States; for that Purpose obstructing the Laws for Naturalization of Foreigners; refusing to pass others to encourage their Migrations hither, and raising the Conditions of new Appropriations of Lands.

He has [suffered] *obstructed* the Administration of Justice [totally to cease in some of these States], *by* refusing his Assent to Laws for establishing Judiciary Powers.

He has made [our] Judges dependent on his Will alone, for the Tenure of their Offices, and the Amount and Payment of their Salaries.

He has erected a Multitude of new Offices [by a self-assumed power], and sent hither Swarms of Officers to harass our People; and eat out their Substance.

He has kept among us, in Times of Peace, Standing Armies [and ships of war], without the consent of our Legislatures.

He has affected to render the Military independent of and superior to the Civil Power.

He has combined with others to subject us to a Jurisdiction foreign to our Constitution, and unacknowledged by our Laws; giving his Assent to their Acts of pretended Legislation:

For quartering large Bodies of Armed Troops among us:

For protecting them, by a mock Trial, from Punishment for any Murders which they should commit on the Inhabitants of these States:

For cutting off our Trade with all Parts of the World:

For imposing Taxes on us without our Consent:

For depriving us, *in many Cases,* of the Benefits of Trial by Jury:

For transporting us beyond Seas to be tried for pretended offences:

For abolishing the free System of English Laws in a neighbouring Province, establishing therein an arbitrary Government, and enlarging its Boundaries, so as to render it at once an Example and fit Instrument for introducing the same absolute Rule into these [States] *Colonies*:

For taking away our Charters, abolishing our most valuable Laws, and altering fundamentally the Forms of our Governments:

For suspending our own Legislatures, and declaring themselves invested with Power to legislate for us in all Cases whatsoever.

He has abdicated Government here, [withdrawing his governors, and declaring us out of his allegiance and protection] *by declaring us out of his Protection and waging War against us.*

He has plundered our Seas, ravaged our Coasts, burnt our Towns, and destroyed the Lives of our People.

He is, at this Time, transporting large Armies of foreign Mercenaries to compleat the Works of Death, Desolation and Tyranny, already begun with circumstances of Cruelty and Perfidy, scarcely paralleled in the most barbarous Ages, and totally unworthy the Head of a civilized Nation.

He has constrained our fellow Citizens taken Captive on the high Seas to bear Arms against their Country, to become the Executioners of their Friends and Brethren, or to fall themselves by their Hands.

He has *excited Insurrections amongst us, and has* endeavoured to bring on the Inhabitants of our Frontiers, the merciless Indian Savages, whose known Rule of Warfare, is an undistinguished Destruction of all Ages, Sexes and Conditions [of existence].

[He has incited treasonable insurrections of our fellow citizens, with the allurements of forfeiture and confiscation of our property.

He has waged cruel war against human nature itself, violating its most sacred rights of life and liberty in the persons of a distant people who never offended him, captivating and carrying them into slavery in another hemisphere, or to incur miserable death in their transportation thither. This piratical warfare, the opprobrium of INFIDEL powers, is the warfare of the CHRISTIAN King of Great Britain. Determined to keep open a market where MEN should be bought and sold, he has prostituted his negative for suppressing every legislative attempt to prohibit or to restrain this execrable commerce. And that this assemblage of horrors might want no fact of distinguished die, he is now exciting those very people to rise in arms among us, and to purchase that liberty of which he has deprived them, by murdering the people on whom he also obtruded them: thus paying off former crimes committed against the LIBERTIES of one people with crimes which he urges them to commit against the LIVES of another.]

IN every stage of these Oppressions we have Petitioned for redress in the most humble Terms: Our repeated Petitions have been answered only by repeated Injury. A Prince, whose Character is thus marked by every act which may define a Tyrant, is unfit to be the Ruler of a *free* People [who mean to be free. Future ages will scarcely believe that the hardiness of one man adventured, within the short compass of twelve years only, to lay a foundation so broad and so undisguised for tyranny over a people fostered and fixed in principles of freedom.]

NOR have we been wanting in Attentions to our British Brethren. We have warned them from Time to Time of Attempts by their Legislature to extend [a] *an unwarrantable* jurisdiction over [these our States] *us.* We have reminded them of the Circumstances of our Emigration and Settlement here [, no one of which could warrant so strange a pretension: that these were effected at the expense of our own blood and treasure, unassisted by the wealth or the strength of Great Britain: that in constituting indeed our several forms of government, we had adopted one common king, thereby laying a foundation for perpetual league and amity with them: but that submission to their parliament was no part of our Constitution, nor ever in idea, if history may be credited: and,]. We *have* appealed to their native Justice and Magnanimity [as well as to] *and we have conjured them by* the Ties of our common Kindred to disavow these Usurpations, which, [were likely to] *would inevitably* interrupt our Connections and Correspondence. They too have been deaf to the Voice of Justice and of Consanguinity [, and when occasions have been given them, by the regular course of their laws, of removing from their councils the disturbers of our harmony, they have, by their free election, reestablished them in power. At this very time too, they are permitting their chief magistrate to send over not only soldiers of our common blood, but Scotch and foreign mercenaries to invade and destroy us. These facts have given the last stab to agonizing affection and manly spirit bids us to renounce forever these unfeeling brethren. We must endeavor to forget our former love for them, and hold them as we hold the rest of mankind, enemies in war, in peace friends. We might have been a free and a great people together; but a communication of grandeur and of freedom, it seems, is below their dignity. Be it so, since they will have it. The road to happiness and to glory is open to us too. We will treat it apart from them, and]. We must, therefore, acquiesce in the Necessity, which denounces our [eternal] Separation, *and hold them, as we hold the rest of Mankind, Enemies in War, in Peace, Friends.*

We therefore the Representatives of the UNITED STATES OF

AMERICA in GENERAL CONGRESS, Assembled, *appealing to the Supreme Judge of the World for the Rectitude of our Intentions,* do, in the Name, and by the Authority of the good People of these [States reject and renounce all allegiance and subjection to the kings of Great Britain and all others who may hereafter claim by, through, or under them; we utterly dissolve all political connection which may heretofore have subsisted between us and the people or parliament of Great Britain: and finally we do assert and declare these Colonies to be free and independent States,] *Colonies, solemnly Publish and Declare, That these United Colonies are, and of Right ought to be,* FREE AND INDEPENDENT STATES; *that they are absolved from all Allegiance to the British Crown, and that all political Connection between them and the State of Great Britain is, and ought to be, totally dissolved;* and that as FREE AND INDEPENDENT STATES, they have full Power to levy War, conclude Peace, contract Alliances, establish Commerce, and to do all other Acts and Things which INDEPENDENT STATES may of right do.

And for the support of this Declaration, *with a firm Reliance on the Protection of divine Providence,* we mutually pledge to each other our Lives, our Fortunes, and our sacred Honor.

Signed by ORDER *and in* BEHALF *of the* CONGRESS,

JOHN HANCOCK, PRESIDENT.

ATTEST.

CHARLES THOMSON, SECRETARY.

JOSEPH II OF AUSTRIA
(1740-1790)

The Hapsburg scion and son of Empress Maria Theresa, was the most sincere of the benevolent despots of his century. During his reign he dealt with two basic problems: the consolidation of the Austrian Empire and the initiation of reform movements in which he strongly believed. His reforms included the establishment of an equitable basis for taxation and the improvement of education. His abolition of serfdom was the most revolutionary decree of this period, but his most lasting reform was the creation of a national court system. Joseph was truly the philosopher-king in action. But many of his reforms appeared premature and he was considered too hasty in adopting new measures. Frederick the Great observed that "Joseph always wishes to take the second step before he has taken the first." He died a broken-hearted man.

---

*To van Swieten; to Count Kollowrat, Grand Chancellor of Bohemia, and First Chancellor of Austria; to a Hungarian Magnat; to Tobias Philip, Baron von Gebler, Bohemian and Austrian Vice-Chancellor**

To van Swieten [*December 1780*].

MON CHER,—I do not know how some monarchs can occupy their minds with such trifles, as to acquire literary accomplishments; to seek a sort of greatness in making verses, in

* Excerpts taken from "Letters of Joseph II," *The Pamphleteer,* London, 1822, XIX, pp. 275-76, 281-83, 287-90, *passim.*

drawing a plan for a theatre, which is to be placed beside the works of Palladio.

I conceive that kings ought not to be entirely unacquainted with the sciences; but that a monarch should pass his time in writing madrigals is, in my opinion, very unnecessary.

The Margrave of Brandenburg has become the head of a sect of kings, who occupy themselves in writing memoirs, poems, and treatises. The Empress of Russia imitated him, studied Voltaire, and wrote dramas and verses to Vanhal; then some odes to her Alcides. Stanislaus Lesczinsky wrote letters of pacification; and, lastly, the King of Sweden letters of friendship.

Their inducements for writing are as singular as their productions. The King of Prussia began his academical occupations at Rheinsberg, whither his father had exiled him, and where he could scarcely live in the style of one of my colonels. When he became king he continued his learned engagements; immediately a number of French champions assembled around him, and sung his victories in Silesia; that is to say, the conquests of a country, which was defended by two regiments of infantry, and which he overran with forty thousand men. At a later period, his passion for making verses induced him to enter into friendship with Voltaire, which, however, was broken off, renewed, again dissolved, and afterwards continued till the death of that watchmaker of Ferney.

The Empress of Russia undertook it from pride; she wished to shine in every thing; time and circumstances, love and friendship, and perhaps a portion of vanity, did the rest. . . .

You see how I think on these matters. The illustrious Greeks and Romans are not unknown to me; I know the history of the German empire, and that of my states in particular; but my time never allowed me to make epigrams, or to write Vaudevilles. I read for instruction; I travelled for the enlargement of my views; and when I patronise men of letters, I do them more service than if I were sitting down with one of them to compose unmeaning sonnets. Adieu!

To Count Kollowrat, Grand Chancellor of Bohemia, and First Chancellor of Austria [*October 1784*].

Sir,—For the encouragement of home productions, and in order to check the progress of luxury and fashion, my commands respecting a general prohibition of foreign merchandise have been made known.

The Austrian commerce has become more passive in consequence of the increasing consumption of foreign productions, and the funds of the state, which has thereby lost more than twenty-four millions annually, would by this time have been nearly exhausted, but for the produce of our excellent mines.

It has been hitherto, one would almost think, the particular object of the Austrian government to benefit the manufacturers and merchants of the French, English, and Chinese, and to deprive itself of all the advantages the state must necessarily enjoy, when it provides for the national wants by national industry.

I know what sensations the prohibition caused among the merchants . . . and I have conversed with Prince Kaunitz on this subject, but I granted them nothing, except that I prolonged the term for their disposing of the foreign merchandise; and more they do not deserve; they are merely the commissioners of the other European merchants.

As to the rest, Prince Kaunitz will give the necessary instructions to the officers of the Custom-houses, that inventories may be made of the stock; that depots may be established; and in general, that such dispositions may be made as will ensure the execution of my orders.

To a Hungarian Magnat [*January 1785*].

Sir,—Every representation which is made to me, whether it concerns the welfare of an individual, or the rights of a whole nation, must be supported by undeniable facts to induce me to alter a resolution previously made.

In the representations, however, of your nation, I see nothing whatever of this. With respect to the new system of taxation for the kingdom, and the German language, which I ordained to be used in the Courts of Justice, I will very briefly give you my sentiments.

The former ensures to the subject his property, fixes the taxes for the crown, and those for the lords of the manor, as has been long customary in my hereditary German dominions, and prevents the nobility from making an arbitrary increase for their own profit. Is this no advantage to the common people? The peasant, who is obliged to bear the greatest burdens of the public wants, has also an especial claim on the protection of his sovereign; and this, Sir, in your country is viewed with dissatisfaction.

The German language is the universal language of my empire; why should the laws be administered, and public affairs transacted, in a single province in its own language? I am Emperor of the German Empire; consequently the other states which I possess are provinces, which, together with the whole state, form one body, of which I am the head. If the kingdom of Hungaria was the most important and the chief of my possessions, I would make its language the principal language of my dominions; but it is otherwise.

Although the orders which I have given in this affair, clearly enough evince my sentiments, I am nevertheless always ready, on proper occasions, more fully to explain the positiveness of my principles, even to individual subjects of my dominions.—My Count! you have here a proof of it.

To Tobias Philip, Baron von Gebler, Bohemian and Austrian Vice-Chancellor [*1785*].

Mr. Vice-Chancellor,—The present system of taxation in my dominions, and the inequality of the taxes which are imposed on the nation, form a subject too important to escape my attention. I have discovered that the principles on which it is founded are unsound, and have become injurious to the industry of the peasant; that there is neither equality, nor equity, between the hereditary provinces with each other, nor between individual proprietors, and therefore it can no longer continue.

With this view I give you the necessary orders to introduce a new system of taxation, by which the contribution, requisite for the wants of the state, may be effected without augmenting the present taxes, and the industry of the peasant, at the same time, be freed from all impediments.

Make these arrangements the principal object of your care, and let them be made conformably to the plan which I have proposed, particularly as I have nominated you President of the Aulic Commission, appointed for that purpose.

Adieu, Gebler! Hasten every thing that brings me nearer to the accomplishment of my plans for the happiness of my people, and, by your zeal, justify the respect which they have always had for your services.

IMMANUEL KANT

(1724-1804)

Actually made no original contribution to political thought, being more interested in analyzing fundamental concepts than in practical questions of politics and administration. But the acceptance of his philosophy promoted liberal ideas and promoted attempts to create representative institutions and national unity (*Metaphysical First Principles of the Theory of Law,* translated 1796; *For Perpetual Peace,* translated 1795). In his famed *Critique of Pure Reason* he propounded that *a priori* knowledge is possible, that by virtue of the forms and categories of the mind, such as space, time and causality, man possesses the presuppositions for coherent and intelligible experience. It is true, however, that we know only by appearances, colors, sounds and the like, never the thing-in-itself. He maintained that true knowledge cannot transcend or go beyond experience; yet, for the sake of religion and morality, we need such concepts as God, soul, freedom and immortality. In the categorical imperative Kant laid a foundation for morality by enjoining man to act in such a way that the maxim of his will may at the same time be raised into a principle of universal law. He inspired many by his treatise on eternal peace; for him, the European system of a balance of power could never create a lasting peace and he favored the subordination of the state to a federal league of nations, creating a "system of international right, founded upon public laws conjoined with power, to which every state must submit." His political concepts were merely elaborations of Rousseau and Montesquieu whose ideas he fitted into the categories of his philosophy. He believed men to be free and equal by nature and that the state represents a contract by which the natural rights of each individual are placed under the guarantee of the whole people. Sovereignty resides in the people, whose general will is the source of law and is expressed by a constitution; the separation of legislative and executive power is basic to liberty. The authority of the people may be represented by elected deputies, or by a king and a nobility. Fearing the influences from revolutionary France, he allowed no right to revolution, insisting that changes in the constitution must be made in a legal way by the sovereign himself (or itself). The abstract principles underlying morals, law and politics include the right of each individual to will and to impose limitations upon himself; mutual limitations upon men living in society are imposed by law, representing the general will. Freedom is basically subjective, and the individual is an end in himself. The supreme value of the rational man is the dominant idea of Kant's philosophy. While Hume claimed that there can be no universal laws which mankind can know, and that there can be no universal foundation for a rational ethics, Kant's position, applied to politics, was to retrieve what was valuable in Rousseau, and to proclaim the moral ultimacy of the individual as the basis of all ethics. On this foundation, subsequent democratic thought, in some cases buttressed by Christian doctrine, has been based ever since.

---

*Perpetual Peace**

SECTION I

Containing the Preliminary Articles for a Perpetual Peace Among States

I. "No treaty of peace shall be esteemed valid, on which is tacitly reserved matter for future war."

A treaty of this sort would be only a truce, a suspension, not a complete cessation of hostilities. To call such a peace perpetual, would be a suspicious pleonasm. By a treaty of

* This excerpt taken from Immanuel Kant, *Perpetual Peace*, with an introduction by Nicholas Murray Butler, New York: Columbia University Press, 1939; copyright 1932 U.S. Library Association, Inc., pp. 2-7.

peace, every subject (at the time perhaps unthought of by the contracting parties) for renewing war, becomes annihilated, even should it, by the most refined cunning, be dug out from the dusty documents of archives. The reservation (*reservatio mentalis*) of ancient pretensions to be declared hereafter, of which neither party makes mention at the time, both too much exhausted to carry on the war, together with the bad design of carrying them into effect at the first favourable opportunity, belongs to the casuistry of a jesuit; estimated in itself, it is beneath the dignity of a sovereign, as the readiness of making deductions of this kind is beneath the dignity of a minister.

But if in consequence of enlightened principles of politics, the glory of the state is placed in its continual aggrandizement, by whatever means; my reasoning will then appear mere scholastic pedantry.

II. "Any state, of whatever extent, shall never pass under the dominion of another state, whether by inheritance, exchange, purchase, or donation."

A state is not, like the soil upon which it is situate, a patrimony. It consists of a society of men, over whom the state alone has a right to command and dispose. It is a trunk which has its own roots. But, like a graft to incorporate it with another state, would be to reduce it from a moral person, to the condition of a thing, which contradicts the idea of a social compact, without which one cannot conceive of a right over a people.

Every one knows to what dangers Europe, the only part of the world where this abuse has existed, has been exposed, even down to our time, by this mercantile precedent, that states may espouse one another; a new kind of contrivance, which obtains, by means of family alliances, and without any repence of forces, excess of power, or an immoderate increase of domain.

By a consequence of the same principle, it is forbidden to every state to let troops to another state, against an enemy not common to both; for this is making one of the subjects as things to be disposed of at pleasure.

III. "Standing armies (*miles perpetuus*) shall in time be totally abolished."

For being ever ready for action, they incessantly menace other states, and excite them to increase without end the number of armed men. This rivalship, a source of inexhaustible expence, renders peace even more burthensome than a short war, and frequently causes hostilities to be commenced with the mere view of being delivered thereby from so oppressive a load. Add to this, that to be paid for killing, or to be killed, is to serve as an instrument or machine in the hands of another (the state) which is incompatible with the right which nature has given to every one his own person.

Very different from this are the military exercises voluntarily undertaken, and at stated times, by the citizens, in order to secure themselves and their country against foreign aggressions.

Treasure, a means of military power, more efficacious perhaps than that of armies or alliances, would produce the same effect as standing armies, and would excite other states to war by menacing them with it, were it less difficult to become acquainted with the extent of the treasure.

IV. "National debts shall not be contracted with a view of maintaining the interests of the state abroad."

Money borrowed, either in the interior of a state or of a foreign nation, would be a resource by no means suspicious, if the sums thus obtained were destined to the economy of the country, such as the repairing of high roads, new colonies, the establishment of magazines against unfruitful years, &c. But what can we think of a system of credit, the ingenious invention of a commercial people of this century, by means of which debts are accumulated without end, and yet cause no embarrassment in their reimbursements, since the creditors never make their demands all at one time. Considered as a political engine, it is a dangerous means of monied power, a treaty for war, superior to that of all other states collectively, and which cannot be exhausted except by a default in the taxes (an exhaustion eventually certain, but long kept off by the favourable reaction credit has upon commerce and industry). This facility of carrying on war, united with the natural inclination men have for it as soon as they possess the power, is an invincible obstacle to a perpetual peace. The abolition of the funding system must therefore be a preliminary article; the more so, as sooner or later a national bankruptcy will take place, by which other states would innocently be involved, and find themselves openly aggrieved. They are therefore justifiable in joining in a confederacy against a state which adopts such obnoxious measures.

V. "No state shall by force interfere with either the constitution or government of another state."

What is there that can authorize such a step? Perhaps the offence given to the subjects of another state; but the example of anarchy may, on the contrary, warn them of the danger they run by exposing themselves to it. Moreover, the bad example one free being gives to another is an offence taken (*scandalum acceptum*) and not a lesion of their rights. Very different would it be, if a revolution should divide a state into two parts, each of which should pretend to the whole. To lend assistance to one of the parties cannot then be esteemed an interference with the government, it being then in a state of anarchy; but so long as these internal dissensions are not to that point, the interferences of a foreign power would be a violation of the rights of an independent nation, struggling with internal evils; it is then an offence given, that would render the autonomy of all states uncertain.

VI. "A state shall not, during war, admit of hostilities of a nature that would render reciprocal confidence in a succeeding peace impossible: such as employing assassins (*per-*

cussores), prisoners (*venefici*), violation of capitulations, secret instigation to rebellion (*perduellio*), &c."

These are dishonourable stratagems. Confidence in the principles of an enemy must remain even during war, otherwise a peace could never be concluded; and hostilities would degenerate into a war of extermination (*bellum internecimum*) since war in fact is but the end resource employed in a state of nature in defence of rights; force standing there in lieu of juridical tribunals. Neither of the two parties can be accused of injustice, since for that purpose a juridical decision would be necessary. But here the event of a battle (as formerly the *judgments of God*) determine the justice of either party; since between states there cannot be a war of punishment (*bellum punitiuum*) no subordination existing between them. . . .

NICOLAI LENIN
(Original Name: Vladimir Ilyich Ulyanov)
(1870-1924)

Was the intellectual architect and organizer of the Russian Revolution, whose writings (*Selected Works,* 12 vols., New York: International Publishers, 1938; *Collected Works,* 7 vols., New York: International Publishers, 1932, and others) have had an effect on countless minds far greater than the tremendous influence he exerted while alive on the history of the world and of Russia in particular. In fact, one of Lenin's major contributions to politics was his insistence, even while he impressed upon his followers the necessity of revolutionary practice, on the immense importance of theory. But Lenin's activities were so related to and influenced by his ideas and so influenced his and others' ideas, that one is reluctant to make a clear-cut distinction between doctrine and practice. Lenin was himself fond of quoting Goethe: "Theory is gray: what is green is the eternal tree of life." Thought divorced from experience was nonsense for him. At the same time, he was equally firm in propounding that there is no revolutionary action without revolutionary theory.

Lenin was born at Simbirsk, son of a college teacher, became a lawyer, joined the Labor movement, adopted the alias of Lenin, became a strict Marxist and led the radical, uncompromising wing of the Russian Socialist party which broke away from the moderate faction in 1903 under the name of "Bolsheviks." Living in exile in Paris, Vienna and Zurich from 1907-1917, he advocated a revolutionary course at Socialist congresses and denounced Socialist support of the war in 1914. After the Russian Revolution in March, 1917, he was transported to Russia by the German General Staff, which saw a chance of getting rid of the Russian enemy. He reached Petersburg in April, 1917, and took the leadership of the Bolshevik party. Together with Trotsky, he organized a first uprising in July (which proved abortive) and a second on November 7, 1919 (October 25 in the Russian calendar), which overthrew the Kerensky government. He became President of the Council of the People's Commissars, as the government was now called. Thereafter, proletarian dictatorship was exercised by the Workers' and Soldiers' Soviets (councils). Civil war followed and Lenin hastened to conclude peace at all costs with Germany and Austria-Hungary so as to have a free hand in the struggle. The civil war lasted till 1921, ending with the victory of the Bolsheviks (who had meanwhile adopted the name of Communists). Lenin organized the Communist (Third) International, combating the moderate Socialists. After the radical "war Communism" he adopted the New Economic Policy, admitting a number of capitalistic elements so as to speed up recovery. In 1922 he was shot at by a woman member of the anti-Bolshevik social revolutionary party and wounded; thereafter his health declined. He fell ill in 1923 and died on January 21, 1924. His body was embalmed and has been permanently exhibited (with that of Stalin, until 1961) in the Lenin mausoleum in Moscow; Petersburg was renamed Leningrad in his honor.

Lenin applied the Marxist approach to the new forms of capitalism which had developed since the conclusion of Marx's work. Following the inevitable concentration of capital, huge trusts and combines have superseded the small producers of the earlier stages of capitalism. Large capital interests and the state have become inextricably interwoven, and the former drove governments to imperialistic policies with a view to securing foreign markets and sources of raw materials. The clash of the various imperialisms leads to war in the interest of big capitalists. Yet imperialism is the very last stage of capitalism; it harbors the inner contradictions of capitalism in an increased degree; these will explode in ever greater crises and wars until the proletarian revolution overthrows capitalism and organizes socialism in its place. Out of colonial extra profits the big monopolists pay higher wages to skilled workers and thus a labor aristocracy arises which dominates the socialist parties and leads them on the way to reformism. The poorer classes of workers, however, continue to adhere to revolutionary socialism. This is the underlying cause of the rift between the moderate and radical factions in the socialist movement. Like Marx, Lenin defines the state as the instrument of the ruling class. The proletariat must destroy it and replace it with a new state machinery of its own. The parliamentary state is but a concealed dictatorship of the capitalistic class; it must be superseded by the Soviet state, the overt dictatorship of the proletariat. As class distinctions vanish and general welfare increases in the socialist society, social conditions will become harmonious and the proletarian state will pass into a stateless Communist society.

---

*The Two Phases of Communist Society**

THE FIRST PHASE of Communist Society. . . .

What we have to deal with here (in analyzing the programme of the workers' party) is a communist society, not as it has *developed* on its own foundations, but, on the contrary, just as it *emerges* from capitalist society; which is thus in every respect, economically, morally and intellectually, still stamped with the birthmarks of the old society from whose womb it emerges.

And it is this communist society—a society which has just emerged into the light of day out of the womb of capitalism and which, in every respect, bears the birthmarks of the old society—that Marx terms the "first," or lower phase of communist society. . . .

Hence, the first phase of communism cannot yet produce justice and equality: differences, and unjust differences, in wealth will still exist, but the *exploitation* of man by man will have become impossible, because it will be impossible to seize the *means of production,* the factories, machines, land, etc., as private property. . . .

Marx not only most scrupulously takes account of the inevitable inequality of men, but he also takes into account the fact that the mere conversion of the means of production

* Excerpts from V. I. Lenin, *The State and Revolution,* Moscow: Foreign Languages Publishing House, n. d., pp. 149-162.

into the common property of the whole of society (commonly called "socialism") *does not remove* the defects of distribution and the inequality of "bourgeois right" which *continues to prevail* as long as products are divided "according to the amount of labour performed." Continuing, Marx says:

. . . But these defects are inevitable in the first phase of communist society as it is when it has just emerged after prolonged birth pangs from capitalist society. Right can never be higher than the economic structure of society and its cultural development conditioned thereby. . . .

And so, in the first phase of communist society (usually called socialism) "bourgeois right" is *not* abolished in its entirety, but only in part, only in proportion to the economic revolution so far attained i.e., only in respect of the means of production. "Bourgeois right" recognizes them as the private property of individuals. Socialism converts them into *common* property. *To that extent*— and to that extent alone—"bourgeois right" disappears.

However, it continues to exist as far as its other part is concerned; it continues to exist in the capacity of regulator (determining factor) in the distribution of products and the allotment of labour among the members of society. The socialist principle: "He who does not work, neither shall he eat" is *already* realized; the other socialist principle: "an equal amount of products for an equal amount of labour," is also *already* realized. But this is not yet communism, and it does not yet abolish "bourgeois right," which gives to unequal individuals, in return for unequal (really unequal) amounts of labour, equal amounts of products.

This is a "defect," says Marx, but it is unavoidable in the first phase of communism; for if we are not to indulge in utopianism, we must not think that having overthrown capitalism people will at once learn to work for society *without any standard of right;* and indeed the abolition of capitalism *does not immediately create* the economic premises for *such* a change. . . . The state withers away in so far as there are no longer any capitalists, any classes, and, consequently, no *class* can be *suppressed.*

But the state has not yet completely withered away, since there still remains the safeguarding of "bourgeois right," which sanctifies actual inequality. For the state to wither away completely complete communism is necessary.

The Higher Phase of Communist Society. Marx continues:

In a higher phase of communist society, after the enslaving subordination of the individual to the division of labour, and therewith also the antithesis between mental and physical labour, has vanished; after labour has become not only a means of life but life's prime want; after the productive forces have also increased with the all-round development of the individual, and all the springs of cooperative wealth flow more abundantly—only then can the narrow horizon of "bourgeois right" be crossed in its entirety and society inscribe on its banners: "From each according to his ability, to each according to his needs!"

The economic basis for the complete withering away of the state is such a high stage of development of communism when the antithesis between mental and physical labour disappears, when there, consequently, disappears one of the principal sources of modern *social* inequality—a source, moreover, which cannot on any account be removed immediately by the mere conversion of the means of production into public property, by the mere expropriation of the capitalists.

This expropriation will create the *possibility* of an enormous development of the productive forces. And when we see how incredibly capitalism is already *retarding* this development, when we see how much progress could be achieved on the basis of the level of technique now already attained, we are entitled to say with the fullest confidence that the expropriation of the capitalists will inevitably result in an enormous development of the productive forces of human society. But how rapidly this development will proceed, how soon it will reach the point of breaking away from the division of labour, of doing away with the antithesis between mental and physical labour, of transforming labour into "the prime necessity of life"—we do not and *cannot* know.

It will become possible for the state to wither away completely when society adopts the rule: "From each according to his ability, to each according to his needs," when people have become so accustomed to observing the fundamental rules of social intercourse and when their labour becomes so productive that they will voluntarily work *according to their ability*. . . .

From the moment all members of society, or even only the vast majority, have learned to administer the state *themselves,* have taken this into their own hands, have set going control over the insignificant minority of capitalists, over the gentry who wish to preserve their capitalist habits and over the workers who have been profoundly corrupted by capitalism—from this moment the need for government of any kind begins to disappear altogether, the more complete the democracy, the nearer the moment approaches when it becomes unnecessary. . . .

For when *all* have learned to administer and actually do independently administer social production, independently keep accounts and exercise control over the idlers, the gentlefolk, the swindlers and suchlike "guardians of capitalist traditions," the escape from this popular accounting and control will inevitably become so incredibly difficult, . . . that the *necessity of observing* the simple, fundamental rules of human intercourse will very soon become a *habit*.

And then the door will be wide open for the transition from the first phase of communist society to its higher phase, and with it to the complete withering away of the state.

ABRAHAM LINCOLN

(1809-1865)

Sixteenth President of the United States, one of the foremost spokesmen of the Republican party before the Civil War, was elected in 1860 by only 40 percent of the popular vote (although he received a large majority in the electoral college). His election and subsequent inauguration touched off the Civil War. There was almost no hope of a peaceful resolution of the North-South tensions over the slavery issue, but as long as there was any at all, Lincoln explored it. In so doing he revealed quite a comprehensive understanding of the nature of political society. The evolution of Lincoln's policy was determined by his need to unite the sentiment of the North behind the administration, his belief that some of the slave states would remain loyal to the federal government, and his refusal to permit secession to disrupt the Union. He attuned the powers of the federal government to meet the exigencies of the war and eventually decided to preserve the union by such steps as the abolition of slavery. His first Inaugural Address (March 4, 1861) and his Second Inaugural Address (March 4, 1865) are classics, showing how Lincoln understood the war and the limitations of military victory. But best known is his Gettysburg Address (November 19, 1863) at the dedication of the National Cemetery at Gettysburg, Pennsylvania; it has been called "the only great prose poem of classical perfection in modern English." As Emerson said in his funeral discourse, Lincoln was a plain man of the people, but a middle-class President. His name is inseparably connected with the cause of popular government, but it took time for the public to recognize his wisdom, the results of a strenuous life, self-education and profound appreciation of the apparently unimportant events and accidents in the lives of small people. His expression of confidence in "government of the people, by the people, for the people" has been quoted time and again.

---

*The Gettysburg Address**

FOUR SCORE and seven years ago our fathers brought forth on this continent, a new nation, conceived in Liberty, and dedicated to the proposition that all men are created equal.

Now we are engaged in a great civil war, testing whether that nation, or any nation so conceived and so dedicated, can long endure. We are met on a great battle-field of that war. We have come to dedicate a portion of that field, as a final resting place for those who here gave their lives that that nation might live. It is altogether fitting and proper that we should do this.

But, in a larger sense, we can not dedicate—we can not consecrate—we can not hallow—this ground. The brave men, living and dead, who struggled here, have consecrated it, far above our poor power to add or detract. The world will little note, nor long remember what we say here, but it can never forget what they did here. It is for us the living, rather, to be dedicated here to the unfinished work which they who fought here have thus far so nobly advanced. It is rather for us to be here dedicated to the great task remaining before us—that from these honored dead we take increased devotion to that cause for which they gave the last full measure of devotion—that we here highly resolve that these dead shall not have died in vain—that this nation, under God, shall have a new birth of freedom—and that government of the people, by the people, for the people, shall not perish from the earth.

The Second Inaugural Address.

Fellow-Countrymen: At this second appearing to take the oath of the Presidential office there is less occasion for an extended address than there was at the first. Then a state-

* Text: Abraham Lincoln, *Complete Works,* John G. Nicolay and John Hay, editors, New York: The Century Co., 1902, II, 439, 656-57.

ment somewhat in detail of a course to be pursued seemed fitting and proper. Now, at the expiration of four years, during which public declarations have been constantly called forth on every point and phase of the great contest which still absorbs the attention and engrosses the energies of the nation, little that is new could be presented. The progress of our arms, upon which all else chiefly depends, is as well known to the public as to myself, and it is, I trust, reasonably satisfactory and encouraging to all. With high hope for the future, no prediction in regard to it is ventured.

On the occasion corresponding to this four years ago all thoughts were anxiously directed to an impending civil war. All dreaded it, all sought to avert it. While the inaugural address was being delivered from this place, devoted altogether to *saving* the Union without war, insurgent agents were in the city seeking to *destroy* it without war–seeking to dissolve the Union and divide effects by negotiation. Both parties deprecated war, but one of them would *make* war rather than let the nation survive, and the other would *accept* war rather than let it perish, and the war came.

One-eighth of the whole population were colored slaves, not distributed generally over the Union, but localized in the southern part of it. These slaves constituted a peculiar and powerful interest. All knew that this interest was somehow the cause of the war. To strengthen, perpetuate, and extend this interest was the object for which the insurgents would rend the Union even by war, while the Government claimed no right to do more than to restrict the territorial enlargement of it. Neither party expected for the war the magnitude or the duration which it has already attained. Neither anticipated that the *cause* of the conflict might cease with or even before the conflict itself should cease. Each looked for an easier triumph, and a result less fundamental and astounding. Both read the same Bible and pray to the same God, and each invokes His aid against the other. It may seem strange that any men should dare to ask a just

God's assistance in wringing their bread from the sweat of other men's faces, but let us judge not, that we be not judged. The prayers of both could not be answered. That of neither has been answered fully. The Almighty has His own purposes. "Woe unto the world because of offenses; for it must needs be that offenses come, but woe to that man by whom the offense cometh." If we shall suppose that American slavery is one of those offenses which, in the providence of God, must needs come, but which, having continued through His appointed time, He now wills to remove, and that He gives to both North and South this terrible war as the woe due to those by whom the offense came, shall we discern therein any departure from those divine attributes which the believers in a living God always ascribe to Him? Fondly do we hope, fervently do we pray, that this mighty scourge of war may speedily pass away. Yet, if God wills that it continue until all the wealth piled by the bondsman's two hundred and fifty years of unrequited toil shall be sunk, and until every drop of blood drawn with the lash shall be paid by another drawn with the sword, as was said three thousand years ago, so still it must be said "the judgments of the Lord are true and righteous altogether."

With malice toward none, with charity for all, with firmness in the right as God gives us to see the right, let us strive on to finish the work we are in, to bind up the nation's wounds, to care for him who shall have borne the battle and for his widow and his orphan, to do all which may achieve and cherish a just and lasting peace among ourselves and with all nations.

JOHN LOCKE

(1632-1704)

English philosopher, known as "The Father of English Empiricism," is even more appreciated for providing the germs of the American Declaration of Independence in the second of his *Two Treatises on Government* (1690), published to justify the British Whig Revolution of two years before. By urging, in his *Letters on Toleration* (1689), the necessity of separating Church and State, he also deeply influenced constitutional and cultural life in the United States. In fact, eighteenth-century Americans could rightly claim to be the true inheritors of Locke's political ideas, which were at first neglected in his native England. His ideas, through the influence of Montesquieu and Voltaire, also conquered France, and subsequently Holland and Scandinavia. Interested in experimental science and philosophy rather than Aristotelian subtleties, his best-known work, *An Essay Concerning Human Understanding* (1690), took him seventeen years to complete, and was the outcome of a talk with friends about morality and religion during which he promised to try to determine what questions the understanding of man was qualified to resolve and what others were outside its province.

Locke's conception of human nature was formed by extensive studies and, even more, by the experiences of his life. The son of a lawyer of Roundhead sympathies, he began to study medicine in 1666, made friends with Boyle, the physicist, and secured the patronage of Anthony Ashley Cooper, Earl of Shaftesbury. He became secretary of Ecclesiastical Presentations to Shaftesbury when the latter was created Chancellor and secretary to the Board of Trade and Plantations in 1673. In 1684 he was exiled because of his connection with Shaftesbury, and took refuge in Holland. On his return to England in 1689, he was made Commissioner of Appeals by William III.

Physically frail, Locke was a giant intellectually. He was probably influenced considerably by Philip Unton's *Treatise of Monarchy* (1643). Locke stressed that philosophy must be of practical use; rather than consciously force a fact to fit his theory he preferred to be accused of inconsistency. He saw the task of inquiring into the faculties and limits of the human mind as a problem with a psychological basis; thus his *Essay* was the first comprehensive study of analytical psychology. It inaugurated the age of empiricism, and directed the thoughts of many philosophers in later periods. In politics, Locke opposed the ecclesiastical and political methods used during the later Stuart period, and attacked both the divine right theory of the Anglicans and Filmer, and the theory of absolutism which Hobbes had derived from the idea of the social contract. In his *Two Treatises on Government* (1690) he attacked the doctrine of royal prerogatives based upon divine rights; in his *Of Civil Government,* he discussed the origin, nature and province of government, acknowledging his indebtedness to Hooker for his leading ideas. He disagreed with Hobbes, insisting that since sovereignty is derived from a compact of the people it must ultimately rest with them. The original state of nature was one in which peace and reason prevailed; it was prepolitical, but not social, and men lived under natural law, which Locke (following Grotius) conceived as a body of rules determined by reason. Under the law of nature, all men are equal and possess equal natural rights, the rights to life, liberty and property. But since there was no agreement as to the law of nature, a social contract was formed, a body politic, whereby individuals gave up their personal right to interpret and administer the law of nature in return for a guarantee that their natural rights to life, liberty and property would be preserved. The power given up was vested in the community as a whole. Such a contract created the need for a majority rule. Since each individual surrendered to the community his right to execute the natural law, the minority was bound by the will of the majority; tacit consent was given by the remaining individuals in the community. Thus the original contract was binding upon subsequent generations. Following the Aristotelian classification of governments into monarchies, aristocracies and democracies, Locke conceived the executive and the judiciary as dependent upon the lawmaking body, and considered democracy, in the hands of delegates provided by popular election, the best form of government. Though the legislature was the supreme organ of government, when injustice to the community's natural rights became obvious, the majority of the people might resist the civil authority, since government must be based upon consent. The state should deal only with the preservation of social order and not with the souls of men; the church is a voluntary society and tolerance in religion must be promoted.

Locke's theory has been of enormous influence. He made philosophy a discipline based on normal powers of empirical observation and common-sense judgment. His idea that private property was derived from primitive communism, where an individual incorporated his labor in some object, stimulated the rise of modern socialism. His "right of revolution" helped to justify the American Revolution. His ideas prompted the separation of church and state; his concept of the right of property was made a fundamental right; and his ideas of human rights are still debated today by the United Nations. Montesquieu developed Locke's concept of the separation of powers, while Rousseau went even further in his concept of social contract, carried to the extreme by the French Revolution. Above all, Locke's ideas are clearly discernible in the American Declaration of Independence and the American Constitution.

---

*Political Power**

TO UNDERSTAND political power aright, and derive it from its original, we must consider what estate all men are naturally in, and that is, a state of perfect freedom to order their actions, and dispose of their possessions and persons as they think fit, within the law of Nature, without asking leave or depending upon the will of any other man.

A state also of equality, wherein all the power and jurisdic-

* This excerpt taken from D. C. Somervell, *Western Civilization: A Course of Selected Reading by Authorities,* London: International University Society, Cultural Publications, 1952, pp. 177-184.

tion is reciprocal, no one having more than another, there being nothing more evident than that creatures of the same species and rank, promiscuously born to all the same advantages of Nature, and the use of the same faculties, should also be equal one amongst another, without subordination or subjection, unless the lord and master of them should, by any manifest declaration of his will, set one above another, and confer on him, by an evident and clear appointment, an undoubted right to dominion and sovereignty.

This equality of men by Nature, the judicious Hooker looks upon as so evident in itself, and beyond all question, that he makes it the foundation of that obligation to mutual love amongst men on which he builds the duties they owe one another, and from whence he derived the great maxims of justice and charity. . . .

The natural liberty of man is to be free from any superior power on earth, and not to be under the will or legislative authority of man, but to have only the law of Nature for his rule. The liberty of man in society is to be under no other legislative power but that established by consent in the commonwealth, nor under the dominion of any will, or restraint of any law, but what that legislative shall enact according to the trust put in it.

If man in the state of Nature be so free as has been said, if he be absolute lord of his own person and possessions, equal to the greatest and subject to nobody, why will he part with this freedom, this empire, and subject himself to the dominion and control of any other power? To which it is obvious to answer, that though in the state of Nature he hath such a right, yet the enjoyment of it is very uncertain and constantly exposed to the invasion of others; for all being kings as much as he, every man his equal, and the greater part no strict observers of equity and justice, the enjoyment of the property he has in this state is very unsafe, very insecure. This makes him willing to quit this condition which, however free, is full of fears and continual dangers; and it is not without reason that he seeks out and is willing to join in society with others who are already united, or have a mind to unite for the mutual preservation of their lives, liberties, and estates, which I call by the general name—property.

The great and chief end, therefore, of men uniting into commonwealths, and putting themselves under government, is the preservation of their property; to which in the state of Nature there are many things wanting.

Firstly: There wants an established, settled, known law, received and allowed by common consent to be the standard of right and wrong, and the common measure to decide all controversies between them. For though the law of Nature be plain and intelligible to all rational creatures, yet men, being biased by their interest, as well as ignorant for want of study of it, are not apt to allow of it as a law binding to them in the application of it to their particular cases.

Secondly: in the state of Nature there wants a known and indifferent judge, with authority to determine all differences according to the established law. For every one in that state being both judge and executioner of the law of Nature, men being partial to themselves, passion and revenge is very apt to carry them too far, and with too much heat in their own cases, as well as negligence and unconcernedness, make them too remiss in other men's.

Thirdly: in the state of Nature there often wants power to back and support the sentence when right, and to give it due execution. They who by any injustice are offended will seldom fail where they are able by force to make good their injustice. Such resistance many times makes the punishment dangerous, and frequently destructive to those who attempt it.

Thus mankind, notwithstanding all the privileges of the state of Nature, being but in an ill condition while they remain in it are quickly driven into society. Hence it comes to pass, that we seldom find any number of men live any time together in this state. The inconveniences that they are therein exposed to by the irregular and uncertain exercise of the power every man has of punishing the transgressions of others, make them take sanctuary under the established laws of government, and therein seek the preservation of their property. It is this that makes them so willingly give up every one his single power of punishing to be exercised by such alone as shall be appointed to it amongst them, and by such rules as the community, or those authorized by them to that purpose, shall agree on. And in this we have the original right and rise of both the legislative and executive power as well as of the governments and societies themselves. . . .

But though men, when they enter into society, give up the equality, liberty, and executive power they had in the state of Nature into the hands of society, to be so far disposed of by the legislative as the good of the society shall require, yet it being only with an intention in every one the better to preserve himself, his liberty and property (for no rational creature can be supposed to change his condition with an intention to be worse), the power of the society or legislative constituted by them can never be supposed to extend farther than the common good, but is obliged to secure every one's property by providing against those three defects above mentioned that made the state of Nature so unsafe and uneasy. And so, whoever has the legislative or supreme power of any commonwealth, is bound to govern by established standing laws, promulgated and known to the people, and not by extemporary decrees, by indifferent and upright judges, who are to decide controversies by those laws; and to employ the force of the community at home only in the execution of such laws, or abroad to prevent or redress foreign injuries and secure the community from inroads and invasion. And all this to be directed to no other end but the peace, safety, and public good of the people.

The great end of men's entering into society being the

enjoyment of their properties in peace and safety, and the great instrument and means of that being the laws established in that society, the first and fundamental positive law of all commonwealths is the establishing of the legislative power; as the first and fundamental natural law, which is to govern even the legislative itself, is the preservation of the society and (as far as will consist with the public good) of every person in it. This legislative is not only the supreme power of the commonwealth, but sacred and unalterable in the hands where the community have once placed it. Nor can any edict of anybody else, in what form soever conceived, or by what power soever backed, have the force and obligation of a law which has not its sanction from that legislative which the public has chosen and appointed; for without this the law could not have that which is absolutely necessary to its being a law, the consent of the society. . . .

Though the legislative, whether placed in one or more, whether it be always in being or only in intervals, though it be the supreme power in every commonwealth; yet, first, it is not, nor can possibly be, absolutely arbitrary over the lives and fortunes of the people. For it being but the joint power of every member of the society given up to that person or assembly which is legislator, it can be no more than those persons had in a state of Nature before they entered into society, and gave it up to the community. For nobody can transfer to another more power than he has in himself, and nobody has an absolute arbitrary power over himself, or over any other, to destroy his own life, or take away the life or property of another. A man, as has been proved, cannot subject himself to the arbitrary power of another; and having, in the state of Nature, no arbitrary power over the life, liberty, or possession of another, but only so much as the law of Nature gave him for the preservation of himself and the rest of mankind, this is all he doth, or can give up to the commonwealth, and by it to the legislative power, so that the legislative can have no more than this. Their power in the utmost bounds of it is limited to the public good of the society. It is a power that hath no other end but preservation, and therefore can never have a right to destroy, enslave, or designedly to impoverish the subjects; the obligations of the law of Nature cease not in society, but only in many cases are drawn closer, and have, by human laws, known penalties annexed to them to enforce their observation. Thus the law of Nature stands as an eternal rule to all men, legislators as well as others. The rules that they make for other men's actions must, as well as their own and other men's actions, be conformable to the law of Nature—*i.e.* to the will of God, of which that is a declaration, and the fundamental law of Nature being the preservation of mankind, no human sanction can be good or valid against it.

Secondly, the legislative or supreme authority cannot assume to itself a power to rule by extemporary arbitrary decrees, but is bound to dispense justice and decide the rights of the subject by promulgated standing laws, and known authorized judges. For the law of Nature being unwritten, and so nowhere to be found but in the minds of men, they who, through passion or interest, shall miscite or misapply it, cannot so easily be convinced of their mistake where there is no established judge; and so it serves not as it ought, to determine the rights and fence the properties of those that live under it. . . .

Thirdly, the supreme power cannot take from any man any part of his property without his consent. For the preservation of property being the end of government, and that for which men enter into society, it necessarily supposes and requires that the people should have property, without which they must be supposed to lose that by entering into society, which was the end for which they entered into it; too gross an absurdity for any man to own. Men, therefore, in society having property, they have such a right to the goods, which by the law of the community are theirs, that nobody hath a right to take them, or any part of them, from them without their own consent; without this they have no property at all. For I have truly no property in that which another can by right take from me when he pleases against my consent. Hence it is a mistake to think that the supreme or legislative power of any commonwealth can do what it will, and dispose of the estates of the subject arbitrarily, or take any part of them at pleasure.

This is not much to be feared in governments where the legislative consists wholly or in part in assemblies which are variable, whose members upon the dissolution of the assembly are subjects under the common laws of their country, equally with the rest. But in governments where the legislative is in one lasting assembly, always in being or in one man as in absolute monarchies, there is danger still, that they will think themselves to have a distinct interest from the rest of the community, and so will be apt to increase their own riches and power by taking what they think fit from the people. For a man's property is not at all secure, though there be good and equitable laws to set the bounds of it between him and his fellow-subjects, if he who commands those subjects have power to take from any private man what part he pleases of his property, and use and dispose of it as he thinks good.

Fourthly. The legislative cannot transfer the power of making laws to any other hands, for it being but a delegated power from the people, they who have it cannot pass it over to others. The people alone can appoint the form of the commonwealth, which is by constituting the legislative, and appointing in whose hands that shall be. And when the people have said, "We will submit, and be governed by laws made by such men, and in such forms", nobody else can say other men shall make laws for them; nor can they be bound by any laws but such as are enacted by those whom they have chosen and authorized to make laws for them.

These are the bounds which the trust that is put in them by the society and the law of God and Nature have set to the legislative power of every commonwealth, in all forms of government. First: They are to govern by promulgated established laws, not to be varied in particular cases, but to have one rule for rich and poor, for the favourite at Court, and the countryman at plough. Secondly: These laws also ought to be designed for no other end ultimately but the good of the people. Thirdly: They must not raise taxes on the property of the people without the consent of the people given by themselves or their deputies. And this properly concerns only such governments where the legislative is always in being, or at least where the people have not reserved any part of the legislative to deputies, to be from time to time chosen by themselves. Fourthly: Legislative neither must nor can transfer the power of making laws to anybody else, or place it anywhere but where the people have.

Magna Carta had put the law above the King. Events in Britain in the seventeenth century had put Parliament above the King. And in the eighteenth century there were times when Parliament thought that it was above the law as well. *If the law is superior to the King, what is above the legislature*—or at least above any whims of the law-makers? Most countries have a written constitution which puts limits on the power of the legislature. But the British constitution is largely unwritten precedent, so what happens then? Listen to the Earl of Chatham, the "Great Commoner", as he explains why the foundations of jurisprudence must be laid in reason. He is speaking in the House of Lords in the famous case of John Wilkes. Wilkes, a most vigorous and outspoken enemy of the Tory government, had been expelled from the Commons in 1764 because of the attack on the King's Speech made in his paper the *North Briton.* He was elected again for Middlesex in 1768, only to be expelled once more, early in 1769. Elected again on February 16, again expelled, re-elected on March 16, once more expelled, and elected for a fourth time on April 13 by 1143 votes to

Luttrell's 296, he was again rejected by the Commons, who declared Luttrell elected.

This action was the signal for a popular outburst of fury. The artisans and lower middle class were all on Wilkes's side, but none of them had votes, so what could they do? "Start agitating for the vote" was the reply, and this they began to do. Democracy started to march forward again after the repose of the early half of the eighteenth century, and it moved not only in England but even more swiftly in America and in France.

NICCOLÒ MACHIAVELLI

(1469-1527)

The celebrated Florentine author of *Il Principe* (*The Prince,* 1513), whose name has been used as an epithet or synonym for the unscrupulous politician, was not actually a diabolical villain, but rather one of the founders of modern realistic political science. He achieved this position by separating politics from ethics and morality, by eliminating theological and moral argument, and by taking the secular state for granted and inquiring scientifically into its behavior. He placed the state at the center of human living and, because he was disillusioned by the corruption of the Church, made even moral and religious life dependent upon it. (He set forth his position also in *The Discourses of Livy*). A thoroughgoing realist, he made an exhaustive study of the measures needed to maintain the power of the state and analyzed the nature of political problems and techniques. Though *The Prince* is dedicated to Lorenzo de Medici, the hero of the book is Cesare Borgia, son of Pope Alexander VI, a Cardinal at seventeen, able military leader, conqueror of Romagna, and a cruel, pitiless dictator, who attained, through duplicity, cruelty and bad faith, temporary success. Machiavelli was a firm partisan of a republican form of government, but when he examined the deplorable condition of Italy, he was persuaded that a Cesare Borgia would be the ideal leader to end the state of chaos. He argued in *The Prince* that the welfare of the state justifies everything and that there are different standards of morals in public life and private life. It is proper for a statesman to commit in the public interest acts of violence and deceit that would be thoroughly reprehensible and even criminal in private transactions: in effect, Machiavelli separates ethics from politics. In politics the highest law is expediency. *The Prince* is a guidebook for princes on how to gain and to hold power—power not for the ruler's sake, but for the good of the people, to provide them with a stable government, secure against revolution or invasion. Because a strong government requires a good army, Machiavelli considered military affairs of the highest importance. A national army composed of citizens is more effective and desirable than mercenaries, and as national survival may depend on armed might, a ruling prince should regard military matters as his principal study and occupation. Several chapters are devoted to how conquered territories are to be governed and to the conduct of princes under various conditions. A prince, for instance, should be unconcerned about gaining a reputation for miserliness, and cruelty ought to be regarded as one of the weapons to keep his subjects united and obedient. No part of *The Prince* has been more denounced than Chapter 18 on "How Princes Should Keep Faith," and the evil connotations of the term "Machiavellian" can be traced to this section. Here he argues that keeping faith is praiseworthy, but that deceit, hypocrisy and perjury are necessary and excusable for the sake of maintaining political power.

Manuscript copies of *The Prince* were passed around during the author's lifetime; its publication in 1532 was approved by Pope Clement VII, cousin of the prince to whom it was dedicated. But the Council of Trent ordered the destruction of Machiavelli's works; he was denounced as an atheist in Rome and his writings were banned; the Jesuits burned him in effigy in Germany, and Catholics and Protestants united against him; in 1559 all of his works were placed on the Index of Prohibited Books. Yet statesmen, philosophers of history and social scientists have often argued that his principles are sound and of basic importance for political success, even for public welfare. For instance, King Frederick II of Prussia wrote a book opposing Machiavelli, yet he acted in accordance with Machiavelli's principles. Mussolini was a great admirer of Machiavelli, but prohibited his subjects from reading his idol's work. Machiavelli's was the most influential political work before Karl Marx and he is today considered the "Founder of the Science of Politics."

---

*The Prince**

CHAPTER V

How such Cities and Principalities are to be governed who lived under their own Laws before they were subdued.

WHEN STATES that are newly conquered have been accustomed to their liberty, and lived under their own laws, to keep them three ways are to be observed: the first is utterly to ruin them; the second, to live personally among them; the third is (contenting yourself with a pension from them) to permit them to enjoy their old privileges and laws, erecting a kind of Council of State, to consist of a few which may have a care of your interest, and keep the people in amity and obedience. And that Council being set up by you, and knowing that it subsists only by your favour and authority, will not omit anything that may propagate and enlarge them. A town that has been anciently free cannot more easily be kept in subjection than by employing its own citizens, as may be seen by the example of the Spartans and Romans. The Spartans had got possession of Athens and Thebes, and settled an oligarchy according to their fancy; and yet they lost them again. The Romans, to keep Capua, Carthage and Numantia, ordered them to be destroyed, and they kept them by that means. Thinking afterwards to preserve Greece, as the Spartans had done, by allowing them their liberty, and indulging their old laws, they found themselves mistaken; so that they were forced to subvert many cities in that province before they could keep it; and certainly that is the safest way which I know; for whoever conquers a free town and does not demolish it commits a great error, and may expect to be ruined himself;

* This excerpt taken from *The Prince,* Introduction by Henry Morley, London: George Routledge & Sons, Broadway, Ludgate Hill; New York: Lafayette Place, n.d., pp. 33-35; 68-71; 77-79.

because whenever the citizens are disposed to revolt, they betake themselves of course to that blessed name of liberty, and the laws of their ancestors, which no length of time nor kind usage whatever will be able to eradicate; and let all possible care and provision be made to the contrary, unless they be divided some way or other, or the inhabitants dispersed, the thought of their old privileges will never out of their heads, but upon all occasions they will endeavour to recover them, as Pisa did after it had continued so many years in subjection to the Florentines. But it falls out quite contrary where the cities or provinces have been used to a prince whose race is extirpated and gone; for being on the one side accustomed to obey, and on the other at a loss for their old family, they can never agree to set up another, and will never know how to live freely without; so that they are not easily to be tempted to rebel, and the prince may oblige them with less difficulty, and be secure of them when he hath done. But in a commonwealth their hatred is more inveterate, their revenge more insatiable; nor does the memory of their ancient liberty ever suffer, or ever can suffer them to be quiet; so that the most secure way is either to ruin them quite, or make your residence among them . . .

CHAPTER X.

How the strength of all Principalities is to be computed.

To any man that examines the nature of principalities, it is worthy his consideration whether a prince has power and territory enough to subsist by himself, or whether he needs the assistance and protection of other people. To clear the point a little better, I think those princes capable of ruling who are able, either by the numbers of their men or the greatness of their wealth, to raise a complete army, and bid battle to any that shall invade them; and those I think depend upon others, who of themselves dare not meet their enemy in the field, but are forced to keep within their bounds and defend them as well they can. Of the first we have spoken already, and shall say more as occasion is presented. Of the second no more can be said, but to advise such princes to strengthen and fortify the capital town in their dominions, and not to trouble themselves with the whole country; and whoever shall do that, and in other things manage himself with the subjects as I have described, and perhaps shall do hereafter, shall with great caution be invaded; for men are generally wary and tender of enterprising anything that is difficult, and no great easiness is to be found in attacking a town well fortified and provided, where the prince is not hated by the people.

The towns in Germany are many of them free; though their country and district be but small, yet they obey the Emperor but when they please, and are in no awe either of him or any other prince of the empire, because they are all so well fortified. Every one looks upon the taking of any one of them as a work of great difficulty and time, their walls being so strong, their ditches so deep, their works so regular and well provided with cannon, and their stores and magazines always furnished for a twelve-month. Besides which, for the aliment and sustenance of the people, and that they may be no burden to the public, they have work-houses where, for a year together, the poor may be employed in such things as are the nerves and life of that city, and sustain themselves by their labour. Military discipline and exercises are likewise in much request there, and many laws and good customs they have to maintain them.

A prince then who has a city well fortified, and the affections of his people, is not easily to be molested, and he that does molest him is like to repent it; for the affairs of this world are so various, it is almost impossible for any army to lie quietly a whole year before a town without interruption. If any objects that the people having houses and possessions out of the town will not have patience to see them plundered and burned, and that charity to themselves will make them forget their prince, I answer, that a wise and dexterous prince will easily evade those difficulties by encouraging his subjects and persuading them, sometimes their troubles will not be long; sometimes inculcating and possessing them with the cruelty of the enemy; and sometimes by correcting and securing himself nimbly of such as appear too turbulent and audacious. Moreover, the usual practice is for the enemy to plunder and set the country on fire at their first coming, whilst every man's spirit is high and fixed upon defence; so that the prince needs not concern himself, nor be fearful of that, for those mischiefs are passed, and inconveniencies received, and when the people in three or four days' time begin to be cool, and consider things soberly, they will find there is no remedy, and join more cordially with the prince, looking upon him as under an obligation to them for having sacrificed their houses and estates in his defence. And the nature of man is such to take as much pleasure in having obliged another as in being obliged himself. Wherefore, all things fairly considered, it is no such hard matter for a prince not only to gain, but to retain, the affection of his subjects, and make them patient of a long siege, if he be wise and provident, and takes care they want nothing either for their livelihood or defence. . . .

. . . The principal foundations of all States—new, old, or mixed—are good laws and good arms; and because there cannot be good laws where there are not good arms, and where the arms are good there must be good laws, I shall pass by the laws and discourse of the arms.

I say the arms, then, with which a prince defends his State are his own, mercenary, auxiliary, or mixed. The mercenary and auxiliary are unprofitable and dangerous, and that prince who founds the duration of his government upon his mercenary forces shall never be firm or secure; for they are divided, ambitious, undisciplined, unfaithful, insolent to their friends, abject to their enemies, without fear of God or faith to men; so the ruin of that person who trusts to them is no longer protracted than the attempt is deferred; in time of peace they divorce you, in time of war they desert you, and the reason is because it is not love nor any principle of honour that keeps them in the field; it is only their pay, and that is not a consideration strong enough to prevail with them to die for you; whilst you have no service to employ them in, they are excellent soldiers; but tell them of an engagement, and they will either disband before or run away in the battle.

And to evince this would require no great pains; seeing the ruin of Italy proceeded from no other cause than that for several years together it had reposed itself upon mercenary arms, which forces it is possible may have formerly done service to some particular person, and behaved themselves well enough among one another; but no sooner were they attacked by a powerful foreigner but they discovered themselves, and showed what they were to the world. Hence it was that Charles VII chalked out his own way into Italy; and that person was in the right who affirmed our own faults were the cause of our miseries. But it was not those faults he believed, but those I have mentioned, which being committed most eminently by princes, they suffered most remarkably in the punishment. But to come closer to the point, and give you a clearer prospect of the imperfection and infelicity of those forces. The great officers of these mercenaries are men of great courage, or otherwise, if the first, you can never be safe, for they always aspire to make themselves great, either by supplanting of you who is their master, or oppressing of other people whom you desired to have preserved; and, on the other side, if the commanders be not courageous, you are ruined again. If it should be urged that all generals will do the same, whether mercenaries or others, I would answer, that all war is managed either by a prince or republic. The prince is obliged to go in person, and perform the office of general himself; the republic must depute some one of her choice citizens, who is to be changed if he carries himself ill; if he behaves himself well he is to be continued, but so straitened and circumscribed by his commission that he may not transgress. And indeed experience tells us that princes alone, and commonwealths alone, with their own private forces have performed great things, whereas mercenaries do nothing but hurt. Besides, a martial commonwealth that stands upon its own legs and maintains itself by its own prowess is not easily usurped, and falls not so readily under the obedience of one of their fellow-citizens as where all the forces are foreign. . . .

JAMES MADISON

(1751-1836)

Fourth President of the United States (1809-1817), collaborated with Hamilton and John Jay in the series of papers known as *The Federalist* (1787-1788), which influenced the adoption by New York, a key state, of the federal Constitution. (*The Federalist* papers were recognized as the best explanation of and defense of the Constitution available, and took their place, almost at once, as a classic. Jefferson—no Federalist himself—pronounced the volume, when it appeared, "the best commentary on the principles of government which has ever been written.") At the Philadelphia Convention of 1787, Madison took the burden of leadership and earned the title "Father of the Constitution," and with Hamilton supplied a rationale for the work of that assembly. In his writings (as in Jefferson's) the doctrine of social contract was presented in its most advanced form. As the leader of the Democratic Republican party, he opposed Hamilton's financial policies. He drafted, with Jefferson, the *Virginia Resolution* (1798), and as President, declared war on Great Britain (1812) (*Madison Papers,* 3 vols., 1840). In the tenth *Federalist,* Madison specifically analyzed the conditions under which freedom and government are possible and found in the new Constitution a set of rules which would contain and direct the eternal conflicts of men. Although he did not appear to comprehend properly the logic of a party system, he understood the nature of pressure groups and reasonably satisfactory ways of dealing with them, while retaining a large measure of individual freedom. He was convinced that it was necessary under the American system to divide power between the national and state governments and attacked those states' righters who were afraid of this grant of power to the national government.

James Madison

*The Federalist No. 47**

THE ACCUMULATION of all powers, legislative, executive, and judiciary, in the same hands, whether of one, a few, or many, and whether hereditary, self-appointed, or elective, may justly be pronounced the very definition of tyranny. Were the federal Constitution, therefore, really chargeable with the accumulation of power, or with a mixture of powers, having a dangerous tendency to such an accumulation, no further arguments would be necessary to inspire a universal reprobation of the system. I persuade myself, however, that it will be made apparent to every one, that the charge cannot be supported, and that the maxim on which it relies has been totally misconceived and misapplied. In order to form correct ideas on this important subject, it will be proper to investigate the sense in which the preservation of liberty requires that the three great departments of power should be separate and distinct.

The oracle who is always consulted and cited on this subject is the celebrated Montesquieu. If he be not the author of this invaluable precept in the science of politics, he has the merit at least of displaying and recommending it most effectually to the attention of mankind. Let us endeavor, in the first place, to ascertain his meaning on this point.

The British Constitution was to Montesquieu what Homer has been to the didactic writers on epic poetry. As the latter have considered the work of the immortal bard as the perfect model from which the principles and rules of the epic art were to be drawn, and by which all similar works were to be judged, so this great political critic appears to have viewed the Constitution of England as the standard, or to use his own expression, as the mirror of political liberty; and to have delivered, in the form of elementary truths, the several characteristic principles of that particular system.

---

* *The Federalist Papers.*

That we may be sure, then, not to mistake his meaning in this case, let us recur to the source from which the maxim was drawn.

On the slightest view of the British Constitution, we must perceive that the legislative, executive, and judiciary departments are by no means totally separate and distinct from each other. The executive magistrate forms an integral part of the legislative authority. He alone has the prerogative of making treaties with foreign sovereigns, which, when made, have, under certain limitations, the force of legislative acts. All the members of the judiciary department are appointed by him, can be removed by him on the address of the two Houses of Parliament, and form, when he pleases to consult them, one of his constitutional councils. One branch of the legislative department forms also a great constitutional council to the executive chief, as, on another hand, it is the sole depositary of judicial power in cases of impeachment, and is invested with the supreme appellate jurisdiction in all other cases. The judges, again, are so far connected with the legislative department as often to attend and participate in its deliberations, though not admitted to a legislative vote.

From these facts, by which Montesquieu was guided, it may clearly be inferred that, in saying "There can be no liberty where the legislative and executive powers are united in the same person, or body of magistrates," or, "if the power of judging be not separated from the legislative and executive powers," he did not mean that these departments ought to have no *partial agency* in, or no *control* over, the acts of each other. His meaning, as his own words import, and still more conclusively as illustrated by the example in his eye, can amount to no more than this, that where the *whole* power of one department is exercised by the same hands which possess the *whole* power of another department, the fundamental principles of a free constitution are subverted. This would have been the case in the constitution examined by him if the king, who is the sole executive magistrate, had possessed also the complete legislative power, or the supreme administration of justice; or if the entire legislative body had possessed the supreme judiciary, or the supreme executive authority. This, however, is not among the vices of that constitution. The magistrate in whom the whole executive power reside cannot of himself make a law, though he can put a negative on every law; nor administer justice in person, though he has the appointment of those who do administer it. The judges can exercise no executive prerogative, though they are shoots from the executive stock; nor any legislative function, though they may be advised with by the legislative councils. The entire legislative can perform no judiciary act, though by the joint act of two of its branches the judges may be removed from their offices, and though one of its branches possessed of the judicial power in the last resort. The entire legislative, again, can exercise no executive prerogative, though one of its branches constitutes the supreme executive magistracy, and another, on the impeachment of a third, can try and condemn all the subordinate officers in the executive department.

The reasons on which Montesquieu grounds his maxim are a further demonstration of his meaning. "When the legislative and executive powers are united in the same person or body," says he, "there can be no liberty, because apprehensions may arise lest *the same* monarch or senate should *enact* tyrannical laws to *execute* them in a tyrannical manner." Again: "Were the power of judging with the legislative, the life and liberty of the subject would be exposed to arbitrary control, for *the judge* would then be *the legislator*. Were it joined to the executive power, *the judge* might behave with all the violence of an *oppressor*." Some of these reasons are more fully explained in other passages; but briefly stated as they are here, they sufficiently establish the meaning which we have put on this celebrated maxim of this celebrated author.

MAO TSE-TUNG

(1893 -)

Chairman of the Central Committee of the Chinese Communist party and Chairman (1949-1959) of the People's Republic of China, is also the ideological revisionist of Marxian doctrines as applied to rural China. He has forced the Chinese, historically the most pacifistic of people, to take up arms and fight for Communist imperialistic motives, and die, by the thousands, in Korea, for a cause not their own. Born in Hunan Province, Mao was the son of a hungry peasant and before he was seven he had to work in the rice fields. Intending to be a teacher, he studied at normal schools in Hunan, then went to the National University at Peking; while a student there, he read Marx, Engels and Lenin and in 1919 was converted to Communism. In 1921, he helped to found the Chinese Communist party and went out recruiting for it; in 1924 he was made a member of its Politbureau. When, in 1927, Chiang Kai-shek turned on his Communist allies, Mao was jailed but bribed his way out. Stalin's policy at the time was to organize immediate broad-scale revolution against Chiang; Mao, for his advocation of "protracted" resistance by the peasants, was ousted from the Politbureau in 1927, and disregarding Stalin's wishes, organized an army of peasants and miners and set up a Chinese Soviet government in the remote province of Kiangsi. By 1934, he was the acknowledged leader of the Chinese Communist party. When Chiang Kai-shek sent a new army against him in 1934, Mao led his 80,000 followers on the "Long March," a 6,000-mile trek on foot to Yenan, where, living with his people in mountain caves, he set up a new Soviet. After the Japanese invasion of China (1937), he waged intensive guerilla warfare and used the patriotic theme to win the Chinese peasants to his side. His armies eventually conquered those of Chiang Kai-shek, and on October 1,

1949, in the great square alongside Peking's Gate of Heavenly Peace, Mao raised the Communist flag, solid red with a cluster of five yellow stars. He then modeled his government along Soviet Union lines, redistributed some land among the peasants, and, until 1961, was subservient to the Kremlin. Under party control, a formidable modern army has been trained, and, for the first time in modern history, China has become once again what she was in ancient days—the foremost power in Asia. With relentless energy and the fanaticism of religious reformers and inquisitors, Mao and his colleagues have tried to remold the thinking of almost a quarter of the human race and imposed the new ideology of Marxism-Leninism, as interpreted by Mao Tse-tung, on a country which has one of the longest unbroken traditions of culture and philosophy on earth (Mao Tse-tung, *Turning Point in China,* 1949; *Selected Works of Mao Tse-tung,* Vol. IV, August, 1945, to September, 1949, Chicago: China Books, 1961; *Mao Tse-tung on Guerrilla Warfare,* New York: Praeger, 1961; Mao Tse-tung, *Selected Works,* I-IV, New York: International Publishers, 1954-56).

Liu Shao-Ch'i, heir apparent to Mao Tse-tung as head of the Chinese Communist party, claimed (1945) that Mao had formulated a "theory" of the revolutionary conquest of power which constituted a new "development" of Communist doctrine. Liu's tribute started what has since proven to be an ambitious effort to exalt "the ideology of Mao" as the sole guide for the Chinese Communist party and people, as well as to propagate an image of the Chinese party leader as the foremost living theorist of the world Communist movement, a point which led to the break with Khrushchev in 1961. In his two essays, "On Practice" and "On Contradictions," written in 1937, but published only in 1950 and 1952, Mao is credited with "a development of the Marxist-Leninist theory of practice," since he "clarifies and develops Engels' and Lenin's famous principle of absolute and relative truth." But Mao's "On Practice" contains little more than paraphrased passages of Lenin's discussion of the theory of knowledge in *Philosophical Notebooks* and *Materialism and Empirico-Criticism,* and Engels' *Anti-Dühring.* In summary, the group around Mao claims that Communism cannot be achieved overnight and that it is necessary to provide for a transitional stage before the advent of communism. This stage called the "New Democracy," will be both capitalistic and socialistic. It must encourage certain forms of capitalism and build up the industries. The New Democracy is democratic and dictatorial at the same time; it is democratic because it serves the interests of "the people"; it is dictatorial in dealing with counterrevolutionaries and enemies of "the people." It must be on guard against ultrademocratism and freedom; freedom and democracy cannot be unrestrained. In the present and transitional stage of the revolution, it is necessary for the proletariat to seek the alliance of nonproletarian classes sympathetic to the proletarian cause. Four "revolutionary classes" are recognized: the workers, the peasants, the petty bourgeoisie and the national bourgeoisie; at the center is the working class, its chief and fundamental ally being the peasant class. The application of this ideology has been proceeding by numerous intermediate stages, each representing a further advance in the direction of full socialism. Thus, in 1949-50, the Communists gave land to peasants and guaranteed the right to private ownership; but in 1951 "cooperativization" was recommended, and in 1958 the communes were introduced. Intermediate stages of transition from private enterprise to socialism have also been prescribed for private industry and commerce, and for the handicrafts. Then, by posing as the leaders in the struggle against imperialism, the Communists have linked themselves with the powerful force of nationalism. Many years ago, Mao declared that "the twin enemies" of the Chinese revolution are imperialism and feudalism, and of the two the first is by far the more deadly enemy.

But the ideological application of the Communist doctrine of Mao had produced difficulties by 1961. At the moment of victory over Chiang Kai-shek in 1949, Mao resolved that, starting from a primitive economy, China must industrialize, not primarily for a better life but so that China could become a military force in world affairs. Out of the turmoil that was uprooting China's ancient society, out of the alternation of hope and terror, of promised reward and present punishment, China worked singlemindedly toward Mao's goal—and achieved comparative miracles. But the hunger resulting from China's economic imbalance forced Mao to vanish discreetly from the public scene by stepping down as head of state (though retaining his all-powerful chairmanship of the Communist party)—the first step in the classic Communist play of disengagement from catastrophe. The cruel rigidity of the commune system has been conspicuously softened.

In November, 1961, the giants of the Communist world, Nikita Khrushchev and Mao were locked in a bitter struggle. At the Party Congress in Moscow, Khrushchev denounced the Red leadership of Albania; Mao, in Peking, went out of his way to declare Red China's "unbreakable friendship" for the Albanian Reds. The difference was one, however, of methods only, since their common aim is a Communist world. The Khrushchev-Mao fight over Stalinist "thought methods" in Albania was part and parcel of the battle Khrushchev won inside the U.S.S.R.; the idea of a Stalinist "tough" line still persists and is kept alive by Mao. Mao's personality has acquired enormous dimensions in the eyes of the Chinese masses; like Stalin's his image has grown beyond the common bounds of humanity and acquired the lineaments of perfection, and the exalted title of "greatest contemporary theoretician of Marxism-Leninism" was bestowed upon him by a member of the Central Committee. While Khrushchev, in order to assert himself after Stalin's death, eliminated his possible rivals, Mao actually conquered China by force of arms, and is therefore in a position to claim Lenin's mantle, and is ever reaching over Stalin's head, let alone Khrushchev's. In the whole body of his doctrine there is scarcely a trace of "peaceful coexistence," and a struggle to the death, an armed contest between Communism and "imperialism," embodied by the U.S., remains the essence of Maoist thought.

---

*On the People's Democratic Dictatorship**

On the basis of the experience of these twenty-eight years, we have reached the same conclusions that Sun Yat-sen, in his will, said he had drawn from "the experience of forty years". That is, "we must awaken the masses of the people and unite

* Foreign Language Press, Peking, 1950.

ourselves in a common struggle with those peoples of the world who treat us on a basis of equality". Sun Yat-sen had a world outlook different from ours and he set off from a different class standpoint in observing and dealing with problems. Nevertheless, on the problem of how to struggle against imperialism in the 1920's, he reached this conclusion which was basically the same as ours.

Twenty-four years have elapsed since Sun Yat-sen's death, and under the leadership of the Chinese Communist Party Chinese revolutionary theory and practice have made tremendous strides forward, fundamentally altering the face of China. The Chinese people have by now accumulated vital and basic experiences along the following two lines.

(1) Internally, the people must be awakened. This means welding the working class, the peasantry, the petty bourgeoisie and the national bourgeoisie into a united front under the leadership of the working class, and from this proceeding to the creation of a state of the people's democratic dictatorship, a state led by the working class and based on the alliance of workers and peasants.

(2) Externally, we must unite in a common struggle with the peoples of all countries and with those nations which treat us as equals. This means allying ourselves with the Soviet Union, with every New Democratic country, and with the proletariat and broad masses in all other countries. This means forming an international united front.

"You incline to one side." That is right. The forty years' experience of Sun Yat-sen and the twenty-eight years' experience of the Chinese Communist Party have convinced us that in order to attain victory and consolidate it, we must incline to one side. According to these experiences, the Chinese people must incline either toward the side of imperialism or toward that of Socialism. There can be no exception to this rule. It is impossible to sit on the fence; there is no third road. We oppose Chiang Kai-shek's imperialism. We also oppose illusions about a third road, without exception, one inclines either toward imperialism or toward Socialism. Neutrality is merely a camouflage; a third road does not exist.

"You are too provocative." Yes, in speaking of our dealing with domestic and foreign reactionaries, that is, imperialists and their running dogs, but not with any other people. In regard to the reactionaries, the question of being provocative or not does not arise. . . .

Internationally we belong to the side of the anti-imperialist front, headed by the Soviet Union. We can only turn to this side for genuine and friendly assistance, not to the side of the imperialist front.

"You are dictatorial." My dear sirs, what you say is correct. That is just what we are. All the experiences of the Chinese people, accumulated in the course of successive decades, tell us to carry out a people's democratic dictatorship.

This means that the reactionaries must be deprived of the right to voice their opinions; only the people have that right.

Who are the "people"? At the present stage in China, they are the working class, the peasantry, the petty bourgeoisie and the national bourgeoisie.

Under the leadership of the working class and the Communist Party, these classes unite to create their own state and elect their own government so as to enforce their dictatorship over the henchmen of imperialism—the landlord class and bureaucratic capitalist class, as well as the reactionary clique of the Kuomintang, which represents these classes, and their accomplices. The people's government will suppress such persons. It will only permit them to behave themselves properly. It will not allow them to speak or act wildly. Should they do so, they will be instantly curbed and punished. The democratic system is to be carried out within the ranks of the people, giving them freedom of speech, assembly and association. The right to vote is given only to the people, not to the reactionaries.

These two things, democracy for the people and dictatorship for the reactionaries, when combined, constitute the people's democratic dictatorship.

Why must things be done in this way? Everyone is very clear on this point. If things were not done like this, revolution would fail, the people would suffer and the state would perish.

"Don't you want to abolish state power?" Yes, we want to, but not at the present time. We cannot afford to abolish state power just now. Why not? Because imperialism still exists. Because, internally, reactionaries still exist and classes still exist.

Our present task is to strengthen the people's state apparatus—meaning principally the people's army, the people's police and the people's courts—thereby safeguarding national defence and protecting the people's interests. Given these conditions, China, under the leadership of the working class and the Communist Party, can develop steadily from an agricultural into an industrial country and from a New Democratic into a Socialist and, eventually, Communist society, eliminating classes and realizing universal harmony.

Such state apparatus as the army, the police and the courts are instruments with which one class oppresses another. As far as the hostile classes are concerned, these are instruments of oppression. They are violent and certainly not "benevolent" things.

"You are not benevolent." Exactly. We definitely have no benevolent policies toward the reactionaries or the counter-revolutionary activities of the reactionary classes. Our benevolent policy does not apply to such deeds or such persons, who are outside the ranks of the people; it applies only to the people.

The people's state is for the protection of the people. Once they have a people's state, the people have the possibility of applying democratic methods on a nationwide and comprehensive scale to educate and reform themselves, so that they may get rid of the influences of domestic and foreign reactionaries. (These influences are still very strong at present and will remain for a long time to come; they cannot be eradicated quickly.) Thus the people can reform their bad habits and thoughts derived from the old society, so that they will not take the wrong road pointed out to them by the reactionaries, but will continue to advance and develop toward a Socialist and then Communist society.

The methods we use in this respect are democratic, that is, methods of persuasion and not of compulsion. If people break the law they will be punished, imprisoned or even sentenced to death. But these will be individual cases, differing in principle from the dictatorship imposed against the reactionaries as a class.

As for those belonging to reactionary classes or groups, after their political power has been overthrown, we will also give them land and work, permitting them to make a living and to reform themselves through labour into new persons—but only on condition that they do not rebel, sabotage or create disturbances. If they do not want to work, the people's state will force them to do so. Furthermore, the propaganda and educational work directed toward them will be carried out with the same care and thoroughness as the work already conducted among captured army officers. This may also be spoken of as a "benevolent policy," but it will be compulsorily imposed upon those originally from enemy classes. This can in no way be compared to our work along self-educational lines among the ranks of the revolutionary people.

This job of reforming the reactionary classes can be handled only by a state having a people's democratic dictatorship. When the work has been completed, China's major exploiting classes—the landlord class and the bureaucratic capitalist class, i.e., the monopoly capitalist class—will have been finally eliminated.

Then there will remain only the national bourgeoisie. In the present stage a great deal of suitable educational work can be done among them. When the time comes to realize Socialism, that is, to nationalise private enterprise, we will go a step further in our work of educating and reforming them. The people have a strong state apparatus in their hands, and they do not fear rebellion on the part of the national bourgeoisie.

The education of the peasantry presents a serious problem. Peasant economy is dispersed. According to the Soviet Union's experience, it takes a long time and much painstaking work before agriculture can be socialised. Without the socialisation of agriculture, there can be no complete and consolidated socialism.

If we wish to socialise agriculture, we must develop a strong industry having state-operated enterprises as its main component. The state of the people's democratic dictatorship must, step by step, solve the problem of industrialising the country. Since this article has no intention of taking up economic questions, I will not go into detail here. . . .

Summarising our experiences and condensing them into one point, we have the people's democratic dictatorship led by the working class (through the Communist Party) and based upon the allegiance of workers and peasants. Our dictatorship must unite with all international revolutionary forces. This then is our formula, our main experience, our main program.

During the long period of its twenty-eight years' existence, our party has done just one thing, and that is, it has attained a basic victory in the revolutionary war. This is worth celebrating because it is a people's victory, and because it is a victory in such a large country as China.

But much work still lies ahead of us. If we were walking down a road, our past work would not seem like more than the first step of a ten-thousand *li* march. The remnants of the enemy must still be wiped out. A grave task of economic construction spreads out before us. Some of the things we are familiar with will soon be laid aside, and we will be compelled to tackle things with which we are not familiar. This means difficulties. The imperialists count upon our not handling our economic problems well. They stand on the side-lines and wait for our failure.

We must overcome all difficulties and learn the things we do not understand. We must learn to do economic work from all who know the ropes (no matter who they are). We must respect them as teachers, learning from them attentively and earnestly. We must not pretend to know when we do not know. We must not put on bureaucratic airs. If one bores into a subject for several months, for one year or two years, it can eventually be mastered.

Some of the Communists in the Soviet Union were also unable to handle economics at the beginning, and the imperialists also waited for their failure. But the Communist Party of the U.S.S.R. emerged victorious. Under Lenin's and Stalin's leadership, the Soviet Communists not only have been able to carry on construction. They have already built up a great and glorious Socialist state.

The Communist Party of the U.S.S.R. is our very best teacher, and we must learn from it. Both the international and the domestic situation are in our favor. There is absolutely no doubt that we can rely upon the weapon of the people's democratic dictatorship, unite all the people throughout the country with the exception of the reactionaries, and march steadily toward our goal.

KARL MARX

(1818-1883)

As a philosopher and ideologist, has not only influenced, as has no other man in contemporary history, subsequent political and social changes, but his teachings, in contrast to those of previous philosophers, have directly affected the minds of the working peoples throughout the world (*Critique of Political Economics,* 1859; *Das Kapital,* 1867, 1885, 1894; *The Communist Manifesto,* in collaboration with Friedrich Engels, 1848). Born in Germany, the son of a Jewish lawyer, into a family that was, in Lenin's words, "well-to-do, cultured, but not revolutionary," he studied law, history and philosophy at Bonn and Berlin, became a doctor of philosophy in 1841, and married happily in 1842. In 1847 he and his friend Engels reorganized a secret propaganda society, the Communist League, in London, at the request of which they drew up the famed *Communist Manifesto,* still the theoretical basis of Communism today. In 1849, having been expelled from Paris, Belgium and Prussia, Marx went to England, where he eked out a frugal existence in Dean Street, Soho, and busied himself in writing books on revolution in the British Museum. (The foundation for Marx's later *Das Kapital* was laid by Engels in 1845 with the publication of his *Condition of the Working Classes in England.*) His wife, Jenny von Westfalen, remained for nearly forty years his faithful partner, sharing with him a life of incredible poverty, privation and misfortune; of their six children, only three survived, and of these, two committed suicide in later life. Unquestionably, these years of extreme hardship influenced Marx's views and account for much of the rancor and bitterness in his ideology; only frequent financial help from Engels saved him from actual starvation. (His only earned income was a guinea a week, received from the New York *Tribune* for a letter on European affairs, and intermittent pay for jobs of hack writing). *Das Kapital* took eighteen years to prepare. He was the power behind the throne of the International Working Men's Association (First International founded in 1864), but which dissolved after the collapse of the Paris Commune (1871).

In his *Theses on Feuerbach* (1845), Marx, who had turned from the political radicalism of the Hegelians to what he then called Communism, and later scientific socialism, declared that the question of absolute truth is not one of theory but a practical one, and that the reality and power of thought must be demonstrated in practice by both interpreting and changing the world; but he also insisted that a vigorous theory is as indispensable to the destruction of a corrupted society and the construction of a new one as drastically disciplined action. When, in his *Critique of Political Economics,* Marx called his method empirical, he did so in order to mark his opposition to abstract spiritualism. He turned Hegel's dialectic upside down because he thought that Hegel's way of proceeding from the abstract to the concrete, from the ideal to the real, could not reach reality, and that Hegel's conception of dialectical motion as the development of consciousness was bound to miss human totality. It is not consciousness that determines the existence of man but the social existence of man that determines his consciousness. Nevertheless, dialectic is the only infallible method of scientific thinking to which all empirical knowledge of facts is subordinated.

Thus Marx was a dialectical materialist, meaning, basically, that the fundamental stuff out of which the universe is made is matter, and that minds, ideas, emotions and so on are either qualitatively the same as matter (which Christianity denies) or, if different from matter, are nevertheless derived from it. Marx looked upon economic conditions as the basis of life, political and ideological systems being merely the "superstructure" erected above them and undergoing changes along with them. The age of the hand-worked weaving loom created feudal society; the age of the steam-driven weaving loom created capitalistic society, with all its ideas, religions and principles (the theory of "historical materialism"). History is a series of class struggles. Capitalism produces within itself its own gravedigger, the proletariat; it will overthrow the bourgeoisie as soon as the capitalistic organization of production becomes obsolete in comparison with the requirements of the productive forces it has developed. The insufficiency of capitalistic methods is based on the inner contradictions of capitalism. All value is a product of labor and the true value of any article is tantamount to the working time required for its production. But capitalists do not pay the worker the full equivalent of the time he works for them; they always pay him less (the "theory of exploitation"), retaining the difference ("surplus value"). The worker must agree to such terms, otherwise his job will be taken by one of the large body of unemployed (the "industrial reserve army") constantly created by technical progress, substituting machines for men; so wages never keep pace with the progress of production, and this discrepancy between buying power and output results in periodic crises. Capitalists become ever richer (the "theory of accumulation") and the big ones swallow the small ones (the "theory of concentration"). Huge combines, equipped for an enormous output, arise, but they use ever more machinery, and ever less hands (the "higher organic composition of capital"), thus increasing permanent unemployment, lowering wages and making crises ever deeper. Despite technical progress the worker becomes poorer and poorer (the "theory of impoverishment"). The accumulation of wealth on the one side of society is accompanied by the accumulation of misery on the other side. Eventually a small number of big capitalists is confronted with a mass of starving proletarians for whom they cannot provide even a slave's existence. This is the hour of revolution, when the victorious proletariat will take the machinery of production from capitalistic ownership as their common property (the "expropriation of the expropriators") to run it for the common benefit.

Marxism has influenced every branch of political and social ideas; even its adversaries have adopted portions of its teachings or methods. Thus Leninism has become a special school of Marxism. His theory of the concentration of wealth, or the condemnation of the "exploitation of man by his fellowman," was borrowed from Saint-Simon, Sismondi and Constantin Pecqueur; his theory of the class struggle was borrowed from French historians of his time, and he owed his theory of surplus value to English economists. "What really dominates the unity of his thinking," remarks Dr. D. D. Runes, "is his conception of history, according to which the forms of economic production determine the formation of human society and the consciousness of its members." While many social thinkers have argued over his concepts and approach, they are ready to admit that he has created a working hypothesis.

---

*The Class Basis of Political Power**

THE HISTORY of all hitherto existing society *is the history of class struggles.*

Freeman and slave, patrician and plebeian, lord and serf, guild-master and journeyman, in a word, oppressor and oppressed, stood in constant opposition to one another, carried on an uninterrupted, now hidden, now open fight, a fight that each time ended, either in a revolutionary re-constitution of society at large, or in the common ruin of the contending classes.

In the earlier epochs of history, we find almost everywhere a complicated arrangement of society into various orders, a manifold gradation of social rank. In ancient Rome we have patricians, knights, plebeians, slaves; in the Middle Ages, feudal lords, vassals, guild-masters, journeymen, apprentices, serfs; in almost all of these classes, again, subordinate gradations.

The modern bourgeois society that has sprouted from the ruins of feudal society has not done away with class antagonisms. It has but established new classes, new conditions of oppression, new forms of struggle in place of the old ones.

Our epoch, the epoch of the bourgeoisie, possesses, however, this distinctive feature: it has simplified the class antagonisms. Society as a whole is more and more splitting up into two great hostile camps, into two great classes directly facing each other: *Bourgeoisie and Proletariat.*

---

* Karl Marx and Friedrich Engels, *The Communist Manifesto.*

Modern industry has established the world-market, for which the discovery of America paved the way. This market has given an immense development to commerce, to navigation, to communication by land. This development has, in its turn, reacted on the extension of industry; and in proportion as industry, commerce, navigation, railways extended, in the same proportion the bourgeoisie developed, increased its capital, and pushed into the background every class handed down from the Middle Ages.

We see, therefore, *how the modern bourgeoisie is itself the product of a long course of development, of a series of revolutions in the modes of production and exchange.*

Each step in the development of the bourgeoisie was accompanied by a corresponding political advance of that class. An oppressed class under the sway of the feudal nobility, an armed and self-governing association in the medieval commune; here independent urban republic (as in Italy and Germany), there taxable "third estate" of the monarchy (as in France), afterwards, in the period of manufacture proper, serving either the semi-feudal of the absolute monarchy as a counter-poise against the nobility, and, in fact, cornerstone of the great monarchies in general, the bourgeoisie has at last, since the establishment of Modern Industry and of the world-market, conquered for itself, in the modern representative State, exclusive political sway. The executive of the modern State is but a committee for managing the common affairs of the whole bourgeoisie.

The bourgeoisie, historically, has played a most revolutionary part.

The bourgeoisie, wherever it has got the upper hand, has put an end to all feudal, patriarchal, idyllic, relations. It has pitilessly torn asunder the motley feudal ties that bound man to his "natural superiors," and has left remaining no other nexus between man and man than naked self-interest, than callous "cash payment." It has drowned the most heavenly ecstasies of religious fervour, of chivalrous enthusiasm, of philistine sentimentalism, in the joy water of egotistical calculation. It has resolved personal worth into exchange value, and in place of the numberless indefeasible chartered freedoms, has set up that single, unconscionable freedom—Free Trade. In one word, for exploitation, veiled by religious and political illusions, it has substituted naked, shameless, direct, brutal exploitation.

The bourgeoisie has stripped of its halo every occupation hitherto honoured and looked up to with reverent awe. It has converted the physician, the lawyer, the priest, the poet, the man of science into its paid wage-labourers.

The bourgeoisie has torn away from the family its sentimental veil, and has reduced the family relation to a mere money relation.

The bourgeoisie has disclosed how it came to pass that the brutal display of vigour in the Middle Ages, which Reactionists so much admire, found its fitting complement in the most slothful indolence. It has been the first to show what man's activity can bring about. It has accomplished wonders far surpassing Egyptian pyramids, Roman aqueducts, and Gothic cathedrals; it has conducted expeditions that put in the shade all former Exoduses of nations and crusades.

The bourgeoisie cannot exist without constantly revolutionising the instruments of production, and thereby the relations of production, and with them the whole relations of society. Preservation of the old modes of production in unaltered form, was, on the contrary, the first condition of existence for all earlier industrial classes. Constant revolutionising of production, uninterrupted disturbance of all social conditions, everlasting uncertainty and agitation distinguish the bourgeois epoch from all earlier ones. All fixed, fast-frozen relations, with their train of ancient and venerable prejudices and opinions, are swept away, all new-formed ones become antiquated before they can ossify. All that is solid melts in the air, all that is holy is profaned, and man is at last compelled to face with sober senses, his real conditions of life, and his relations with his kind.

The need of a constantly expanding market for its products chases the bourgeoisie over the whole surface of the globe. It must nestle everywhere, settle everywhere, establish connexions everywhere.

The bourgeoisie has through its exploitation of the world-market given a cosmopolitan character to production and consumption in every country. . . .

The bourgeoisie, by the rapid improvement of all instruments of production, by the immensely facilitated means of communication, draws all, even the most barbarian, nations into civilization. The cheap prices of its commodities are the heavy artillery with which it batters down all Chinese Walls, with which it forces the barbarians' intensely obstinate hatred of foreigners to capitulate. It compels all nations, on pain of extinction, to adopt the bourgeois mode of production; it compels them to introduce what it calls civilization into their midst, i.e., to become bourgeois themselves. In one word, it creates a world after its own image.

The bourgeoisie has subjected the country to the rule of the towns. It has created enormous cities, has greatly increased the urban population as compared with the rural, and has thus rescued a considerable part of the population from the idiocy of rural life. Just as it has made the country dependent on the towns, so it has made barbarian and semi-barbarian countries dependent on the civilized ones, nations of peasants on nations of bourgeois, the East on the West.

The bourgeoisie keeps more and more doing away with the scattered state of the population, of the means of production, and of property. It has agglomerated population, centralized means of production, and has concentrated property in a few hands. The necessary consequence of this was political centralization. Independent, or but loosely connected provinces, with separate interests, laws, governments and systems of taxation, became lumped together into one nation, with one government, one code of laws, one national class-interest, one frontier and one customs-tariff.

The bourgeoisie, during its rule of scarce one hundred years, has created more massive and more colossal productive forces than have all preceding generations together. . . .

We see then: the means of production and of exchange, on whose foundation the bourgeoisie built itself up, were generated in feudal society. At a certain stage in the development of these means of production and of exchange, the conditions under which feudal society produced and exchanged, the feudal organization of agriculture and manufacturing industry, in one word, the feudal relations of property became no longer compatible with the already developed productive forces; they became so many fetters. They had to be burst asunder; they were burst asunder.

Into their place stepped free competition, accompanied by a social and political constitution adapted to it, and by the economical and political sway of the bourgeois class.

A similar movement is going on before our own eyes. Modern bourgeois society with its relations of production, of exchange and of property, a society that has conjured up such gigantic means of production and of exchange, is like the sorcerer who is no longer able to control the powers of the nether world whom he has called up by his spells. For many a decade past the history of industry and commerce is but the history of the revolt of modern productive forces against modern conditions of production, against the property relations that are the conditions for the existence of the bourgeoisie and of its rule. It is enough to mention the commercial crises that by their periodical return put on its trial, each time more threateningly, the existence of the entire bourgeoisie society. In these crises a great part not only of the existing products, but also of the previously created productive forces, are periodically destroyed. In these crises there breaks out an epidemic that, in all earlier epochs, would have seemed an absurdity—the epidemic of overproduction. Society suddenly finds itself put back into a state of momentary barbarism; it appears as if a famine, a universal war of devastation had cut off the supply of every means of subsistence; industry and commerce seem to be destroyed; and why? Because there is too much civilization, too much means of subsistence, too much industry, too much commerce. The productive forces at the disposal of society no longer tend to further the development of the conditions of bourgeois property; on the contrary, they have become too powerful for these conditions, by which they are fettered, and so soon as they overcome these fetters, they bring disorder into the whole of bourgeois society, endanger the existence of bourgeois property. The conditions of bourgeois society are too narrow to comprise the wealth created by them. And how does the bourgeoisie get over these crises? On the one hand by enforced destruction of a mass of productive forces; on the other, by the conquest of new markets, and by the more thorough exploitation of the old ones. That is to say, by paving the way for more extensive and more destructive crises, and by diminishing the means whereby crises are prevented.

The weapons with which the bourgeoisie felled feudalism to the ground are now turned against the bourgeoisie itself.

But not only has the bourgeoisie forged the weapons that bring death to itself; it has also called into existence the men who are to wield those weapons—the modern working class—the proletarians.

In proportion as the bourgeoisie, i.e., capital, is developed, in the same proportion is the proletariat, the modern working class, developed—a class of labourers, who live only so long as they find work, and who find work only so long as their labour increases capital. These labourers, who must sell themselves piecemeal, are a commodity, like every other article of commerce, and are consequently exposed to all the vicissitudes of competition, to all the fluctuations of the market.

Owing to the extensive use of machinery and to division of labour, the work of the proletarians has lost all individual character, and, consequently, all charm for the workman. He becomes an appendage of the machine, and it is only the most simple, most monotonous, and most easily acquired knack, that is required of him. Hence, the cost of production of a workman is restricted, almost entirely, to the means of subsistence that he requires for his maintenance, and for the propagation of his race. But the price of a commodity, and therefore also of labour, is equal to its cost of production. In proportion, therefore, as the repulsiveness of the work increases, the wage decreases. Nay more, in proportion as the use of machinery and division of labour increase, in the same proportion the burden of toil also increases, whether by prolongation of the working hours, by increase of the work exacted in a given time or by increased speed of the machinery, etc.

Modern industry has converted the little workshop of the patriarchal master into the great factory of the industrial capitalist. Masses of labourers, crowded into the factory, are organized like soldiers. As privates of the industrial army they are placed under the command of a perfect hierarchy of officers and sergeants. Not only are they slaves of the bourgeois class, and of the bourgeois State; they are daily and hourly enslaved by the machine, by the overlooker, and, above all, by the individual bourgeois manufacturer himself. The more openly this despotism proclaims gain to be its end and aim, the more petty, the more hateful and the more embittering it is.

The lower strata of the middle class—the small tradespeople, shopkeepers, and retired tradesmen generally, the handicraftsmen and peasants—all these sink gradually into the proletariat, partly because their diminutive capital does not suffice for the scale on which Modern Industry is carried on, and is swamped in the competition with the large capitalists, partly because their specialized skill is rendered worthless by new methods of production. Thus the proletariat is recruited from all classes of the population.

The proletariat goes through various stages of development. With its birth begins its struggle with the bourgeoisie. At first the contest is carried on by individual labourers, then by the workpeople of a factory, then by the operatives on one trade, in one locality, against the individual bourgeois who directly exploits them. They direct their attacks not against the bourgeois conditions of production, but against the instruments of production themselves; they destroy imported wares that compete with their labour, they smash to pieces machinery, they set factories ablaze, they seek to restore by force the vanished status of the workman of the Middle Ages.

At this stage the labourers still form an incoherent mass scattered over the whole country, and broken up by their mutual competition. If anywhere they united to form more compact bodies, this is not yet the consequence of their own active union, but of the union of the bourgeoisie, which class, in order to attain its own political ends, is compelled to set the whole proletariat in motion, and is moreover yet, for a time, able to do so. At this stage, therefore, the proletarians do not fight their enemies, the remnants of absolute monarchy, the landowners, the non-industrial bourgeois, the petty bourgeoisie. Thus the whole historical movement is concentrated in the hands of the bourgeoisie; every victory so obtained is a victory for the bourgeoisie.

But with the development of industry the proletariat not only increases in number; it becomes concentrated in greater masses, its strength grows and it feels that strength more. The various interests and conditions of life within the ranks of the proletariat are more and more equalized in proportion, as machinery obliterates all distinctions of labour, and nearly everywhere reduces wages to the same low level. The growing competition among the bourgeois, and the resulting commercial crises, make the wages of the workers ever more fluctuating. The unceasing improvement of machinery, ever more rapidly developing, makes their livelihood more and more precarious; the collisions between individual workmen and individual bourgeois take more and more the character of collisions between two classes. Thereupon the workers begin to form combinations (Trades' Unions) against the bourgeois; they club together in order to keep up the rate of wages; they found permanent associations in order to make provision beforehand for these occasional revolts. Here and there the contest breaks out into riots.

Now and then the workers are victorious, but only for a time. The real fruit of their battles lies, not in the immediate result, but in the ever-expanding union of the workers. This union is helped on by the improved means of communication that are created by modern industry and that place the workers of different localities in contact with one another. It was just this contact that was needed to centralize the numerous local struggles, all of the same character, into one national struggle between classes. But every class struggle is a political struggle. And that union, to attain which the burghers of the Middle Ages, with their miserable highways, required centuries, the modern proletarians, thanks to railways, achieve in a few years.

This organization of the proletarians into a class, and consequently into a political party is continually being upset again by the competition between the workers themselves. But it ever rises up again, stronger, firmer, mightier. It compels legislative recognition of particular interests of the workers, by taking advantage of the divisions among the bourgeoisie itself. Thus the ten-hours' bill in England was carried.

Altogether collisions between the classes of the old society further, in many ways, the course of development of the proletariat. The bourgeoisie finds itself involved in a constant battle. At first with the aristocracy; later on with those portions of the bourgeoisie itself, whose interests have become antagonistic to the progress of industry; at all times, with the bourgeoisie of foreign countries. In all these battles it sees itself compelled to appeal to the proletariat, to ask for its help, and thus, to drag it into the political arena. The bourgeoisie itself, therefore, supplies the proletariat with its own elements of political and general education, in other words, it furnishes the proletariat with weapons for fighting the bourgeoisie.

Further, as we have already seen, entire sections of the ruling classes are by the advance of industry, precipitated into the proletariat, or are at least threatened in their conditions of existence. These also supply the proletariat with fresh elements of enlightenment and progress.

Finally, in times when the class struggle nears the decisive hour, the process of dissolution going on within the ruling class, in fact within the whole range of old society, assumes such a violent, glaring character, that a small section of the ruling class cuts itself adrift, and joins the revolutionary class, the class that holds the future in its hands. Just as, therefore, at an earlier period, a section of the nobility went over to the bourgeoisie, so now a portion of the bourgeoisie goes over to the proletariat, and in particular, a portion of the bourgeois ideologists, who have raised themselves to the level of comprehending theoretically the historical movement as a whole.

Of all the classes that stand face to face with the bourgeoisie today, the proletariat alone is a really revolutionary class. The other classes decay and finally disappear in the face of modern industry; the proletariat is its special and essential product.

All preceding classes that got the upper hand, sought to fortify their already acquired status by subjecting society at large to their conditions of appropriation. The proletarians cannot become masters of the productive forces of society, except by abolishing their own previous mode of appropriation. They have nothing of their own to secure and to fortify; their mission is to destroy all previous securities for, and insurances of, individual property.

All previous historical movements were movements of minorities. The proletarian movement is the self-conscious, independent movement of the immense majority, in the interests of the immense majority. The proletariat, the lowest stratum of our present society, cannot stir, cannot raise itself up, without the whole superincumbent strata of official society being sprung into the air.

Though not in substance, yet in form, the struggle of the proletariat with the bourgeoisie is at first a national struggle. The proletariat of each country must, of course, first of all settle matters with its own bourgeoisie.

In depicting the most general phases of the development of the proletariat, we trace more or less veiled civil war, ranging within existing society, up to the point where that war breaks out into open revolution, and where the violent overthrow of the bourgeoisie lays the foundation for the sway of the proletariat.

Hitherto, every form of society has been based, as we have already seen, on the antagonism of oppressing and oppressed classes. But in order to oppress a class, certain conditions must be assured to it under which it can, at least, continue its slavish existence. The serf, in the period of serfdom, raised himself to membership in the commune, just as the petty bourgeois, under the yoke of feudal absolutism managed to develop into a bourgeois. The modern labourer, on the contrary, instead of rising with the progress of industry, sinks deeper and deeper below the conditions of existence of his own class. He becomes a pauper, and pauperism develops more rapidly than population and wealth. And here it becomes evident, that the bourgeoisie is unfit any longer to be the ruling class in society, and to impose its conditions of existence upon society as an overriding law. It is unfit to rule because it is incompetent to assure an existence to its slave within his slavery, because it cannot help letting him sink into such a state, that it has to feed him, instead of being fed by him. Society can no longer live under this bourgeoisie, in other words, its existence is no longer compatible with society.

The essential condition for the existence, and for the sway of the bourgeois class, is the formation and augmentation of capital; the condition for capital is wage-labour. Wage labour rests exclusively on competition between the labourers. The advance of industry, whose involuntary promoter is the bourgeoisie, replaces the isolation of the labourers, due to competition, by their revolutionary combination, due to association. The development of Modern Industry, therefore, cuts from under its feet the very foundation on which the bourgeoisie produces and appropriates products. What the bourgeoisie, therefore, produces, above all is its own grave-diggers. Its fall and the victory of the proletariat are equally inevitable.

Position of the Communists in relation to the various existing opposition parties. The Communists fight for the attainment of the immediate aims, for the enforcement of the momentary interests of the working class; but in the movement of the present, they also represent and take care of the future of that movement.

In short, the Communists everywhere support every revolutionary movement against the existing social and political order of things.

In these movements they bring to the front, as the leading question in each, the property question, no matter what its degree of development at the time.

Finally, they labour everywhere for the union and agreement of the democratic parties of all countries.

The Communists disdain to conceal their views and aims. They openly declare that their ends can be attained only by the forcible overthrow of all existing social conditions. Let the ruling classes tremble at a Communistic revolution. The proletarians have nothing to lose but their chains. They have a world to win.

Workingmen of all countries, unite! . . .

JOHN STUART MILL
(1806-1873)

An English political economist and philosopher, led the trend in liberal thought away from the extreme individualism of the utilitarians toward greater governmental action, reflecting the major dilemmas of modern democracy (*On Liberty,* 1859; *Considerations on Representative Government,* 1860; *System of Logic,* Book VI, 1843; *Thoughts on Parliamentary Reform,* 1859; *Utilitarianism,* 1863; and *The Subjection of Women,* 1869). His theory resembled that of Tocqueville, since both thinkers feared tyranny by the majority, but Mill did not use the aristocratic approach to evaluating democracy; he saw democratic government as a positive good to be sought and not a mixed blessing. He believed that the greater number of society should be free to elect and control their governors (the principle of political equality of Rousseau); but he also insisted that the autonomous individual, whether alone or part of a social minority, should be allowed to think and act according to his conscience. He was also critical of the philosophy cherished by his father, James Mill, the stern utilitarian who educated him as his son's sole teacher. At the age of three, John Stuart learned Greek; at seven he studied Plato's dialogues; at eight he had to teach his sister Latin; when fifteen years of age, he was initiated into Bentham's doctrine of the greatest happiness of the greatest number, which struck him as a revelation and made him a lifetime convert to utilitarianism.

Mill was also influenced by Comte and Guizot, and combined British utilitarianism with French positivism. Thus he remained a staunch defender of individual liberty because he was convinced of its social usefulness; but he was ready to sacrifice individual property rights when they endangered the common good. He remained the advocate of representative government, but he considered social questions of increasing importance and became more and more devoted to the cause of the working class, without idealizing the workers. When he campaigned for a seat in Parliament, he warned his constituents that he would do nothing for their special interest but only what he thought to be right. He also fought for women's suffrage and for the rights of colored people. During the second half of the nineteenth century, his influence on the spirit of European philosophy was immense, and many of the noted reforms of that century can be traced to it. Since then it has withered. But many of those who belittle him are, in fact, obligated to him. What he said of Bentham may be also true of Mill himself: "He was not a great philosopher but a great reformer in philosophy."

---

*The Proper Limits of Government**

THE OBJECTIONS to government interference, when it is not such as to involve infringement of liberty, may be of three kinds.

The first is, when the thing to be done is likely to be better done by individuals than by the government. Speaking generally, there is no one so fit to conduct any business, or to determine how or by whom it shall be conducted, as those who are personally interested in it. This principle condemns the interferences, once so common, of the legislature, or the officers of government, with the ordinary processes of industry. But this part of the subject has been sufficiently enlarged upon by political economists, and is not particularly related to the principles of this essay.

The second objection is more nearly allied to our subject. In many cases, though individuals may not do the particular thing so well, on the average, as the officers of government, it is nevertheless desirable that it should be done by them rather than by the government, as a means to their own

* This excerpt taken from John Stuart Mill, *On Liberty,* London: John W. Parker & Son, 1859, pp. 186-207, *passim.*

mental education—a mode of strengthening their active faculties, exercising their judgment, and giving them a familiar knowledge of the subjects with which they are thus left to deal. This is a principal, though not the sole, recommendation of jury trial (in cases not political); of free and popular local and municipal institutions; of the conduct of industrial and philanthropic enterprises by voluntary associations. These are not questions of liberty, and are connected with that subject only by remote tendencies; but they are questions of development. It belongs to a different occasion from the present to dwell on these things as parts of national education; as being, in truth, the peculiar training of a citizen, the practical part of the political education of a free people, taking them out of the narrow circle of personal and family selfishness, and accustoming them to the comprehension of joint interests, the management of joint concerns—habituating them to act from public or semi-public motives, and guide their conduct by aims which unite instead of isolating them from one another. Without these habits and powers, a free constitution can neither be worked nor preserved; as is exemplified by the too often transitory nature of political freedom in countries where it does not rest upon a sufficient basis of local liberties. The management of purely local business by the localities, and of the great enterprises of industry by the union of those who voluntarily supply the pecuniary means, is further recommended by all the advantages which have been set forth in this essay as belonging to individuality of development, and diversity of modes of action. Government operations tend to be everywhere alike. With individuals and voluntary associations, on the contrary, there are varied experiments, and endless diversity of experience. What the State can usefully do is to make itself a central depository, and active circulator and diffuser, of the experience resulting from many trials. Its business is to enable each experimentalist to benefit by the experiments of others, instead of tolerating no experiments but its own.

The third and most cogent reason for restricting the interference of government is the great evil of adding unnecessarily to its power. Every function superadded to those already exercised by the government causes its influence over hopes and fears to be more widely diffused, and converts, more and more, the active and ambitious part of the public into hangers-on of the government or of some party which aims at becoming the government. If the roads, the railways, the banks, the insurance offices, the great joint-stock companies, the universities, and the public charities, were all of them branches of the government; if, in addition, the municipal corporations and local boards, with all that now devolves on them, became departments of the central administration; if the employees of all these different enterprises were appointed and paid by the government, and looked to the government for every rise in life; not all the freedom of the press and popular constitution of the legislature would make this or any other country free otherwise than in name. And the evil would be greater, the more efficiently and scientifically the administrative machinery was constructed—the more skillful the arrangements for obtaining the best qualified hands and heads with which to work it. . . . If indeed all the high talent of the country *could* be drawn into the service of the government, a proposal tending to bring about that result might well inspire uneasiness. If every part of the business of society which required organized concert, or large and comprehensive views, were in the hands of the government, and if government offices were universally filled by the ablest men, all the enlarged culture and practiced intelligence in the country, except the purely speculative, would be concentrated in a numerous bureaucracy, to whom alone the rest of the community would look for all things: the multitude for direction and dictation in all they had to do; the able and aspiring for personal advancement. To be admitted into the ranks of this bureaucracy, and when admitted, to rise therein, would be the sole object of ambition. Under this *regime,* not only is the outside public ill-qualified, for want of practical experience, to criticize or check the mode of operation of the bureaucracy, but even if the accidents of despotic or the natural working of popular institutions occasionally raise to the summit a ruler or rulers of reforming inclinations, no reform can be effected which is contrary to the interest of the bureaucracy. . . . [T]he public, accustomed to expect everything to be done for them by the State, or at least to do nothing for themselves without asking from the State not only leave to do it, but even how it is to be done, naturally hold the State responsible for all evil which befalls them, and when the evil exceeds their amount of patience, they rise against the government, and make what is called a revolution; whereupon somebody else, with or without legitimate authority from the nation, vaults into the seat, issues his orders to the bureaucracy, and everything goes on much as it did before; the bureaucracy being unchanged, and nobody else being capable of taking their place. . . .

It is not, also, to be forgotten, that the absorption of all the principal ability of the country into the governing body is fatal, sooner or later, to the mental activity and progressiveness of the body itself. Banded together as they are—working a system which, like all systems, necessarily proceeds in a great measure by fixed rules—the official body are under the constant temptation of sinking into indolent routine, or if they now and then desert that mill-horse round, of rushing into some half-examined crudity which has struck the fancy of some leading member of the corps; and the sole check to these closely allied, though seemingly opposite, tendencies, the only stimulus which can keep the ability of the body itself up to a high standard, is liability to the watchful criticism of equal ability outside the body. It is indispensable, therefore, that the means should exist, independently of the government, of forming such ability, and furnishing it with the opportunities and experience necessary for a correct judgment of great practical affairs. If we would possess permanently . . . a body able to originate and willing to adopt improvements; if we would not have our bureaucracy degenerate into a pedantocracy, this body must not engross all the occupations which form and cultivate the faculties required for the government of mankind.

To determine the point at which evils, so formidable to human freedom and advancement, begin, or rather at which they begin to predominate over the benefits attending the collective application of the force of society, under its recognized chiefs, for the removal of the obstacles which stand in the way of its well-being; to secure as much of the advantages of centralized power and intelligence as can be had without turning into governmental channels too great a proportion of the general activity—is one of the most difficult and complicated questions in the art of government. It is, in a great measure, a question of detail, in which many and various considerations must be kept in view, and no absolute rule can be laid down. But I believe that the practical principle in which safety resides, the ideal to be kept in view, the standard by which to test all arrangements intended for overcoming the difficulty, may be conveyed in these words: the greatest dissemination of power consistent with efficiency; but the greatest possible centralization of information, and diffusion of it from the center. . . . This central organ should have a right to know all that is done, and its special duty should be that of making the knowledge acquired in one place available for others. Emancipated from the petty prejudices and narrow views of a locality by its elevated position and comprehensive sphere of observation, its advice would naturally carry much authority; but its actual power, as a permanent institution, should, I conceive, be limited to compelling the local officers to obey the laws laid down for their guidance. . . . A government cannot have too much of the kind of activity which does not impede, but aids and stimulates, individual exertion and development. The mischief begins when, instead of calling forth the activity and powers of individuals and bodies, it substitutes its own activity for theirs; when, instead of informing, advising, and, upon occasion, denouncing, it makes them work in fetters, or bids them stand aside and does their work instead of them. The worth of a State, in the long run, is the worth of the individuals composing it: and a State which postpones the interest of *their* mental expansion and elevation to a little more of administrative skill, or of that semblance of it which practice gives, in the details of business; a State which dwarfs its men, in order that they may be more docile instruments in its hands even for beneficial purposes—will find that with small men no great thing can really be accomplished; and that the perfection of machinery to which it has sacrificed everything will in the end avail it nothing, for want of the vital power which, in order that the machine might work more smoothly, it has preferred to banish.

MONTESQUIEU, BARON DE LA BRÈDE
(Charles Louis de Secordat)
(1689-1755)

Was a French historian and aristocrat whose political ideas, especially the principle of separation of powers, or of checks and balances, deeply influenced Jefferson, Hamilton, Adams, Madison and the other founders of the United States. He spent much of his life as a high judge in Bordeaux, at the same time engaging in study and presenting papers on philosophy, politics and natural science to the academy there. In his early writings he satirized, anonymously, the social and literary conditions of his day. Then he traveled extensively through Europe, observing men and society, and in 1784 published his chief work, *Esprit des Lois* (*Spirit of the Law*), the purpose of which was to show how the laws of a country are related to its social and geographical characteristics, such as the government, customs, climate, religion and commerce. It was a notable attempt at the empiric approach in the study of actual conditions. His *Persian Letters* (1721) was a thinly veiled satirical criticism of French life; his *Reflections on the Causes of the Greatness and the Decadence of the Romans* (1734) is considered one of the most important monuments of modern historical literature. He especially admired England; for him English institutions guaranteed and realized the highest possible degree of freedom, and he attributed this to the application of the principle of checks and balances (although this view is not shared by modern constitutional historians or jurists, least of all concerning the England of Montesquieu's day). But his influence has been of most lasting value on the rise of methods of analyzing political, social and legal conditions. Next to John Locke, Montesquieu was the most influential champion of liberalism in the eighteenth century. Montesquieu himself was influenced by Giambattista Vico (1668-1744), who believed that political institutions and ideas pass through transitions in accordance with their environment and with the national character of the people who practice them. Thus, for Montesquieu, no form of government was basically good; its value was relative, and if the spirit which characterized each form underwent change, a revolution necessarily followed. He was mainly interested in liberty (deriving his ideas from Locke), stressing natural rights or individualism; liberty was possible only where governmental powers were subject to limitations, and the essential safeguard was the separation of the executive, legislative and judicial powers of government (such as he thought existed in England). His inductive and historical method was that of Aristotle, Machiavelli and Bodin. His confidence in the validity of natural reason simplified his approach. The confidence and serenity of his writing recall the poise of the Hellenistic and Augustan ages, mingled with the French eighteenth century's optimism.

---

*The Nature of Laws**

LAWS, in their most general signification, are the necessary relation arising from the nature of things. In this sense all beings have their laws: the Deity His laws, the material world its laws, the intelligences superior to man their laws, the beasts their laws, man his laws.

They who assert that a blind fatality produced the various effects we behold in this world talk very absurdly; for can anything be more unreasonable than to pretend that a blind fatality could be productive of intelligent beings?

There is, then, a prime reason; and laws are the relations subsisting between it and different beings, and the relations of these to one another.

God is related to the universe, as Creator and Preserver; the laws by which He created all things are those by which

* Excerpts taken from Dagobert D. Runes, ed., *Treasury of Philosophy*, New York: Philosophical Library, 1955, pp. 834-839.

He preserves them. He acts according to these rules, because He knows them; He knows them, because He made them; and He made them, because they are in relation to His wisdom and power.

Since we observe that the world, though formed by the motion of matter, and void of understanding, subsists through so long a succession of ages, its motions must certainly be directed by invariable laws, and could we imagine another world, it must also have constant rules, or it would inevitably perish.

Thus the creation, which seems an arbitrary act, supposes laws as invariable as those of the fatality of the Atheists. It would be absurd to say that the Creator might govern the world without those rules, since without them it could not subsist.

These rules are a fixed and invariable relation. In bodies moved, the motion is received, increased, diminished, or lost, according to the relations of the quantity of matter and velocity; each diversity is *uniformity,* each change is *constancy.*

Particular intelligent beings may have laws of their own making, but they have some likewise which they never made. Before there were intelligent beings, they were possible; they had therefore possible relations, and consequently possible laws. Before laws were made, there were relations of possible justice. To say that there is nothing just or unjust but what is commanded or forbidden by positive laws, is the same as saying that before the describing of a circle all the radii were not equal.

We must therefore acknowledge relations of justice antecedent to the positive law by which they are established: as, for instance, if human societies existed, it would be right to conform to their laws; if there were intelligent beings that had received a benefit of another being, they ought to show their gratitude; if one intelligent being had created another intelligent being, the latter ought to continue in its original state of dependence; if one intelligent being injures another, it deserves a retaliation; and so on.

But the intelligent world is far from being so well governed as the physical. For though the former has also its laws, which of their own nature are invariable, it does not conform to them so exactly as the physical world. This is because, on the one hand, particular intelligent beings are of a finite nature, and consequently liable to error; and on the other, their nature requires them to be free agents. Hence they do not steadily conform to their primitive laws; and even those of their own instituting they frequently infringe.

Whether brutes be governed by the general laws of motion, or by particular movement, we cannot determine. Be that as it may, they have not a more intimate relation to God than the rest of the material world; and sensation is of no other use to them than in the relation they have either to other particular beings or to themselves.

By the allurement of pleasure they preserve the individual, and by the same allurement they preserve their species. They have natural laws, because they are united by sensation; positive laws they have none, because they are not connected by knowledge. And yet they do not invariably conform to their natural laws; these are better observed by vegetables, that have neither understanding nor sense.

Brutes are deprived of the high advantages which we have; but they have some which we have not. They have not our hopes, but they are without our fears; they are subject like us to death, but without knowing it; even most of them are more attentive than we to self-preservation, and do not make so bad a use of their passions.

Man, as a physical being, is like other bodies governed by invariable laws. As an intelligent being, he incessantly transgresses the laws established by God, and changes those of his own instituting. He is left to his private direction, though a limited being, and subject, like all finite intelligences, to ignorance and error: even his imperfect knowledge he loses; and as a sensible creature, he is hurried away by a thousand impetuous passions. Such a being might every instant forget his Creator; God has therefore reminded him of his duty by the laws of religion. Such a being is liable every moment to forget himself; philosophy has provided against this by the laws of morality. Formed to live in society, he might forget his fellow-creatures; legislators have therefore by political and civil laws confined him to his duty.

Antecedent to the above-mentioned laws are those of nature, so called, because they derive their force entirely from our frame and existence. In order to have a perfect knowledge of these laws, we must consider man before the establishment of society: the laws received in such a state would be those of nature.

The law which, impressing on our minds the idea of a Creator, inclines us towards Him, is the first in importance, though not in order, of natural laws. Man in a state of nature would have the faculty of knowing, before he had acquired any knowledge. Plain it is that his first ideas would not be of a speculative nature; he would think of the preservation of his being, before he would investigate its origin. Such a man would feel nothing in himself at first but impotency and weakness; his fears and apprehensions would be excessive; as appears from instances (were there any necessity of proving it) of savages found in forests, trembling at the motion of a leaf, and flying from every shadow.

In this state every man, instead of being sensible of his equality, would fancy himself inferior. There would therefore be no danger of their attacking one another; peace would be the first law of nature.

The natural impulse or desire which Hobbes attributes to mankind of subduing one another is far from being well founded. The idea of empire and dominion is so complex, and depends on so many other notions, that it could never be the first which occurred to the human understanding.

Hobbes inquires, *For what reason go men armed, and*

have locks and keys to fasten their doors, if they be not naturally in a state of war? But is it not obvious that he attributes to mankind before the establishment of society what can happen but in consequence of this establishment, which furnishes, them with motives for hostile attacks and self-defense?

Next to a sense of his weakness man would soon find that of his wants. Hence another law of nature would prompt him to seek for nourishment.

Fear, I have observed, would induce men to shun one another; but the marks of this fear being reciprocal would soon engage them to associate. Besides, this association would quickly follow from the very pleasure one animal feels at the approach of another of the same species. Again, the attraction arising from the difference of sexes would enhance this pleasure, and the natural inclination they have for each other would form a third law.

Besides the sense or instinct which man possesses in common with brutes, he has the advantage of acquired knowledge; and thence arises a second tie, which brutes have not. Mankind have therefore a new motive of uniting; and a fourth law of nature results from the desire of living in society.

As soon as man enters into a state of society he loses the sense of his weakness; quality ceases, and then commences the state of war.

Each particular society begins to feel its strength, whence arises a state of war between different nations. The individuals likewise of each society become sensible of their force; hence the principal advantages of this society they endeavor to convert to their own emolument, which constitutes a state of war between individuals.

These two different kinds of states give rise to human laws. Considered as inhabitants of so great a planet, which necessarily contains a variety of nations, they have laws relating to their mutual intercourse, which is what we call the *law of nations.* As members of a society that must be properly supported they have laws relating to the governors and the governed and this we distinguish by the name of *political law.* They have also another sort of laws, as they stand in relation to each other; by which is understood the *civil law.*

The law of nations is naturally founded on this principle, that different nations ought in time of peace to do one another all the good they can, prejudicing their real interests.

The object of war is victory; that of victory is conquest; and that of conquest preservation. From this and the preceding principle all those rules are derived which constitute the *law of nations.*

All countries have a law of nations, not excepting the Iroquois themselves, though they devour their prisoners: for they send and receive ambassadors, and understand the rights of war and peace. The mischief is that their law of nations is not founded on true principles.

Besides the law of nations relating to all societies, there is a polity or civil constitution for each particularly considered. No society can subsist without a form of government. *The united strength of individuals,* as Gravina well observes, *constitutes what we call the body politic.*

The general strength may be found in the hands of a single person, or of many. Some think that nature having established paternal authority, the most natural government was that of a single person. But the example of paternal authority proves nothing. For if the power of a father relates to a single government, that of brothers after the death of a father, and that of cousin-germans after the decease of brothers, refer to a government of many. The political power necessarily comprehends the union of several families.

Better is it to say, that the government most conformable to nature is that which best agrees with the humor and disposition of the people in whose favor it is established.

The strength of individuals cannot be united without a conjunction of all their wills. *The conjunction of those wills,* as Gravina again very justly observes, *is what we call the civil state*.

Law in general is human reason, inasmuch as it governs all the inhabitants of the earth: the political and civil laws of each nation ought to be only the particular case in which human reason is applied.

They should be adapted in such a manner to the people for whom they are framed that it should be a great chance if those of one nation suit another.

They should be in relation to the nature and principle of each government; whether they form it, as may be said of political laws; or whether they support it, as in the case of civil institutions.

They should be in relation to the climate of each country, to the quality of its soil, to its situation and extent, to the principal occupation of the natives, whether husbandmen, huntsmen, or shepherds: they should have relation to the degree of liberty which the constitution will bear; to the religion of the inhabitants, to their inclinations, riches, numbers, commerce, manners, and customs. . . .

SIR THOMAS MORE
(1478-1535)

An outstanding representative of Renaissance humanism, was an English statesman and author, a friend of Erasmus, Colet and other leading scholars of the time. He wrote in both Latin and English, his most famous work being *Utopia* (1516), written in Latin. His English works include a biography, *Pice Della Mirandela* (1515); a *History of Richard III* (1543); *Supplication of Souls* (1529); and *An Apology of Sir Thomas More* (1533). He held numerous important positions in the government of his time, being a member of Parliament, an envoy on several missions abroad, a court official, and ultimately Lord Chancellor (succeeding Cardinal Wolsey in 1529). He was also a staunch Catholic, engaging in vigorous controversies with the Protestant "heretics" of the time. Although he had been a friend of King Henry VIII, he would not take an oath to the Act of Supremacy acknowledging the King to be chief authority over the English Church as against the Pope, and for this refusal was beheaded as a traitor. In his *Utopia,* after which numerous utopias have been named, More described an imaginary island where a perfectly wise and happy people had established the best imaginable commonwealth by means of ideal institutions, living in peace and abhorring war and oppression of any kind. He advocated the willing subordination of the individual to the commonwealth, the community ownership of goods, national education and the employment of all; magistrates were elective, and the glories of war were renounced. He found the chief evil in society to be the institution of private property, and pictured a new regime of peace and plenty under a system of communism. The word "Utopia" has become one of the most attractive symbolic words since his time and Utopianism has become an essential component of our civilization, producing a series of projects for a truly rational society, a logic which imposed itself on all subsequent reformers, and a pure expression of the spirit of the Renaissance which would bring reason into every aspect of life and the universe. More's hopes were based on a universal theism of Platonic inspiration.

---

*Utopia**

. . . THE CHIEF, and almost the only business of the syphogrants, is to take care that no man may live idle, but that every one may follow his trade diligently; yet they do not wear themselves out with perpetual toil, from morning to night, as if they were beasts of burden, which as it is indeed a heavy slavery, so it is everywhere the common course of life among all mechanics except the Utopians; but they, dividing the day and night into twenty-four hours, appoint six of these for work; three of which are before dinner; and three after. They then sup, and at eight o'clock, counting from noon, go to bed and sleep eight hours. The rest of their time besides that taken up in work, eating and sleeping, is left to every man's discretion; yet they are not to abuse that interval to luxury and idleness, but must employ it in some proper exercise according to their various inclinations, which is for the most part reading. It is ordinary to have public lectures every morning before daybreak; at which none are obliged to appear but those who are marked out for literature; yet a great many, both men and women of all ranks, go to hear lectures of one sort or other, according to their inclinations. But if others, that are not made for contemplation, choose rather to employ themselves at that time in their trades, as many of them do, they are not hindered, but are rather commended, as men that take care to serve their country. After supper, they spend an hour in

---

* This excerpt taken from Charles M. Andrews, ed., *Ideal Empires and Republics,* Washington & London: M. Walter Dunne, Publishers, 1901, pp. 169-170.

some diversion, in summer in their gardens, and in winter in the halls where they eat; where they entertain each other, either with music or discourse. They do not so much as know dice, or any such foolish and mischievous games; they have, however, two sorts of games not unlike our chess; the one is between several numbers, in which one number, as it were, consumes another; the other resembles a battle between the virtues and the vices, in which the enmity in the vices among themselves, and their agreement against virtue is not unpleasantly represented; together with the special oppositions between the particular virtues and vices; as also the methods by which vice either openly assaults or secretly undermines virtue; and virtue on the other hand resists it. But the time appointed for labor is to be narrowly examined, otherwise you may imagine, that since there are only six hours appointed for work, they may fall under a scarcity of necessary provisions. But it is so far from being true, that this time is not sufficient for supplying them with plenty of all things, either necessary or convenient; that it is rather too much; and this you will easily apprehend, if you consider how great a part of all other nations is quite idle. . . .

GAETANO MOSCA
(1858-1941)

The contemporary of both Marx and Mussolini, was one of the earliest and most brilliant exponents of the doctrine of "elitism," a dominant theme in the history of Western thought in the last three generations. The idea that the Many do not and never will dominate the Few has become common parlance among those belonging to the school of Toynbee's "Creative Minorities." A disappointed Socialist, Mosca claimed (*The Ruling Class*) that no matter what the form of a political society, there are always those who rule and those who are ruled; this small minority dominates in spite of all the legal and political devices to prevent it. This minority rule is carried on not only by force but especially by appealing to the vanities, prejudices and self-interests of the many. The ruling class is seldom solidly united, but is divided into segments or groups which struggle for pre-eminence in the state, and through participation in this fight achieve positions of power. Although the basic motivation is always the same—pre-eminence and power—this is never openly admitted, each ruling class offering a "political formula" to justify its aspirations or its actual exercise of power (using such platitudes as "divine right," "popular will," "social contract," "democracy," "social justice," etc.). Some of these ruling cliques are liberal and others democratic, depending on the elements conditioning their tenure of power and the formula used to justify it. Pareto first berated Mosca's ideas, and then adopted them in his works. Mosca was also interested in the works of C. E. Merriam, H. D. Lasswell, Lord Bryce, Ostrogorski and Benoist. But Mosca considered Machiavelli impractical and unscientific, although he admired the Florentine's clear mind and direct style. Mosca's ideas (and those of Pareto), laying stress on the predominant role of the elite in society, were seized upon by the Nazi and Fascist thinkers to support their concepts of the "leadership" principle and the rule of the elite.

---

*The Bureaucratic State**

Among the constant facts and tendencies that are to be found in all political organisms, one is so obvious that it is apparent to the most casual eye. In all societies—from societies that are very meagerly developed and have barely attained the dawnings of civilization down to the most advanced and powerful societies—two classes of people appear—a class that rules and a class that is ruled. The first class, always the less numerous, performs all political functions, monopolizes power and enjoys the advantages that power brings, whereas the second, the more numerous class, is directed and controlled by the first, in a manner that is now more or less legal, now more or less arbitrary, and violent, and supplies the first in appearance at least, with material means of subsistence and with the instrumentalities that are essential to the vitality of the political organism. . . .

. . . The man who is at the head of the state would certainly not be able to govern without the support of a numerous class to enforce respect for his orders and to have them carried out; and granting that he can make one individual, or indeed many individuals, in the ruling class feel the weight of his power, he certainly cannot be at odds with the class as a whole or do away with it. Even if that were possible, he would at once be forced to create another class, without the support of which action on his part would be completely paralyzed. On the other hand, granting that the discontent of the masses might succeed in deposing a ruling class, inevitably, as we shall later show, there would have to be an-

---

* Excerpts from Gaetano Mosca, *The Ruling Class,* translated by Hannah D. Kahn, edited and revised by Arthur Livingston, New York: McGraw-Hill Book Co., 1939, pp. 50-87, 404-409.

other organized minority within the masses themselves to discharge the functions of a ruling class. Otherwise all organization, and the whole social structure, would be destroyed. . . .

Everywhere—in Russia and Poland, in India and Medieval Europe—the ruling warrior classes acquire almost exclusive ownership of the land. Land, as we have seen, is the chief source of production and wealth in countries that are not very far advanced in civilization. But as civilization progresses, revenue from land increases proportionately. With the growth of population there is, at least in certain periods, an increase in rent, in the "Ricardian" sense of the term, largely because great centers of consumption arise—such at all times have been the great capitals and other large cities, ancient and modern. Eventually, if other circumstances permit, a very important social transformation occurs. Wealth rather than military valor comes to be the characteristic feature of the dominant class: the people who rule are the rich rather than the brave.

The condition that in the main is required for this transformation is that social organization shall have concentrated and become perfected to such an extent that the protection offered by public authority is considerably more effective than the protection offered by private force. In other words, private property must be so well protected by the practical and real efficacy of the laws as to render the power of the proprietor superfluous. This comes about through a series of gradual alterations in the social structure whereby a type of political organization, which we shall call the "feudal," is transformed into an essentially different type, which we shall term the "bureaucratic state." We are to discuss these types at some length hereafter, but we may say at once that the evolution here referred to is as a rule greatly facilitated by progress in pacific manners and customs and by certain moral habits which societies contract as civilization advances.

Once this transformation has taken place, wealth produces

political power just as political power has been producing wealth. In a society already somewhat mature—where, therefore, individual power is curbed by the collective power—if the powerful are as a rule the rich, to be rich is to become powerful. And, in truth, when fighting with the mailed fist is prohibited whereas fighting with pounds and pence is sanctioned, the better posts are inevitably won by those who are better supplied with pounds and pence.

There are, to be sure, states of a very high level of civilization which in theory are organized on the basis of moral principles of such a character that they seem to preclude this overbearing assertiveness on the part of wealth. But this is a case—and there are many such—where theoretical principles can have no more than a limited application in real life. In the United States all powers flow directly or indirectly from popular elections, and suffrage is equal for all men and women in all the states of the Union. What is more, democracy prevails not only in institutions but to a certain extent also in morals. The rich ordinarily feel a certain aversion to entering public life, and the poor a certain aversion to choosing the rich for elective office. But that does not prevent a rich man from being more influential than a poor man, since he can use pressure upon the politicians who control public administration. It does not prevent elections from being carried on to the music of clinking dollars. It does not prevent whole legislatures and considerable numbers of national congressmen from feeling the influence of powerful corporations and great financiers.

In China, too, down to a few years ago, though the government had not accepted the principle of popular elections, it was organized on an essentially equalitarian basis. Academic degrees gave access to public office, and degrees were conferred by examination without any apparent regard for family or wealth. According to some writers, only barbers and certain classes of boatmen, together with their children, were barred from competing for the various grades of the mandarinate. But though the moneyed class in China was less numerous, less wealthy, less powerful than the moneyed class in the United States is at present, it was none the less able to modify the scrupulous application of this system to a very considerable extent. Not only was the indulgence of examiners often bought with money. The government itself sometimes sold the various academic degrees and allowed ignorant persons, often from the lowest social strata, to hold public office.

In all countries of the world those other agencies for exerting social influence—personal publicity, good education, specialized training, high rank in church, public administration, and army—are always readier of access to the rich than to the poor. The rich invariably have a considerably shorter road to travel than the poor, to say nothing of the fact that the stretch of road that the rich are spared is often the roughest and more difficult. . . .

. . . All ruling classes tend to become hereditary in fact if not in law. All political forces seem to possess a quality that in physics used to be called the force of inertia. They have a tendency, that is, to remain at the point and in the state in which they find themselves. Wealth and military valor are easily maintained in certain families by moral tradition and by heredity. Qualification for important office—the habit of, and to an extent the capacity for, dealing with affairs of consequence—is much more readily acquired when one has had a certain familiarity with them from childhood. Even when academic degrees, scientific training, special aptitudes as tested by examinations and competitions, open the way to public office, there is no eliminating the special advantage in favor of certain individuals which the French call the advantage of *positions déjà prises*. In actual fact, though examinations and competitions may theoretically be open to all, the majority never have the resources for meeting the expense of long preparation, and many others are without the connections and kinships that set an individual promptly on the right road, enabling him to avoid the gropings and blunders that are inevitable when one enters an unfamiliar environment without any guidance or support.

The democratic principle of election by broad-based suffrage would seem at first glance to be in conflict with the tendency toward stability which, according to our theory, ruling classes show. But it must be noted that candidates who are successful in democratic elections are almost always the ones who possess the political forces above enumerated, which are very often hereditary. In the English, French and Italian parliaments we frequently see the sons, grandsons, brothers, nephews and sons-in law of members and deputies, ex-members and ex-deputies.

In the second place, when we see a hereditary caste established in a country and monopolizing political power, we may be sure that such a status *de jure* was preceded by a similar status *de facto*. Before proclaiming their exclusive and hereditary right to power the families or castes in question must have held the scepter of command in a firm grasp, completely monopolizing all the political forces of that country at that period. Otherwise such a claim on their part would only have aroused the bitterest protests and provoked the bitterest struggles. . . .

Before we proceed any further, it might be wise to linger briefly on the two types into which, in our opinion, all political organisms may be classified, the feudal and the bureaucratic.

This classification, it should be noted, is not based upon essentially unchanging criteria. It is not our view that there is any psychological law peculiar to either one of the two types and therefore alien to the other. It seems to us, rather, that the two types are just different manifestations, different phases, of a single constant tendency whereby human societies become less simple, or, if one will, more complicated in political organization, as they grow in size and are perfected in civilization. Level of civilization is, on the whole, more important in this regard than size, since, in actual fact, a literally huge state may once have been feudally organized. At bottom, therefore, a bureaucratic state is just a feudal state that has advanced and developed in organization and so grown more complex; and a feudal state may derive from a once bureaucratized society that has decayed in civilization and reverted to a simpler, more primitive form of political organization, perhaps falling to pieces in the process.

By "feudal state" we mean that type of political organization in which all the executive functions of society—the economic, the judicial, the administrative, the military—are exercised simultaneously by the same individuals, while at the same time the state is made up of small social aggregates, each of which possesses all the organs that are required for self-sufficiency. The Europe of the Middle Ages offers the most familiar example of this type of organization—that is why we have chosen to designate it by the term "feudal;" but as one reads the histories of other peoples or scans the accounts of travelers of our own day one readily perceives that the type is widespread. Just as the medieval baron was simultaneously owner of the land, military commander, judge and administrator of his fief, over which he enjoyed both a pure and a mixed sovereignty, so the Abyssinian *ras* dispensed justice, commanded the soldiery and levied taxes—or rather extorted from the farmer everything over and above the bare necessaries of subsistence. . . .

In the bureaucratic state not all the executive functions need to be concentrated in the bureaucracy and exercised by it. One might even declare that so far in history that has never been the case. The main characteristic of this type of social organization lies, we believe, in the fact that, wherever it exists, the central power conscripts a considerable portion of the social wealth by taxation and uses it first to maintain a military establishment and then to support a more or less extensive number of public services. The greater the number of officials who perform public duties and receive their salaries from the central government or from its local agencies, the more bureaucratic a society becomes.

In a bureaucratic state there is always a greater specialization in the functions of government than in a feudal state. The first and most elementary division of capacities is the withdrawal of administrative and judiciary powers from the military element. The bureaucratic state, furthermore, assures a far greater discipline in all grades of political, administrative and military service. To gain some conception of what this means, one has only to compare a medieval count, hedged about by armed retainers and by vassals who have been attached for centuries to his family and supported by the produce of his lands, with a modern French or Italian prefect or army general, whom a telegram can suddenly shear of authority and even of stipend. The feudal state, therefore, demands great energy and a great sense of statemanship in the man, or men, who stand on the top rung of the social ladder, if the various social groups, which would otherwise tend to disorganization and autonomy, are to be kept organized, compact and obedient to a single impulse. So true is this that often with death of an influential leader the power of a feudal state itself comes to an end. Only great moral unity—the presence of a sharply defined social type—can long save the political existence of a people that is feudally organized. Nothing less than Christianity was required to hold the Abyssinian tribes together amid the masses of pagans and Mohammedans that encircled them, and to preserve their autonomy for over two thousand years. But when the estranging force is feeble, or when the feudal state comes into contact with more soundly organized peoples, then such a state may very easily be absorbed and vanish in one of the frequent periodical crises to which its central power is irremediably exposed—the example of Poland comes immediately to mind. On the other hand, the personal qualities of the supreme head exert relatively little influence on the destinies of a bureaucratic state. A society that is bureaucratically organized may retain its freedom even if it repudiates an old political formula and adopts a new one, or even if it subjects its social type to very far-reaching modifications. This was the case with the Roman Empire. It survived the adoption of Christianity in the West for a century and a half, and in the East for more than eleven centuries. So our modern nations have nearly all shifted at one time or another from a divine-right formula to parliamentary systems of government.

Bureaucratic organization need not necessarily be centralized, in the sense commonly given to that expression. Often bureaucratization is compatible with a very liberal provincial autonomy, as in China, where the eighteen strictly Chinese provinces preserved broad autonomous privileges and the capital city of each province looked after almost all provincial affairs.

States of European civilization—even the most decentralized of them—are all bureaucratized. As we have already indicated, the chief characteristic of a bureaucratic organization is that its military functions, and other public services in numbers more or less large, are exercised by salaried employees. Whether salaries are paid exclusively by the central government or in part by local bodies more or less under the control of the central government is a detail that is not as important as it is often supposed to be. History is not lacking in cases of very small political organisms which have accomplished miracles of energy in every branch of human activity with the barest rudiments of bureaucratic organization or with practically none at all. The ancient Hellenic cities and the Italian communes of the Middle Ages are examples that flock to mind. But when vast human organisms, spreading over huge territories and comprising millions and millions of individuals, are involved, nothing short of bureaucratic organization seems capable of uniting under a single impulse the immense treasures of economic power and moral and intellectual energy with which a ruling class can in a measure modify conditions within a society and make its influence effective and powerful beyond its own frontiers. Under a feudal organization the authority which a given member of the ruling class exerts over individuals of the subject class, few or many, may be more direct, oppressive, and arbitrary. Under a bureaucratic organization society is influenced less by the given individual leader than by the ruling class as a whole.

Egypt was bureaucratized in the golden ages of the seventeenth and eighteenth dynasties, when the civilization of the Pharaohs had one of its most lustrous periods of renascence, and the Egyptian battalions pushed their conquests from the Blue Nile to the foothills of the Caucasus. In the ancient Egypt, as in China, the coinage of precious metals was unknown. Taxes therefore were collected in kind or were calculated in precious metals, which were weighed out on scales. This was no inconsiderable obstacle to the functioning of the bureaucratic system. The difficulty was overcome by a complicated and very detailed system of bookkeeping. It is interesting also to note, on the psychological side, that with social conditions equal, man is always the same, even in little things, through the ages. Letters surviving from those days show Egyptian officers detailing the hardships of their faraway garrisons in Syria, and functionaries who are bored in their little provincial towns soliciting the influence of their superiors to procure transfers to the gayer capital. Such letters could be drawn from the archives of almost any department in any modern European government.

The Roman Empire was a highly bureaucratized state, and its sound social organism was able to spread Greco-Roman civilization and the language of Italy over large portions of the ancient world, accomplishing a most difficult task of social assimilation. Another bureaucracy was czarist Russia, which despite a number of serious internal weaknesses, had great vitality and carried its expansion deep into the remote fastness of Asia. . . .

BENITO MUSSOLINI

(1883-1945)

Italy's dictator and Fascist Prime Minister (1922-1943), came from humble stock (his father was a blacksmith and his mother a schoolteacher); largely self-educated, he spent his early years as a manual laborer. Then embarking on a Socialist career, he tried his luck at journalism. Shortly after the outbreak of World War I he deserted the Socialist party and advocated Italy's intervention on the side of the Allies. (Whether he changed his principles or French francs made it worth while for him to desert the pacifist program is not clear). He joined Italy's armed forces and became corporal, was wounded by an Italian gun explosion, and returned to civilian life. Back in his newspaper office, he gained know-how in a crusade against defeatism and the peace treaties. Disavowed by the Socialists, he organized ex-soldiers and nationalists into what was to become the Fascist party (the name stems from the Latin "fasces," meaning a bundle or bunch of sticks tied around an ax—a symbol of authority in ancient Rome). Elections in 1921 placed only 35 Fascists in the Chamber of Deputies. What the Party lacked in numbers and support, it gained by the use of force; its superpatriotic and nationalistic members, wearing black shirts, armed and organized into a party militia, roamed the streets terrorizing and beating up political opponents or forcing large doses of castor oil down their throats: their bag of tricks (uniforms, songs, and symbols—such as the ancient Roman salute) appealed to young bully boys, the ignorant and the disillusioned. In the autumn of 1922 fear of a general communist uprising permeated the upper and middle classes; this enabled Mussolini's Party to find support among industrialists. When King Victor Emmanuel summoned Mussolini to Rome (October 28, 1922, the "March on Rome"), Mussolini, called "Il Duce" (Leader) by his followers, demanded the power; the weak Facta Government gave way and Mussolini was appointed Prime Minister. Step by step he eliminated his opponents and reorganized Italy along Fascist lines, featuring order and national efficiency (at the expense of liberty). In 1935, Mussolini conquered Abyssinia; half-hearted sanctions by the League of Nations drove Mussolini to join forces with Hitler in the Axis policy but eventually he had to learn to be a subordinate to Hitler. In 1943, while Allied forces fought in Sicily, his dictatorship fell apart and he was executed (with his mistress). The ideology of Mussolini's party seems to have been somewhat nebulous, but showed the influence of Pareto, Machiavelli, Sorel, Hegel, and Nietzsche. He was opposed to communism, internationalism, pacifism, and the class war; favored rehabilitating capitalism and of uniting the various strata of Italy's society into a powerful state; among his published works we may cite various collections of speeches, such as *Discorsi Politici* (1921), *Discorsi del 1925, Discorsi del 1926, Discorsi della Rivoluzione* (1927); his autobiography appeared in 1928. Probably the most important statement of his ideology is contained in his article, "The Political and Social Doctrine of Fascism," contributed to the *Encyclopedia Italiana,* Vol. XIV, in 1932. Of the many writers who devoted their talents to the Fascist cause we may cite Alfredo Rocco and Giovanni Gentile.

---

*The Doctrine of Fascism**

THE KEYSTONE OF Fascist doctrine is the conception of the State, of its essence, of its tasks, of its ends. For Fascism the State is an absolute before which individuals and groups are relative. Individuals and groups are "thinkable" in so far as they are within the State. The Liberal State does not direct the interplay and the material and spiritual development of the groups, but limits itself to registering the results; the Fascist State has a consciousness of its own, a will of its own, on this account it is called an "ethical" State. In 1929, at the

* Excerpt taken from Michael Oakeshott, *The Social and Political Doctrines of Contemporary Europe,* London: Cambridge University Press, 1939, pp. 175-179.

first quinquennial assembly of the regime, I said: "For Fascism, the State is not the night-watchman who is concerned only with the personal security of the citizens; nor is it an organization for purely material ends, such as that of guaranteeing a certain degree of prosperity and a relatively peaceful social order, to achieve which a council of administration would be sufficient, nor is it a creation of mere politics with no contact with the material and complex reality of the lives of individuals and the life of peoples. The State, as conceived by Fascism and its acts, is a spiritual and moral fact because it makes concrete the political, juridical, economic organization of the nation and such an organization is, in its origin and in its development, a manifestation of the spirit. The State is the guarantor of internal and external security, but it is also the guardian and the transmitter of the spirit of the people as it has been elaborated through the centuries in language, custom, faith. The State is not only present, it is also past, and above all, future. It is the State which transcending the brief limit of individual lives, represents the immanent conscience of the nation. The forms in which States express themselves change, but the necessity of the State remains. It is the State which educates citizens for civic virtue, makes them conscious of their mission, calls them to unity; harmonizes their interests in justice; hands on the achievements of thought in sciences, the arts, in law, in human solidarity; it carries men from the elementary life of the tribe to the highest human expression of power which is Empire; it entrusts to the ages the names of those who died for its integrity or in obedience to its laws; it puts forward as an example and recommends to the generations that are to come the leaders who increased its territory and the men of genius who gave it glory. When the sense of the State declines and the disintegrating and centrifugal tendencies of individuals and groups prevail, national societies move to their decline.

From 1929 up to the present day these doctrinal positions

have been strengthened by the whole economico-political evolution of the world. It is the State alone that grows in size, in power. It is the State alone that can solve the dramatic contradiction of capitalism. What is called the crisis cannot be overcome except by the State, within the State. Where are the shades of Jules Simons who, at the dawn of liberalism, proclaimed that "the State must strive to render itself unnecessary and to prepare for its demise"; of the MacCullochs who, in the second half of the last century, affirmed that the State must abstain from too much governing? And faced with the continual, necessary and inevitable interventions of the State in economic affairs what would the Englishman Bentham now say, according to whom industry should have asked of the State only to be left in peace? Or the German Humboldt, according to whom the "idle" State must be considered the best? It is true that the second generation of liberal economists was less extremist than the first, and already Smith himself opened, even though cautiously, the door to State intervention in economics. But when one says liberalism, one says the individual; when one says Fascism, one says the State. But the Fascist State is unique; it is an original creation. It is not reactionary, but revolutionary in that it anticipates the solutions of certain universal problems. These problems are no longer seen in the same light: in the sphere of politics they are removed from party rivalries from the supreme power of parliament, from the irresponsibility of assemblies; in the sphere of economics they are removed from the sphere of the syndicates' activities—activities that were ever widening their scope and increasing their power, both on the workers' side and on the employers'—removed from their struggles and their designs; in the moral sphere they are divorced from ideas of the need for order, discipline and obedience, and lifted into the plane of the moral commandments of the fatherland. Fascism desires the State to be strong, organic and at the same time founded on a wide popular basis. The Fascist State has also claimed for itself the field of economics and, through the corporative, social and educational institutions which it has created, the meaning of the State reaches out to and includes the farthest off-shoots; and within the State, framed in their respective organizations, there revolve all the political, economic and spiritual forces of the nation. A State founded on millions of individuals who recognize it, feel it, are ready to serve it, is not the tyrannical State of the medieval lord. It has nothing in common with the absolutist States that existed either before or after 1789. In the Fascist State the individual is not suppressed, but rather multiplied, just as in a regiment a soldier is not weakened but multiplied by the number of his comrades. The Fascist State organizes the nation, but it leaves sufficient scope to individuals; it has limited useless or harmful liberties and has preserved those that are essential. It cannot be the individual who decides in this matter, but only the State.

The Fascist State does not remain indifferent to the fact of religion in general and to that particular positive religion which is Italian Catholicism. The State has no theology, but it has an ethic. In the Fascist State religion is looked upon as one of the deepest manifestations of the spirit; it is, therefore, not only respected, but defended and protected. The Fascist State does not create a "God" of its own, as Robespierre once, at the height of the Convention's foolishness, wished to do; nor does it vainly seek, like Bolshevism, to expel religion from the minds of men; Fascism respects the God of the ascetics, of the saints, of the heroes, and also God as seen and prayed to by the simple and primitive heart of the people.

The Fascist State is a will to power and to government. In it the tradition of Rome is an idea that has force. In the doctrine of Fascism Empire is not only a territorial, military or mercantile expression, but spiritual or moral. One can think of an empire, that is to say a nation that directly or indirectly leads other nations, without needing to conquer a single square kilometre of territory. For Fascism the tendency to Empire, that is to say, to the expansion of nations, is a manifestation of vitality; its opposite, staying at home, is a sign of decadence: peoples who rise or re-rise are imperialist, peoples who die are renunciatory. Fascism is the doctrine that is most fitted to represent the aims, the states of mind, of a people, rising again after many centuries of abandonment or slavery to foreigners. But Empire calls for discipline, coordination of forces, duty and sacrifice; this explains many aspects of the practical working of the regime and the direction of many of the forces of the State and the necessary severity shown to those who would wish to oppose this spontaneous and destined impulse of the Italy of the twentieth century, to oppose it in the name of the superseded ideologies of the nineteenth, repudiated wherever great experiments of political and social transformation have been courageously attempted: especially when, as now, peoples thirst for authority, for leadership, for order. If every age had its own doctrine, it is apparent from a thousand signs that the doctrine of the present age is Fascism. That it is a doctrine of life is shown by the fact that it has resuscitated a faith. That this faith has conquered minds is proved by the fact that Fascism has had its dead and its martyrs.

Fascism henceforward has in the world the universality of all those doctrines which, by fulfilling themselves, have significance in the history of the human spirit. . . .

NAPOLEON BONAPARTE

(1769-1821)

Emperor of the French (1804-1815), "The Little Corporal," was hardly a philosopher, but his military victories in Europe promoted the rise of nationalism, and his reforms produced the centralized nation-state, with its unified system of law, bureaucracy and education in the spirit of the eighteenth-century enlightened despots. His over-all ambition was to renew Charlemagne's or Caesar's empires. He is often quoted: "Ability is of little account without opportunity." "Forethought we may have, undoubtedly, but not foresight." "What is history but a fable agreed upon?" "The human race is governed by imagination." "Impossible is a word to be found only in the dictionary of fools." "Do you know what is harder to bear than the reverses of fortune? It is the baseness, the hideous ingratitude, of man." "I fear three newspapers more than a hundred thousand bayonets." "Soldiers, forty centuries are looking down upon you from those pyramids." "If they want peace, nations should avoid the pin-pricks that precede cannon-shots." "Victory belongs to the most persevering." "There is only one step from the sublime to the ridiculous." "It requires more courage to suffer than to die."

---

*Proclamation, 19th Brumaire**

To the people:

Frenchmen, on my return to France I found division reigning among all the authorities. They agreed only on this single

* This excerpt taken from James Harvey Robinson and Charles A. Beard, *Readings in Modern European History,* Boston: Ginn & Co., 1908, I, pp. 322-323.

point, that the constitution was half destroyed and was unable to protect liberty.

Each party in turn came to me, confided to me their designs, imparted their secrets, and requested my support. But I refused to be the man of any party.

The Council of Elders appealed to me. I answered their appeal. A plan of general restoration had been conspired at by men whom the nation has been accustomed to regard as the defenders of liberty, equality, and property. This plan required calm deliberation, free from all influence and all fear. The Elders therefore resolved upon the removal of the legislative bodies to St. Cloud. They placed at my disposal the force necessary to secure their independence. I was bound, in duty to my fellow-citizens, to the soldiers perishing in our armies, and to the national glory acquired at the cost of so much blood, to accept the command.

The Council assembled at St. Cloud. Republican troops guaranteed their safety from without, but assassins created terror within. Many deputies in the Council of Five Hundred, armed with stilettos and pistols, spread the menace of death around them.

The plans which ought to have been developed were withheld. The majority of the Council was disorganized, the boldest orators were disconcerted, and the futility of submitting any salutary proposition was quite evident.

I proceeded, filled with indignation and chagrin, to the Council of the Elders. I besought them to carry their noble designs into execution. I directed their attention to the evils of the nation, which were their motives for conceiving those designs. They concurred in giving me new proofs of their unanimous good will.

I presented myself before the Council of the Five Hundred alone, unarmed, my head uncovered, just as the elders had received and applauded me. My object was to restore to the majority the expression of its will and to secure to it its power.

The stilettoes which had menaced the deputies were instantly raised against their deliverer. Twenty assassins rushed upon me and aimed at my breast. The grenadiers of the legislative body, whom I had left at the door of the hall, ran forward and placed themselves between me and the assassins. One of these brave grenadiers had his clothes pierced by a stiletto. They bore me out.

At the same moment cries of "Outlaw him!" were raised against the defender of the law. It was the horrid cry of assassins against the power destined to repress them. They crowded around the president, uttering threats. With arms in their hands, they commanded him to declare me outlawed. I was informed of this. I ordered him to be rescued from their fury, and six grenadiers of the legislative body brought him out. Immediately afterwards some grenadiers of the legislative body charged the hall and cleared it.

The seditious, thus intimidated, dispersed and fled. The majority, freed from their assailants, returned freely and peaceably into the hall, listened to the propositions for the public safety, deliberated, and drew up the salutary resolution which will become the new and provisional law of the republic.

Frenchmen, you will doubtless recognize in this conduct the zeal of a soldier of liberty, of a citizen devoted to the republic. Conservative, judicial and liberal ideas resumed their sway upon the dispersion of those seditious persons who had domineered in the councils and who proved themselves the most odious and contemptible of men.

BONAPARTE

THOMAS PAINE

(1737-1809)

Whom historians regard as the literary-politico guide of the American Revolution, articulated the thoughts that helped kindle the fire of freedom in the days of indecision prior to the Revolution. Yet in many ways, of all the leading figures of the early revolutionary movement in the U.S., Paine is the most enigmatic—a figure whose real personality has been obscured by generations who remember him for the enemies he made rather than for the causes he so eloquently espoused. The son of a Quaker staymaker, Paine came from England to the New World in 1774–sponsored by his idol, Benjamin Franklin. He had only the rudiments of an education, but by the time he reached America, he had become one of the master bridge engineers of his era, as well as a self-taught literary stylist. His early writings (*Common Sense,* 1776; *The Forester's Letters,* 1776; *The American Crisis,* 1776-1783) did much to stir Americans to fight for their liberty and exerted a vast influence during the period of colonial indecision in putting forward a concrete call for independence. His fervent arguments for freedom were evident in his pamphlet, *Common Sense;* in an era when pamphleteering was a more polished and influential art than it is today, its publication made Paine at once a prime enunciator of the argument for independence. He was the kind of prickly nonconformist who was certain to be in hot water most of the time. A great man with huge flaws, he has been accorded uncritical eulogistic treatment at the hands of his own biographers and has been savagely denounced by the biographers of his political opponents. As a popular journalist, Paine was never excellent; as a political thinker he lacked both the scholarship and the originality of some of his contemporaries. But he had a wonderful talent for timing, which was matched by a priceless gift for marshaling arguments for his own side and a stout-hearted courage in challenging formidable opponents. Unfortunately, his private life was less than exemplary, and his whole career was a mass of contradictions.

As a middle-class entrepreneur, he came out of the American Revolution financially independent; but as a thoroughgoing revolutionary, Paine disappointed American radicals in the 1780's by supporting the claims of land companies, opposing paper money and giving the plan for a big bank his enthusiastic endorsement. Once more committed to the cause of revolution (this time in France, *The Rights of Man,* 1791-1792), he was repudiated by extremist circles when he opposed the Reign of Terror and by a seeming miracle escaped liquidation. But in the eyes of the pious, Paine was always the archradical because of his attacks on organized religion; he ended his career back in America as a thorough Jeffersonian partisan, and some of his later writings are among his least inspired pieces.

Paine believed in the constant upward advance of human culture and deduced from this that "the higher a culture stands, the less is the need for government." He asserted that man is inherently social and that social organization is a natural development. He always argued on behalf of the rule of reason in all things (including religion). Together with Ethan Allen, Thomas Jefferson and other Founding Fathers, he held, as a Freethinker and Deist, that there is a natural or rational morality and religion which reason can find out, and that divine revelation can add nothing important to it. His *Common Sense* (1776) abandoned the worshipful approach of other colonial literature toward the British Constitution and provided the arguments for cutting loose from the King. Distinguishing between society and government, he found the former produced by our wants, the latter by our wickedness. "Society in every state is a blessing, but government even in its best state is but a necessary evil." He urged the colonists to declare their independence, arguing that foreign nations would not intervene on the side of the colonists so long as they accepted allegiance to the British crown. In defense of the French Revolution he declared that each generation must be free to act for itself and that there is nothing sacred about the existing forms of political institutions. He also opposed that formal democracy which sees in the will of the majority the last word of wisdom. He criticized the checks-and-balances system that Montesquieu had praised, and stated that there are but two functions of government, the creation of law and the execution of law; and that the judiciary exercises merely one phase of executive power. Writing on the French Revolution in defense of Burke, he distinguished between state and government (which Burke had confused): the state was the necessary result of man's nature and needs, while government was an artificial creation, needed to restrain man's vices, and even the best form of government was a necessary evil, whose activities were to be restricted.

---

*Common Sense**

. . . As MUCH has been said of the advantages of reconciliation, which, like an agreeable dream, has passed away and left us as we were, it is but right that we should examine the contrary side of the argument, and inquire into some of the many material injuries which these colonies sustain, and always will sustain, by being connected with and dependent on Great Britain. To examine that connection and dependence on the principles of nature and common sense; to see what we have to trust to, if separated, and what we are to expect, if dependent.

I have heard it asserted by some, that as America hath flourished under her former connection with Great Britain, the same connection is necessary towards her future happiness, and will always have the same effect. Nothing can be more fallacious than this kind of argument. We may as well assert that because a child has thriven upon milk, that it is never to have meat, or that the first twenty years of our lives is to become a precedent for the next twenty. But even this is admitting more than is true; for I answer roundly, that America would have flourished as much, and probably much

* This excerpt taken from Richard Hofstadter, ed., *Common Sense,* New York: Vintage Books, 1958, pp. 54-56.

more, had no European power taken any notice of her. The commerce by which she hath enriched herself are the necessaries of life, and will always have a market while eating is the custom of Europe.

But she has protected us, say some. That she hath engrossed us is true, and defended the continent at our expense as well as her own is admitted; and she would have defended Turkey from the same motive, viz., for the sake of trade and dominion.

Alas! we have been long led away by ancient prejudices, and made large sacrifices to superstition. We have boasted the protection of Great Britain without considering that her motive was *interest,* not *attachment;* and that she did not protect us from *our enemies* on *our account,* but from her enemies on her own account, from those who had no quarrel with us or any *other account,* but who will always be our enemies on the *same account.* Let Britain waive her pretensions to the continent, or the continent throw off the dependence, and we should be at peace with France and Spain were they at war with Britain. The miseries of Hanover's last war ought to warn us against connections.

It hath lately been asserted in parliament, that the colonies have no relation to each other but through the parent country, *i.e.,* that Pennsylvania and the Jerseys, and so on for the rest, are sister colonies by way of England; this is certainly a very roundabout way of proving relationship, but it is the nearest and only true way of proving enmity (or enemyship, if I may so call it). France and Spain never were, nor perhaps ever will be our enemies as *Americans,* but as our being the *subjects of Great Britain.*

But Britain is the parent country, say some. Then the more shame upon her conduct. Even brutes do not devour their young, nor savages make war upon their families; wherefore, the assertion, if true, turns to her reproach; but it happens not to be true, or only partly so, and the phrase *parent* or *mother country* hath been jesuitically adopted by the king and his parasites, with a low papistical design of gaining an unfair bias on the credulous weakness of our minds. Europe, and not England, is the parent country of America. This new world hath been the asylum for the persecuted lovers of civil and religious liberty from *every part* of Europe. Hither have they fled, not from the tender embraces of a mother, but from the cruelty of the monster; and it is so far true of England, that the same tyranny which drove the first emigrants from home, pursues their descendants still.

In this extensive quarter of the globe, we forget the narrow limits of three hundred and sixty miles (the extent of England) and carry our friendship on a larger scale; we claim brotherhood with every European Christian, and triumph in the generosity of the sentiment. . . .

I challenge the warmest advocate for reconciliation to show a single advantage that this continent can reap, by being connected with Great Britain. I repeat the challenge, not a single advantage is derived. Our corn will fetch its price in any market in Europe, and our imported goods must be paid for, buy them where we will.

But the injuries and disadvantages we sustain by that connection are without number; and our duty to mankind at large, as well as to ourselves, instructs us to renounce the alliance: because any submission to, or dependence on, Great Britain, tends directly to involve this continent in European wars and quarrels, and sets us at variance with nations who would otherwise seek our friendship, and against whom we have neither anger nor complaint. As Europe is our market for trade, we ought to form no partial connection with any part of it. 'Tis the true interest of America to steer clear of European contentions, which she never can do while by her dependence on Britain she is made the makeweight in the scale of British politics.

Europe is too thickly planted with kingdoms to be long at peace, and whenever a war breaks out between England and any foreign power, the trade of America goes to ruin, *because of her connection with Britain.* The next war may not turn out like the last, and should it not, the advocates for reconciliation now will be wishing for separation then, because neutrality in that case would be a safer convoy than a man of war. Everything that is right or natural pleads for separation. The blood of the slain, the weeping voice of nature cries, 'TIS TIME TO PART. Even the distance at which the Almighty hath placed England and America is a strong and natural proof that the authority of the one over the other, was never the design of heaven. The time likewise at which the continent was discovered, adds weight to the argument, and the manner in which it was peopled, increases the force of it. The Reformation was preceded by the discovery of America, as if the Almighty graciously meant to open a sanctuary to the persecuted in future years, when home should afford neither friendship nor safety.

VILFREDO PARETO

(1848-1923)

Portrayed by some as the ideological father of Fascism ("the Marx of the bourgeoisie") exerted considerable influence (with Gaetano Mosca) through his concept that in reality all social organizations are led and governed by a "ruling class" (an elite or oligarchy), which, possessed of greater social vitality and usefulness than the other classes, guides and dominates them until it is in turn overpowered by another elite more vigorous, alert and capable (circulation of elites). No regime is, per se, better than another and none is essentially different except for the social composition of the minority, which always governs. This interpretation of political history, which reduces it to a conflict of social groups without ideal values and in which ideologies play but a secondary role, derives in part from the thesis of Hippolyte Taine's *Origines de la France Contemporaine.* Central to Pareto's theoretical work (*Tratto di Sociologia Generale,* 1916, translated as *The Mind and Society,* 1935, 4 vols.) is his conception of logical and nonlogical action. By logical actions Pareto means those which use means appropriate to ends determined by logic and experience. They are actions determined by some real aim and he singles out scientific and economic activities as examples. (Although Pareto does not explicitly include the struggle for political power in this category, nevertheless it can be surmised from his work that he so included it.) Nonlogical actions, on the other hand, are those which do not use means appropriate to their ends; they are actions opposed to science, to economic activities and to the real interests of the individual as interpreted by experience and logic. They are determined by some impulse which is inaccessible to further explanation, and are essentially irrational. Nonlogical actions overwhelmingly predominate in society and thus, in the last analysis, human behavior is irrational; man is a bundle of irrational sentiments and instincts. The instinct glorified by Pareto above all others, as indicative of strength, virility and excellence, is brute force—force used by an elite as an instrument to gain and exercise power.

Pareto also developed a number of special or subsidiary theories, such as the theories of utility, revolution, demagogic plutocracy, etc. He made a real contribution to European sociology and joins Durkheim and a few others in setting the pace for political sociology. His ideas have been used in Fascist movements and regimes opposed to intellectualism and in favor of vigorous, natural sentiments, and in economics favoring corporate states and managed economies.

---

*The Elite**

THERE ARE PEOPLE who worship Napoleon Bonaparte as a god. There are people who hate him as the lowest of criminals. Which are right? We do not choose to solve that question in connexion with a quite different matter. Whether Napoleon was a good man or a bad man, he was certainly not an idiot, nor a man of little account, as millions of others are. He had exceptional qualities, and that is enough for us to give him a high ranking, though without prejudice of any sort to questions that might be raised as to the ethics of his qualities or their social utility.

In short, we are here as usual resorting to scientific analysis, which distinguishes one problem from another and studies each one separately. As usual, again, we are replacing imperceptible variations in absolutely exact numbers with the sharp variations corresponding to groupings by class, just as in examinations those who are passed are sharply and arbitrarily distinguished from those who are "failed," and

---

* **This excerpt taken from Vilfredo Pareto, *The Mind and Society,* edited by Arthur Livingston, New York: Harcourt, Brace, 1935, pp. 1422-1427.**

just as in the matter of physical age we distinguish children from young people, the old from the aged.

So let us make a class of the people who have the highest indices in their branch of activity, and to that class give the name of *élite.*

For the particular investigation with which we are engaged, a study of the social equilibrium, it will help if we further divide that class into two classes: a *governing élite,* comprising individuals who directly or indirectly play some considerable part in government, and a *non-governing élite,* comprising the rest.

A chess champion is certainly a member of the *élite,* but it is no less certain that his merits as a chess-player do not open the doors to political influence for him; and hence unless he has other qualities to win him that distinction, he is not a member of the governing *élite.* Mistresses of absolute monarchs have oftentimes been members of the *élite,* either because of their beauty or because of their intellectual endowments; but only a few of them, who have had, in addition, the particular talents required by politics, have played any part in government.

So we get two strata in a population: (1) A lower stratum, the *non-élite,* with whose possible influence on government we are not just here concerned; then (2) a higher stratum, *the élite,* which is divided into two: (a) a governing *élite;* (b) a non-governing *élite.*

In the concrete, there are no examinations whereby each person is assigned to his proper place in these various classes. That deficiency is made up for by other means, by various sorts of labels that serve the purpose after a fashion. Such labels are the rule even where there are examinations. The label "lawyer" is affixed to a man who is supposed to know something about the law and often does, though sometimes again he is an ignoramus. So, the governing *élite* contains individuals who wear labels appropriate to political offices of a certain altitude—ministers, Senators, Deputies, chief justices, generals, colonels, and so on—making the apposite exceptions for those who have found their way into that exalted company without possessing qualities corresponding to the labels they wear.

Such exceptions are much more numerous than the exceptions among lawyers, physicians, engineers, millionaires (who have made their own money), artists of distinction, and so on; for the reason, among others, that in these latter departments of human activity the labels are won directly by each individual, whereas in the *élite* some of the labels—the label of wealth, for instance—are hereditary. In former times there were hereditary labels in the governing *élite* also—in our day hardly more than the label of king remains in that status; but if direct inheritance has disappeared, inheritance is still powerful indirectly; and an individual who has inherited a sizable patrimony can easily be named Senator in certain countries, or can get himself elected to the parliament by buying votes or, on occasion, by wheedling voters with assurances that he is a democrat of democrats, a Socialist, an Anarchist. Wealth, family, or social connections also help in many other cases to win the label of the *élite* in general, or of the governing *élite* in particular, for persons who otherwise hold no claim upon it.

In societies where the social unit is the family the label worn by the head of the family also benefits all other members. In Rome, the man who became Emperor generally raised his freedmen to the higher class, and oftentimes, in fact, to the governing *élite*. For that matter, now more, now fewer, of the freedmen taking part in the Roman government possessed qualities good or bad that justified their wearing the labels which they had won through imperial bounty. In our societies, the social unit is the individual; but the place that the individual occupies in society also benefits his wife, his children, his friends.

If all these deviations from type were of little importance, they might be disregarded, as they are virtually disregarded in cases where a diploma is required for the practice of a profession. Everyone knows that there are persons who do not deserve their diplomas, but experience shows that on the whole such exceptions may be overlooked.

One might, further, from certain points of view at least, disregard deviations if they remained more or less constant quantitatively—if there were only a negligible variation in proportions between the total of a class and the people who wear its label without possessing the qualities corresponding.

As a matter of fact, the real cases that we have to consider in our societies differ from those two. The deviations are not so few that they can be disregarded. Then again, their number is variable, and the variations give rise to situations having an important bearing on the social equilibrium. We are therefore required to make a special study of them.

Furthermore, the manner in which the various groups in a population intermix has to be considered. In moving from one group to another an individual generally brings with him certain inclinations, sentiments, attitudes, that he has acquired in the group from which he comes, and that circumstance cannot be ignored.

To this mixing, in the particular case in which only two groups, the *élite* and the non-*élite*, are envisaged, the term "circulation of élites" has been applied—in French, *circulation des élites* [or in more general terms "class circulation"].

In conclusion we must pay special attention (1), in the case of one single group, to the proportions between the total of the group and the number of individuals who are nominally members of it but do not possess the qualities requisite for effective membership; and then (2), in the case of various groups, to the ways in which transitions from one group to the other occur, and to the intensity of that movement—that is to say, to the velocity of the circulation.

Velocity in circulation has to be considered not only absolutely but also in relation to the supply of and the demand for certain social elements. A country that is always at peace does not require many soldiers in its governing class, and the production of generals may be overexuberant as compared with the demand. But when a country is in a state of continuous warfare many soldiers are necessary, and though production remains at the same level it may not meet the demand. That, we might note in passing, has been one of the causes for the collapse of many aristocracies.

Another example. In a country where there is little industry and little commerce, the supply of individuals possessing in high degree the qualities requisite for those types of activity exceeds the demand. Then industry and commerce develop and the supply, though remaining the same, no longer meets the demand.

We must not confuse the state of law with the state of fact. The latter alone, or almost alone, has a bearing on the social equilibrium. There are many examples of castes that are legally closed, but into which, in point of fact, new-comers make their way, and often in large numbers. On the other hand, what difference does it make if a caste is legally open, but conditions *de facto* prevent new accessions to it? If a person who acquires wealth thereby becomes a member of the governing class, but no one gets rich, it is as if the law erected serious barriers against access to the caste. Something of that sort was observable towards the end of the Roman Empire. People who acquired wealth entered the order of the curials. But only a few individuals made any money. Theoretically we might examine any number of groups. Practically we have to confine ourselves to the most important. We shall proceed by successive approximations, starting with the simple and going on to the complex.

Higher class and lower class in general. The least we can do is to divide society into two strata: a higher stratum, which usually contains the rulers, and a lower stratum, which usually contains the ruled. That fact is so obvious that it has always forced itself even upon the most casual observation, and so for the circulation of individuals between the two strata. Even Plato had an inkling of class-circulation and tried to regulate it artificially. The "new man," the upstart, the *parvenu,* has always been a subject of interest, and literature has analyzed him unendingly. Here, then, we are merely giving a more exact form to things that have long been perceived more or less vaguely. Above, we noted a varying distribution of residues in the various social groupings, and chiefly in the higher and the lower class. Such heterogeneousness is a fact perceived by the most superficial glance. . . .

Aristocracies do not last. Whatever the causes, it is an incontestable fact that after a certain length of time they pass away. History is a graveyard of aristocracies. The Athenian "People" was an aristocracy as compared with the remainder of a population of resident aliens and slaves. It vanished without leaving any descent. The various aristocracies of Rome vanished in their time. So did the aristocracies of the Barbarians. Where, in France, are the descendants of the Frankish conquerors? The genealogies of the English nobility have been very exactly kept; and they show that very few families still remain to claim descent from the comrades of William the Conqueror. The rest have vanished. In Germany the aristocracy of the present day is very largely made up of descendants of vassals of the lords of old. The populations of European countries have increased enormously during the past few centuries. It is as certain as certain can be that the aristocracies have not increased in proportion.

They decay not in numbers only. They decay also in quality, in the sense that they lose their vigour, that there is a decline in the proportions of the residues which enabled them to win their power and hold it. The governing class is restored not only in numbers, but—and that is the most important thing— in quality, by families rising from the lower classes and bringing with them the vigour and the proportions of residue necessary for keeping themselves in power. It is also restored by the loss of its more degenerate members.

If one of those movements comes to an end, or worse still,

if they both come to an end, the governing class crashes to ruin and often sweeps the whole of a nation along with it. Potent causes of disturbance in the equilibrium is the accumulation of superior elements in the lower classes and, conversely, of inferior elements in the higher classes. If human aristocracies were like thorough-breds among animals, which reproduce themselves over long periods of time with approximately the same traits, the history of the human race would be something altogether different from the history we know.

In virtue of class-circulation, the governing *élite* is always in a state of slow and continuous transformation. It flows on like a river, never being today what it was yesterday. From time to time sudden and violent disturbances occur. There is a flood—the river overflows its banks. Afterwards, the new governing *élite* again resumes its slow transformation. The flood has subsided, the river is again flowing normally in its wonted bed.

Revolutions come about through accumulations in the higher strata of society—either because of a slowing-down in class-circulation or from other causes—of decadent elements no longer possessing the residues suitable for keeping them in power, and shrinking from the use of force; while meantime in the lower strata of society elements of superior quality are coming to the fore, possessing residues suitable for exercising the functions of government and willing enough to use force.

In general, in revolutions the members of the lower strata are captained by leaders from the higher strata, because the latter possess the intellectual qualities required for outlining a tactic, while lacking the combative residues supplied by the individuals from the lower strata.

WILLIAM PENN

(1644-1718)

Famous founder of Pennsylvania, influenced the acceptance of the principle of freedom of conscience in America. He was willing to sacrifice his own liberty for his faith, and while in prison he told his jailer that he "scorned that religion which is not worth suffering for, and able to sustain those that are afflicted for it." This son of a distinguished seafaring father, Admiral Sir William Penn, "great captain commander" of the fleet, after serving with him in the war against the Dutch, studied law and was sent to Ireland to look after one of his father's estates. He had been attracted earlier to the Society of Friends (Quakers) and on his return to London at the age of twenty-three became an open convert. Quakers had no easy time of it, and young William was twice jailed. When his father died, the younger Penn was left well-to-do and bought into the Jerseys proprietorship, but wished to have a colony of his own where he could put his ideas into practice. The Duke of York was heavily indebted to the Penns and agreed to pay the debt with a grant of land in America, which the Duke named "Pennsylvania" (1681). The charter of the new colony gave the proprietor less kingly powers than any proprietor thus far. Penn drafted the first laws on a consciously moral basis. The local institutions were remarkably free. The proprietor was the governor and appointed a deputy-governor to act for him. Pennsylvania was well governed when Penn was present, but several of his deputy-governors were inferior men. When James II was ousted (1688), the new English government confiscated Pennsylvania because Penn and King James had been close friends. Penn's rights were restored under Queen Anne, but Penn never profited from the colony and spent time in prison for debt. At any rate, he was able to experiment in the colony in accordance with his religious and political ideas, and his treaties with the Indians aroused the admiration even of Voltaire, who praised them because they were "not ratified by an oath and were never infringed." Religious tolerance was the cornerstone of Penn's political system, in which fundamental and circumstantial laws are distinguished (*Charter of Liberties,* 1701). He prepared charters for New Jersey (1676) and Pennsylvania (1683) in which he utilized Harrington's *Oceana.* Pennsylvania especially became famous in Europe and Montesquieu wrote of it with admiration, while the Italian jurist and publicist Gaetano Folangieri (1752-1788) compared its founder with Lycurgus and Solon. The internationalists also remember Penn for his scheme of creating a European parliament before which international disputes could be brought, and states refusing to arbitrate or to abide by the award of the international body would be coerced by joint action of the other states (*Essay Towards the Present and Future Peace of Europe,* 1693).

---

*Religion and Society**

THE WORLD is the stage in which all men do act for eternity, and every venture of this brings its true weight of eternal life or death.

By revelation we understand the discovery and illumination of the light and spirit of God relating to those things that properly and immediately concern the daily information and satisfaction of our souls in the way of our duty to Him and our neighbors.

As there is this natural and intelligent spirit by which man is daily informed of the concerns of mortal life, so is a divine principle communicated to him, which we call the Light and that does illuminate and discover to his understanding the condition of his soul, and gives him a true knowledge of what is required at his hands, either in obeying or suffering.

---

* This excerpt taken from Dagobert D. Runes, ed., *Treasury of Philosophy,* New York: Philosophical Library, 1955, p. 916.

William Penn

I know no religion that destroys courtesy, civility and kindness.

All men have reason, but not all men are reasonable. Is it the fault of the grain in the granary that it yields no increase, or of the talent in the napkin that it is not improved?

Conscience, truly speaking, is no other than the sense a man has, or judgment he makes of his duty to God, according to the understanding God gives him of his will.

Justice is the means of peace betwixt the government and the people and one man and company and another.

Liberty without obedience is confusion, and obedience without liberty is slavery.

Liberty of conscience is every man's natural right, and he who is deprived of it is a slave in the midst of the greatest liberty.

PERICLES
(495-429 B.C.)

Is famed for the funeral oration delivered by him (as reported by Thucydides, II, 34-35) at the burial of the Athenians killed in the first campaign of the Peloponnesian War, a statement of the ideals of the Athenian democracy, which declares that the government of Athens is called a democracy because its administration is in the hands of the many.

---

*The Democratic Way of Life**

I WILL speak first of our ancestors, for it is right and becoming that now, when we are lamenting the dead, a tribute should be paid to their memory. There has never been a time when they did not inhabit this land, which by their valor they have handed down from generation to generation, and we have received from them a free state. But if they were worthy of praise, still more worthy were our fathers, who added to their inheritance, and after many a struggle transmitted to us, their sons, this great empire. And we ourselves, assembled here today, who are still most of us in the vigor of life, have richly endowed our city with all things, so that she is sufficient for herself both in peace and war. Of the military exploits by which our various possessions were acquired, or of the energy with which we or our fathers drove back the tide of war, Hellenic or Barbarian, I will not speak,

* Reprinted from "Pericles," pp. 917-920, in Dagobert D. Runes, ed., *Treasury of Philosophy*, New York: Philosophical Library, 1955.

for the tale would be long and is familiar to you. But before I praise the dead, I should like to point out by what principles of action we rose to power, and under what institutions and through what manner of life our empire became great. For I conceive that such thoughts are not unsuited to the occasion, and that this numerous assembly of citizens and strangers may profitably listen to them.

Our form of government does not enter into rivalry with the institutions of others. We do not copy our neighbors, but are an example to them. It is true that we are called a democracy, for the administration is in the hands of the many and not of the few. But while the law secures equal justice to all alike in their private disputes, the claim of excellence is also recognized; and when a citizen is in any way distinguished, he is preferred to the public service, not as a matter of privilege but as the reward of merit. Neither is poverty a bar, but a man may benefit his country whatever be the obscurity of his condition. There is no exclusiveness in our public life, and in our private intercourse we are not suspicious of one another, nor angry with our neighbor if he does what he likes; we do not put on sour looks at him which, though harmless, are not pleasant. While we are thus unconstrained in our private intercourse, a spirit of reverence pervades our public acts; we are prevented from doing wrong by respect for authority and for the laws, having an especial regard to those which are ordained for the protection of the injured as well as to those unwritten laws which bring upon the transgressor of them the reprobation of the general sentiment.

And we have not forgotten to provide for our weary spirits many relaxations from toil; we have regular games and sacrifices throughout the year; at home the style of our life is refined; and the delight which we daily feel in all these things helps to banish melancholy. Because of the greatness of our city the fruits of the whole earth flow in upon us; so that we enjoy the goods of other countries as freely as our own.

We are lovers of the beautiful, yet simple in our tastes, and we cultivate the mind without loss of manliness. Wealth we employ, not for talk and ostentation, but when there is a real use for it. To avow poverty with us is no disgrace; the true disgrace is in doing nothing to avoid it. An Athenian citizen does not neglect the state because he takes care of his own household; and even those of us who are engaged in business have a very fair idea of politics. We alone regard a man who takes no interest in public affairs, not as a harmless, but as a useless character; and if few of us are originators, we are all sound judges of a policy. The great impediment to action is, in our opinion, not discussion, but the want of that knowledge which is gained by discussion preparatory to action. For we have a peculiar power of thinking before we act and of acting too, whereas other men are courageous from ignorance, but hesitate upon reflection. And they are surely to be esteemed the bravest spirits who, having the clearest sense both of the pains and pleasures of life, do not on that account shrink from danger. In so doing, again, we are unlike others—we make our friends by conferring, not receiving favors.

To sum up: I say that Athens is the school of Hellas, and that the individual Athenian in his own person seems to have the power of adapting himself to the most varied forms of action with the utmost versatility and grace. This is no passing and idle word, but truth and fact; and the assertion is verified by the position to which these qualities have raised the state. For in the hour of trial, Athens alone among her contemporaries is superior to the report of her. No enemy who comes against her is indignant at the reverses which he sustains at the hands of such a city; no subject complains that his masters are unworthy of him. And we shall assuredly not be without witnesses; there are mighty monuments of our power which will make us the wonder of all ages.

We have compelled every land and every sea to open a path for our valor, and have everywhere planted eternal memorials of our friendship and of our enmity. Such is the city for whose sake these men fought and died; they could not bear to think that she might be taken from them; and every one of us who survive should gladly toil on her behalf. . . .

WILLIAM PITT

(First Earl of Chatham, 1708-1778)

English statesman and orator, called "The Great Commoner," used his influence on behalf of the cause of the American colonies though he was unwilling to recognize their independence from England. When repealing the Stamp Act in March, 1766, Parliament passed the Declaratory Act, which declared that the King and Parliament could bind the colonists in all cases whatsoever. Because Pitt had opposed the tax and King George III had agreed to the repeal of it, they were both complimented by the erection of statues; Pitt's is still standing. In his speech of November 18, 1777, he declared: "You cannot conquer America."

Speech on the Stamp Act, January 14, 1765*

GENTLEMEN,—Sir [to the speaker], I have been charged with giving birth to sedition in America. They have spoken their sentiments with freedom against this unhappy act, and that freedom has become their crime. Sorry I am to hear the liberty of speech in this house, imputed as a crime. But the imputation shall not discourage me, It is a liberty I mean to exercise. No gentleman ought to be afraid to exercise it. It is a liberty by which the gentleman who calumniates it might have profited, by which he ought to have profited. He ought to have desisted from his project. The gentleman tells us, America is obstinate; America is almost in open rebellion. I rejoice that America has resisted, Three millions of people

* This excerpt taken from Richard Hofstadter, ed., *Speech on the Stamp Act, January 14, 1765,* New York: Vintage Books, Inc., 1958, pp. 17-18.

so dead to all feelings of liberty, as voluntarily to submit to be slaves, would have been fit instruments to make slaves of the rest. I come not here armed at all points, with law cases and acts of parliament, with the statute book doubled down in dogs'-ears, to defend the cause of liberty: if I had, I myself would have cited the two cases of Chester and Durham. I would have cited them, to have shown that even under former arbitrary reigns, parliaments were ashamed of taxing a people without their consent, and allowed them representatives. Why did the gentleman confine himself to Chester and Durham? He might have taken a higher example in Wales; Wales, that never was taxed by parliament till it was incorporated. I would not debate a particular point of law with the gentleman. I know his abilities. I have been obliged to his diligent researches: but, for the defence of liberty, upon a general principle, upon a constitutional principle, it is a ground upon which I stand firm; on which I dare meet any man. The gentleman tells us of many who are taxed, and are not represented. The India Company, merchants, stock-holders, manufacturers. Surely many of these are represented in other capacities, as owners of land, or as freemen of boroughs. It is a misfortune that more are not equally represented: but they are all inhabitants, and as such, are they not virtually represented? . . . they have connections with those that elect, and they have influence over them. The gentleman mentioned the stock-holders: I hope he does not reckon the debts of the nation as a part of the national estate. Since the accession of King William, many ministers, some of great, others of more moderate abilities, have taken the lead in government. (He then went through the list of them, bringing it down till he came to himself, giving a short sketch of the characters of each of them.)

None of these thought, or even dreamed, of robbing the colonies of their constitutional rights. That was reserved to mark the era of the late administration: not that there were wanting some, when I had the honour to serve his Majesty, to propose to me to burn my fingers with an American stamp-act. With the enemy at their back, with our bayonets at their breasts, in the day of their distress, perhaps the Americans would have submitted to the imposition; but it would have been taking an ungenerous and unjust advantage. . . .

PLATO

(427-347 B.C.)

Whose real name was Aristocles, the son of Ariston, a man of influential ancestry, studied mostly with Socrates. After traveling about the Mediterranean region, he founded his own school in Athens (387 B.C.) in the Grove of Academus ("The Academy"). Following the general ideas of Socrates, he developed his theory of knowledge and his ethical concepts into comprehensive metaphysical and ethical systems. *The Republic* is his greatest work, one of the three dialogues (along with *The Statesman,* and *The Laws*) which have earned him the reputation as the first writer to address himself to political philosophy. In *The Republic,* as in the other dialogues, the principal themes are developed through the telling of myths, tales in which the external circumstances are fabulous but which carry significant implications. As a proponent of reason, keeping apart from the stresses of contemporary political life, Plato tried to create a blueprint of a world in which the political imperfections of the existing world would be obviated. Thus his *Republic* is really a Utopia, a complete philosophy, a picture of the nature of human personality and of the universe in which it lives. He attempted to formulate a philosophic conception of justice, setting forth his ideas about an ideal state in which justice prevailed; he viewed the state as a magnified individual and drew analogies between individual and political ideals. While he did not view the state as having an existence apart from the individuals composing it, his abstract idea of the state endowed it with an existence of its own. He found the origin of the state in the differences of men's needs and desires, and the need to cooperate in order to satisfy them. He denounced morality as an invention of the weak to neutralize the strength of the strong; the real virtues of a man are courage (*andreia*) and intelligence (*phronesis*). Men are not content with a simple life; they are acquisitive, ambitious, competitive and jealous; they soon tire of what they have, and pine for what they have not and seldom desire anything unless it belongs to others. The result is the rivalry of groups for the resources of the soil, and then war. Trade and finance develop, and bring new class divisions. The changes in the distribution of wealth produce adjustments of policy to growth, which are replaced by politics, which is the strategy of party and the lust for the spoils of office. Every form of government tends to perish through the excess of its basic principle; even democracy ruins itself by excess of democracy. Plato is astounded at the folly of leaving to mob caprice and gullibility the selection of political officials. To devise a method barring incompetence and knavery from public office, and of selecting and preparing the best to rule for the common good —that is the problem of political philosophy. Governing authority must be associated with the broadest knowledge and culture; the philosopher should be the statesman. Although most of Plato's ideals are Utopian, some of his theories were developed by such thinkers as Burke, Hegel and Marx.

The Republic*

JUSTICE, then, my friend, can be no very important matter, if it is useful only in respect of things not to be used. But let us consider this matter: is not he who is the cleverest at striking in a fight, whether with the fists or some other way, the cleverest likewise, in self-defense? Certainly. And as to the person who is clever in warding off and escaping from a distemper, is he not very clever also in bringing it on? So I suppose. And he too the best guardian of a camp, who can steal the counsels, and the other operations of the enemy? Certainly. Of whatever, then, any one is a good guardian, of

* Excerpts taken from *The Republic*: *The States of Plato,* Part I. *The Republic,* translated by Henry Davis, M.A.; Part II. *The Statesman,* translated by George Burges, M.A., Washington & London: D. Walter Dunne, publisher, 1901.

that likewise he is a clever thief. It seems so. If, therefore, the just man be clever in guarding money, he is clever likewise in stealing. So it would seem, said he, from this reasoning. The just man, then, has been shown to be a sort of thief; and it is likely you have learned this from Homer; for he not only admires Autolycus, the maternal grandfather of Ulysses, but says, that he was distinguished beyond all men for thievishness and swearing. Justice, then, seems in your opinion as well as in that of Homer and Simonides, to be a sort of thieving carried on for the benefit of our friends on the one hand, and for the injury of our enemies on the other: did not you say so? No, by Zeus, I did not; nor, indeed, do I any longer know what I was saying: yet it is still my opinion, that justice benefits friends, but injures foes. But [tell me] whether you pronounce such to be friends, as seem to be honest; or such merely as are so, though not seeming so; and in the same way as to enemies? It is reasonable, said he, to love those whom one deems honest, and to hate those [one deems] wicked. But do not men fall into error on this point, so that many appear to them honest who are not so, and many the contrary? Yes, they do. To such as these, then, the good are enemies, and the bad friends? Certainly. But still is it, in that case, just for them to benefit the wicked, and hurt the good? So it seems. The good, moreover, are just, and incapable of doing any ill. True. According to your argument, then, is it just to do those harm who do no harm [themselves]? By no means [think that], Socrates, replied he; for that opinion seems to be vicious. With respect to the unjust, then, said I, is it right to injure these but to do good to the just? This opinion seems fairer than the other. To many, then, it will occur [to think] Polemarchus,—that is, to as many as have formed wrong opinions of men,—that they may justly hurt their friends (for they are wicked to them), and, on the other hand, benefit their enemies, inasmuch as they are good: and thus we shall state the very reverse of what we alleged Simonides to say. That is precisely the case, said he: but, let us change our definition; for we seem not to have rightly defined a friend and a foe. How were they defined, Polemarchus? That he who seems honest is a friend. How then are we now to alter our definition, said I? That the person, replied he, who seems, and also is honest, is a friend; but that he who is apparently honest, but not really so, seems to be, yet is not [really] a friend: the definition, too, respecting an enemy, exactly corresponds. The good man, according to this reasoning, will, it seems, be a friend; and the wicked man a foe? . . .

Now tell me, Thrasymachus; was this what you meant by justice,—namely, the advantage of the more powerful, such as appeared so to the more powerful, whether it really were so, or not: shall we say that you mean this? Not at all, said he: for, think you, I call him who errs, the more powerful, at the time he errs? For my part, said I, I thought you meant this, when you acknowledged that governors were not infallible, but that in some things even they erred. You are a sycophant, said he, in reasoning, Socrates! For, for instance, do you call him a physician who errs about the treatment of the sick, in respect of that very thing in which he errs; or him a reasoner, who errs in reasoning, at the very time he errs, and with reference to that very error? But, we say, in common language, I fancy, that the physician erred, the reasoner erred and the grammarian likewise; but in fact, I think, each of these, so far as he is what we designate him, never errs; so that, strictly speaking (especially as you are a strict reasoner), no artist errs; for he who errs, errs through defect of science, in what he is not an artist; and hence no artist, or wise man, or governor, errs, in so far as he is a governor. Yet every one would say "the physician erred," and "the governor erred." You must understand, then, that it was in this way I just now answered you. But the most accurate answer is this: that the governor, in as far as he is governor, errs not; and as he does not err, he enacts that which is best for himself, and this must be observed by the governed. So that as I said at the beginning, I call justice the doing that which is for the advantage of the strongest [*i. e.,* the best]. . . .

An extremely small number is left, said I, Adimantus, of those who engage worthily in philosophy, men of that noble and well-cultivated nature, which somehow seeks retirement, and naturally persists in philosophic study, through the absence of corrupting tendencies; or it may be, in a small state, some mighty soul arises, who has despised and wholly neglected civil honors; and there may be some small portion perhaps, who, having a naturally good disposition, hold other arts in just contempt, and then turn to philosophy. These the bridle of our friend Theages will probably be able to restrain; for all other things are calculated to withdraw Theages from philosophy, while the care of his health occupies him to the exclusion of politics: and as to what concerns myself, namely the sign of my demon, it is not worth while to mention that; for I think it has heretofore been met with only by one other, if any at all. And even of these few [they are] such as taste, and have tasted, how sweet and blessed is the acquisition of philosophy, and have withal sufficiently observed the madness of the multitude, and that none of them, as I may say, does what is wholesome in state matters, and that a man can get none to aid him in securely succoring the just, but is like one falling among wild beasts, neither willing nor able to aid them in doing wrong, as one only against a host of wild creatures, and so without doing any good either to the state or his friends, perishes unprofitably to all the world. Quietly reasoning on all these things, and attending to his own affairs, like a man sheltered under a wall in a storm of dust and foam borne along on the wind, by which he sees all about him overwhelmed in disorder, such a one is content anyhow to pass his life pure from injustice and unholy deeds, and to effect his exit hence with good hopes cheerful and agreeable. Aye, and he will make his exit, said he, without having done even the least of them.

Nor the greatest either, said I; because he has not found a suitable form of government; for in one that suits him, he will both make greater progress himself, and together with the affairs of private persons, will preserve those of the public also.

As respects philosophy, then, for what reasons it has been traduced, and that it has been so unjustly, we have, I think, sufficiently stated unless you have anything else to allege. Nay, said he; I can say nothing further about this point: but which of the present forms of government do you conceive to be suited to philosophy? None whatever, said I; and this particularly is what I complain of, that no existing constitution of a state is worthy of the philosophic nature; and in this account therefore it is turned and altered, just as a foreign seed sown in an improper soil becomes worthless, and has a tendency to fall under the influence of the soil in which it is placed; so this race likewise has not at present its proper power, but degenerates to some pattern foreign to it; but in case that it does meet with the best form of government, being itself also best, it will then be evident that this is really divine, and all others only human, both as to their natures and pursuits; but as a matter of course you are evidently about to ask what is this form of government? You are mistaken, said he, for this I was not going to ask; but whether it be this, which we have described in establishing our state, or some other. As regards all other things, said I, it is this one; and this very thing was then mentioned, that there must always be in our state something having the same regard for the government, which you the legislator had in establishing the laws. Aye,—that was mentioned, said he. Yes, but, said I, it was not made sufficiently clear, owing to the fear of what you objected when you showed also that the illustration of the thing would be both tedious and difficult; for indeed it is not on the whole quite easy to discuss what remains. What is that? In what manner a state is to undertake the study of philosophy, so as not itself to be destroyed;

for all great pursuits are dangerous; and, as the saying is, those noble even are truly difficult. But still, rejoined he, let our demonstration be completed by making this evident. Want of inclination, said I, will not hinder, though possibly want of power may; and now you shall at once be assured of my readiness. Consider indeed, how readily and adventurously I am about to assert, that a state ought to attempt this study in a way opposite to what it does at present. How? At present, said I, those who engage in it are striplings, who, quite from childhood, amidst their domestic affairs and lucrative employments, betake themselves to most abstruse inquiries, considering themselves consummate philosophers, (and I call what respects reasoning, the most difficult of all); and should they in aftertime be invited by others practicing this art, they are pleased to become hearers, and think it a great condescension, reckoning they ought to do it as a by-work, but toward old age, with the exception indeed of some few, they are extinguished even more than the Heraclitean sun, because they are never again rekindled. But how should they act? said he. Quite the reverse of what they do; while they are lads and youths they should study youthful learning and philosophy, and, take special care of the body, during its growth and strengthening by inviting its services to the aid of philosophy; and then, as that time of life progresses, during which the soul is attaining its perfection, they should vigorously apply to her exercises; but when strength decays, and is no longer suited for civil and military employments, they should then be dismissed, and live at pleasure, with the exception of a by-work, [that is, studying philosophy], if indeed they propose to live happy, and, when they die, possess in the other world, a destiny suited to the life which they have led in this.

How truly do I think, Socrates, said he, that you speak with ready zeal: I think, however, that most of your hearers will still more zealously oppose you, and by no means be persuaded, and Thrasymachus even first. Do not divide

Thrasymachus and me, said I, who are now become friends, though not enemies heretofore; for we will not at all relax our efforts, till we either persuade both him and the rest, or make some advances toward that life, on attaining which they will again meet with such discourses as these. You have spoken, said he, only for a short time. No time at all, said I, as compared at least with the whole of time: but that the multitude are not persuaded by what is said, is no wonder; for they have never as yet seen that what was mentioned actually come to pass, but rather, that they were certain mere words cleverly fitted to each other, and not as now coming out spontaneously: and as regards the man, who is, as completely as possible, squared and made consistent with virtue both in word and deed, holding power in a state of such different character; they have never at all seen either one or more of the kind. Do you think they have? By no means. And again, as respects arguments, my excellent friend, they have not sufficiently listened to what are fair and liberal, such as persevere in the search for truth, by every method, for the mere sake of knowledge, saluting at a distance such intricate and contentious questions, as tend only to opinion and strife, either in their law-courts or private meetings. Not even as respects these, he replied. On these accounts, then, said I, and foreseeing these things, we, although with fear, still asserted (compelled by truth), that neither state nor government, nor even a man in the same way, could ever become perfect, till some need of fortune should compel those few philosophers, who at present are termed not depraved but useless, to take the government of the state, whether they will or not, and oblige it to be obedient to them; or till the sons of those who are now in high offices and magistracies, or they themselves, be by some divine inspiration filled with a true love of sincere philosophy: and I am sure that no one can reasonably suppose either or both of these to be impossible; for thus might we justly be derided, as saying things which otherwise are only like wishes: is it not so? It is. If then, in the infinite series of past ages, absolute necessity has compelled men who have reached the summit of philosophy to take the government of a state, or even if such is now the case in some barbarous region, remote from our observation, or is likely to be the case hereafter, we are ready, in that case, to advance in argument, that this form of government just described has existed and now exists [in possibility], and will actually arise, when this our muse shall obtain the government of the state: for this is neither impossible to happen, nor do we speak of impossibilities, though we ourselves confess that they are difficult. I too, said he, am of the same opinion. But you will say, replied I, that the multitude are not of that opinion? Very likely, said he. My excellent friend, said I, do not thus altogether condemn the multitude; and do not upbraid them for their opinion, but rather encourage them, remove the reproach thrown on philosophy, and point out to them the persons you call philosophers, defining distinctly, as at present, both their genius and pursuits, that they may not think that you speak of such as they themselves call philosophers. Indeed, if they talk of the same men, will you not say that they have conceived a different opinion of the men from what you have, and give very different replies from yours; and think you that one man can be angered at another, who is not angry himself; or that a man will envy the envious, who is himself free from envy, and of a gentle temper? I will anticipate you by saying, that I think some few, though not the great mass of mankind, have naturally so bad a temper as you have described. I am quite of that opinion also, said he. Are you then of my opinion in this also, namely, that, as regards the ill-feeling of the populace toward philosophy, those people from without [*i.e.*, the sophists] are the real cause of it, by making an indecent and turbulent irruption thereinto, insulting and showing a downright hatred of philosophers, ever directing their discourses at particular men, and so doing what least of all becomes philosophy? Certainly, said he.

In fact, Adimantus, the man who really applies his intellect to reflect on true being, probably has no leisure to look down on the little affairs of mankind, and by fighting with them, become filled with envy and ill-nature; but on the other hand, beholding and contemplating objects that are orderly, always self-consistent and stable, such as neither injure nor are injured by each other, but are in all respects beautiful and consonant with reason, these he imitates and resembles as far as possible: what, think you it at all possible, that a man will not imitate what he admires as soon as he is conversant therewith? Impossible, he replied. The philosopher, then, who is occupied with what is divine and orderly, becomes himself divine and orderly, as far as lies in man's power: yet in all there is great room for blame. . . . It is our business then, said I, to compel those of the inhabitants, who possess the greatest talent, to devote themselves to that learning which we formerly considered most important, both to contemplate the good and go in search of it; and when they have gained it, and taken a sufficient view thereof, yet they are not to be allowed what is now allowed them. What is that? To abide there, said I, and show an unwillingness to descend again to those captives of whom we were speaking; or share with them both their labors and honors, whether trifling or more important. In that case, said he, are we to do them injustice, and make them live a worse life, when they could have lived a better?

You have forgotten again, said I, that this is not the lawgiver's concern, how any one class in a state may be especially happy, but to contrive rather that happiness shall be generated throughout the state, uniting the citizens both by persuasion and compulsion, making them share each other's services, such as they can confer on the community at large; and when he introduces such men as these into the state, he does so, not that he may dismiss them and let them turn whichever way each likes, but that he may employ them as a bond of the state. True indeed, said he, for I had forgotten that. Anxiously consider then, Glaucon, that we must do no injustice to the philosophers born among us, but tell them what is just, when we compel them to take charge of and guard the remainder: for we will assert, that those who in all other states become such [philosophers] do not probably take a share in the labors going on therein, as they spring up of their own accord without the consent of the government in each; and it is just that what is voluntary, inasmuch as it owes its nurture to none, should willingly pay no one the price of its nurture; but as for you, we brought into being both yourselves and the rest of the state, as leaders and kings in beehives, brought up better and more perfectly than the others, and better able to take a share in both [public life and philosophical pursuits]. Each must then in turn descend to the dwelling of the rest, and accustom himself to behold obscure objects; for, when once used to them, you will perceive the individual images of each, what they are and whence sprung, ten thousand times better from having already seen the truth concerning what is beautiful, and just, and good: and thus the state will be settled as a real vision, both by us and yourselves, and not as a dream, like most of those inhabited by persons fighting about shadows, and quarreling about government, as if it were some great good. The truth, however, is as follows: in whatever state those about to rule are least anxious to take the government, this must necessarily be the best and most peacefully governed, while one that has governors of an opposite character, must of course be the opposite. Certainly, said he. Think you then, that those under our charge, when they hear these things, will disobey us, and be unwilling to take their individual share in the labors of the state, and spend the greater part of their time with one another in a state of leisure? Impossible, said he; for we will prescribe what is just to just men, and each of them will enter on his office from this consideration above all others, that he should act in a manner directly contrary from those who now govern individual states. Yes, for so it is, my friend; if you find the life of those appointed to official stations superior to the dignity of their office, then your state may possibly be well settled; as in that alone will the really wealthy govern, not those rich in gold, but as happy men should be rich, in a life of virtue and good sense; whereas, should they be poor, and destitute of property of their own, and then come into public life, thinking that they ought to plunder the public of its property, it is not possible [that such a state can be rightly settled]: for as the contest is about the possession of the ruling power, such a war being domestic and intestine, is destructive to themselves as well as the rest of the state. Most true, he replied. Do you conceive then that any other kind of life despises political offices except that of true philosophy? No, by Zeus, said he. But still it is fitting, at least, that those should enter upon it who are not fond of governing, otherwise the rivals will fight about it. Of course, it cannot be otherwise. Whom else, then, would you compel to enter on the guardianship of a state, except such as are most intelligent in what concerns the best establishment of a state, and possess other honors, and a mode of life superior to that of a mere politician? . . .

Well, then, Glaucon, these things have been agreed on, that in a state that is to be perfectly administered the women are to be in common, the children in common, and their education also,—so likewise their employments both in war and peace in common, and their kings the best possible both in philosophy and warfare. It has been so agreed, he replied. And this, moreover, we agreed on, that when the commanders are appointed and leading their soldiers, they should dwell in habitations, such as we have described, containing nothing particularly belonging to any individual, but common to all. . . .

Democracy, as it seems, must next be considered, how it arises, and when once arisen, what kind of man it produces; in order that understanding the nature of such a man, we may at once bring him to trial. Yes, said he; that would be our consistent course. Well then, said I, is not the change from oligarchy to democracy produced in some such way as this, through the insatiable desire of the proposed good, *viz.*, the desire of becoming as rich as possible? How? Inasmuch as its governors govern through the possession of great wealth, they will have no wish, methinks, to restrain by law the profligate portion of the young men from squandering and wasting their property at pleasure; because, by purchasing such persons' effects, and lending on usury, they will not only be still more enriched, but held in higher repute. Far more so than any other. This, then, is already quite clear in our state, that to honor riches, and at the same time practice temperance, is impossible, since either the one or the other must necessarily be neglected. Of course, that is quite plain, said he. While, therefore, they are neglectful in oligarchies, and allow the youths to indulge in licentiousness, they must necessarily sometimes bring men to poverty, even those that are not ignoble. Quite so. And these, I suppose, stand in our state both spurred, and in armor; some in debt, others in disgrace, others in both, hating and conspiring against those who have got what belonged to them, and against others also, for mere love of change. Aye, such is the case. These usurers, however, bent on their own interests, and apparently unobservant of these, wound all that ever yield to them by advancing them money, and so, by getting multiplied interest for the parent principal, fill the state with many a drone and pauper. Aye, with many a one, he replied. And even when such an evil is raging in the state, said I, they are not willing to extinguish it, not even by restraining people from spending their property at pleasure, nor yet in this way by making another law to destroy such disorders. What law? One that shall follow the other, compelling the citizens to cultivate virtue; for if they were bidden to engage in voluntary contracts chiefly at their own hazard, their usurers would create less scandal in the state, and fewer also of the evils now mentioned would arise therein. Far fewer, said he. At present, however, said I, it is by all these means that the governors in the state thus dispose of the governed; and both as to themselves and those belonging to them, do they not render the youths luxurious and idle as respects all bodily and mental exercises, effeminate in bearing pleasure and pains, and indolent likewise? What else? And as to themselves, they neglect everything but the acquisition of wealth, and pay no more regard to virtue than the poor. No, surely. Having then been thus trained up, when the governors and their subjects are thrown together, either on a journey along the road, or in other meetings, either at public spectacles, or on warlike expeditions, either as fellow-sailors or fellow-soldiers, or when they see one another in real dangers, the poor in this case are by no means despised by the rich; but very often a robust fellow, poor and sunburnt, whose post in battle is by the side of a rich man bred up in the shade, and swollen with much unnecessary fat, if he should see him panting for breath and in agony, think you not, he will consider such persons to grow rich to their own injury, and will say to his fellow, when meeting in private, that our rich men are good for nothing? Of course, I well know, said he, that they do so. Well then, as a diseased body needs but the smallest shock from without to give it pain, and is sometimes thrown into disorder without any interference from without, so also the state that resembles it will, on the smallest occasion from without, either when one party forms an alliance with an oligarchal, or the other with a democratic state, become disordered, and fight with itself, and also rise in revolt without any external interference. Yes, certainly. A democracy then, I think, arises, when the poor prevailing over the rich, kill some, and banish others, and share the state offices and magistracies equally among the remainder; and for the most part the magistracies therein are disposed of by lot. . . .

. . . Aye, for excessive liberty seems only to degenerate into excessive slavery, either in private individuals or states. It is probable, indeed. Probably then, said I, tyranny is established out of no other form than democracy; out of the highest degree of liberty, methinks, the greatest and fiercest slavery. Yes, it is reasonable, said he. This, however, methinks, said I, was not what you asked: but what is that same disease which arises in an oligarchy and a democracy, and reduces each to slavery? Your remark is true, replied he. I meant, said I, that there was a race of idle and profuse men, the bravest of whom were the leaders, and the more cowardly their followers, whom, indeed, we compared to drones; some to those with stings, others to those without stings. . . .

The Statesman

Guest.—After a certain manner it is evident that legislation is a part of the science of a king: but it is best, not for the laws to prevail, but for a man, who has with prudence the power of a king. Do you know in what way?

Soc. jun.—In what way do you mean?

Guest.—Because the law cannot, by comprehending that which is the best and most accurately just in all cases, at the same time ordain what is the best. For the inequalities of men and their actions, and the fact that not a single atom, so to say, of human affairs, enjoys a state of rest, do not permit any art whatever to exhibit in any case any thing simple (without exception) respecting all matters and through all time. Shall we admit this?

Soc. jun.—How not?

Guest.—And yet we see the law tending nearly to this very point; and, like a certain self-willed and ignorant man, it does not suffer any person to do any thing contrary to its own orders, nor to put a question, not even should something new happen to be in some case better as compared with the decree it had ordained.

Soc. jun.—True. For the law does really so, as you have just now said, to each of us.

Guest.—Is it not then impossible for that, which is under all cases simple, to do well in cases which are never at any time simple?

Soc. jun.—It appears so nearly.

[34] *Guest.*—Why then is it necessary to lay down laws? Since law is not a thing of the greatest rectitude. Of this we must inquire the cause.

Soc. jun.—How not?

Guest.—Are there not then amongst us, as in other cities likewise, certain exercises of men collected together for the sake of competition relating to running or something else?

Soc. jun.—Yes. There are very many.

Guest.—Come then, let us again recall to our memory the orders of those who practice scientifically exercises in meetings of this kind.

Soc. jun.—What is this?

Guest.—They do not conceive it is requisite to be very fine in ordering, according to each individual, what is suited to the body of each; but think more stupidly, that they ought to make their arrangements of what benefits the body, suited to the majority of circumstances and persons.

Soc. jun.—Excellent.

Guest.—On which account assigning now equal labors to persons collected together, they urge them on together, and stop them together in the race, and wrestling, and all the labors of the body.

Soc. jun.—Such is the fact.

Guest.—Let us hold then, that the legislator who would preside over his herds in matters of justice, and their contracts with each other, will never be sufficient for all collectively, by accurately enjoining upon each individual what is fitting.

Soc. jun.—This is likely.

Guest.—But I think he will establish laws suited to the

majority of persons and circumstances, and somehow thus in more stupid way for each, delivering them in writings, and in an unwritten (form), and legislating according to the customs of the country. . . .

Guest.—Let us say then that this is the end of the web of the statesman's doing, (so as for him) to weave with straight weaving the manners of manly and temperate men, when the kingly science shall by bringing together their common life, through a similarity in sentiment and friendship, complete the most magnificent and excellent of all webs, [so as to be common,] and enveloping all the rest in the state, both slaves and freemen, shall hold them together by this texture, and, as far as it is fitting for a state to become prosperous, shall rule and preside over it, deficient in that point not one jot.

Soc. jun.—You have brought, O guest, most beautifully, on the other hand, the characters of the king and statesman to a finish.

PIERRE JOSEPH PROUDHON

(1809-1865)

Was a French philosophic anarchist, whose most famous work, *What Is Property?* (1840), starts out with the answer, "Property is theft!" Of all the socialist theorists of the nineteenth century, Proudhon was the most fruitful in his ideas but the least capable of mastering them. For him philosophy was only a means of changing the thoughts of men. He was born in Besançon (the birthplace of Fourier); his parents were poor and he earned his way through school by taking care of cows, acting as a waiter in restaurants and at similar occupations. At school he earned numerous awards. At nineteen, obliged to leave college, he became a printer, but continued reading, especially the contents of volumes on theology printed by his firm. Subsequently he received a pension of 1500 francs from the Académie de Besançon, given to promising students in the field of literature and science. In 1840, he wrote his famed *Qu'est-ce que la Propriété?*, a pioneering work which tried to prove the inequity of private property per se, and expounded the doctrine of labor time as a measure of value (an idea which later helped the socialist movement and provided a philosophic background for the anarchist movement). In 1846 he published his *Système des Contradictions Economiques ou Philosophie de la Misère (The System of Economic Contradictions or the Philosophy of Misery)*, in which he criticized socialist and communist theories, but failed to formulate a constructive philosophy. After the 1848 Revolution he was elected to the Constituent Assembly; later served three years in prison for breaking a censorship law, and, on his release, was again sentenced to a prison term for attacking the church. He escaped to Belgium, however, and returned to France in 1860. He lived a life of simplicity and self-sacrifice, was devoted to his family, and often rebuked some of the early Utopians for their immorality.

Pierre Joseph Proudhon

In approaching the social problem, he sought a science of society based on liberty, equality and fraternity. He distinguished between the ultimate goal and the transition to that goal. The state was his chief enemy: "Governments are the scourge of God." Nothing less than annihilation of the whole mechanism of authority is needed to reclaim society. In order to free the French workers and peasants from their industrial and financial slavery, he urged the establishment of cooperative credit banks where money could be had without interest and where goods could be exchanged at cost value by means of a "labor currency" representing the hours of work needed to produce each commodity. (An American disciple of his, Josiah Warren, for a time conducted a group of "Equity Stores," using labor-exchange currency as their sole medium.) At first friendly with Marx, they became bitter enemies, although Marx adopted Proudhon's view that the philosopher has not only to interpret the world but to change it. Solidarity, according to Proudhon, is a natural and original characteristic of human beings, and egoism is the result of a deviation from natural conditions. Man must be guided back from his state of isolation to a community in which the equilibrium between the rights of the individual and "public" or "collective" reason must be established anew, and too great inequality of wealth must be prohibited. He was opposed to the assumption that ideas of justice and morality are dependent on economic or social conditions (being, in this respect, a Platonist). His ultimate society would be devoid of government, for "the highest perfection is found in the union of order and anarchy." The control of man by man is oppression. The ideal society would contain no private property (although he was not opposed to private possession, providing it was secured by labor). He took issue with Communists on the ground that their system would lead to the oppression of the strong by the weak. His aim was not primarily to bring to men equality of compensation, but equality of means for producing wealth. Some of his ideas were derived from William Godwin's *Inquiry Concerning Political Justice* (1793), and were later developed by Bakunin, Kropotkin and Reclus (and along different lines by Stirner, Tolstoy and Nietzsche).

*The Complexity of Human Nature**

HUMAN society is *complex* in its nature. Though this expression is inaccurate, the fact to which it refers is none the less true; namely, the classification of talents and capacities. But who does not see that these talents and capacities, owing to their infinite variety, give rise to an infinite variety of wills, and that the character, the inclinations, and if I may venture to use the expression—the form of the ego are necessarily changed; so that in the order of liberty, as in the order of intelligence, there are as many types of individuals, as many characters as heads, whose tastes, fancies, and propensities, being modified by dissimilar ideas, must necessarily conflict? Man, by his nature and his instinct, is predestined to society; but his personality, ever varying, is adverse to it.

In societies of animals, all the members do exactly the same things. The same genius directs them; the same will animates them. A society of beasts is a collection of atoms, round, hooked, cubical, or triangular, but always perfectly identical. These personalities do not vary, and we might say that a single ego governs them all. The labors which animals perform whether alone or in society are exact reproductions of their character. Just as the swarm of bees is composed of individual bees, alike in nature and equal in value, so the honeycomb is formed of individual cells, constantly and invariably repeated.

But man's intelligence, fitted for his social destiny and his personal needs, is of a very different composition, and therefore gives rise to a wonderful variety of human wills. In the bee, the will is constant and uniform, because the instinct which guides it is invariable, and constitutes the animal's whole life and nature. In man, talent varies, and the mind wavers; consequently, his will is multiform and vague.

* This excerpt taken from Dagobert D. Runes, ed., *Treasury of Philosophy*, New York: Philosophical Library, 1955, pp. 977-979.

He seeks society, but dislikes constraint and monotony; he is an imitator, but fond of his own ideas, and passionately in love with his works.

If, like the bees, every man were born possessed of talent, perfect knowledge of certain kinds, and, in a word, an innate acquaintance with the functions he has to perform, but destitute of reflective and reasoning faculties, society would organize itself. We should see one man plowing a field, another building houses; this one forging metals, that one cutting clothes; and still others storing the products and superintending their distribution. Each one, without inquiring as to the object of his labor, and without troubling himself about the extent of his task, would obey orders, bring his product, receive his salary, and would then rest for a time; keeping meanwhile no accounts, envious of nobody, and satisfied with the distributor, who never would be unjust to any one. Kings would govern, but would not reign, for to reign is to be a *proprietor à l'engrais,* as Bonaparte said: and having no commands to give, since all would be at their posts, they would serve rather as rallying centers than as authorities or counsellors. It would be a state of ordered communism, but not a society entered into deliberately and freely.

But man acquires skill only by observation and experiment. He reflects, then, since to observe orders and experiment is to reflect; he reasons, since he cannot help reasoning. In reflecting, he becomes deluded; in reasoning, he makes mistakes, and, thinking himself right, persists in them. He is wedded to his opinions; he esteems himself, and despises others. Consequently, he isolates himself; for he could not submit to the majority without renouncing his will and his reason,—that is, without disowning himself, which is impossible. And this isolation, this intellectual egotism, this individuality of opinion, lasts until the truth is demonstrated to him by observation and experience. . . .

MAXIMILIEN FRANCOIS ROBESPIERRE

(1758-1794)

Known as "The Sea-Green Incorruptible," was a leader of the French Revolution who was practically the prime minister of the Committee of Public Safety (1793-1794). He was mainly responsible for the Reign of Terror (1793-1794), which sent Marie Antoinette to her death on October 16, 1793, the Girondin leaders two weeks later, and then the Dantonists. But despite victories by the French armies during this period, he showed no signs of relaxing governmental controls and, in fact, the tempo of the Terror accelerated. Finally, the enemies of Robespierre, fearing they might face the guillotine at any moment, decided to collaborate against him; on July 27, 1794 (the 9 Thermidor), the Convention shouted Robespierre down and voted his arrest, and on the following day he and his close associates were executed.

---

*Proposed Declaration of Rights**

THE representatives of the French people, met in National Convention, recognizing that human laws which do not flow from the eternal laws of justice and reason are only the outrages of ignorance and despotism upon humanity; convinced that neglect and contempt of the natural rights of man are the sole causes of the crimes and misfortunes of the world, have resolved to set forth in a solemn declaration these sa-

*** This excerpt is taken from Frank Maloy Anderson, *The Constitutions and Other Select Documents Illustrative of the History of France 1789-1901*, Minneapolis, 1904, pp. 160-164.**

cred and inalienable rights, in order that all citizens, being enabled to compare constantly the acts of the government with the purpose of every social institution, may never permit themselves to be oppressed and discouraged by tyranny; and in order that the people may always have before their eyes the foundations of their liberty and their welfare; the magistrate, the rule of his duties; the legislator, the purpose of his mission.

In consequence, the National Convention proclaims in the face of the world and under the eyes of the Immortal Legislator the following declaration of the rights of man and citizen.

1. The purpose of every political association is the maintenance of the natural and imprescriptible rights of man and the development of all his faculties.

2. The principal rights of man are those of providing for the preservation of his existence and his liberty.

3. These rights belong equally to all men whatever may be the difference of their physical and mental powers.

4. Equality of rights is established by nature: society, far from impairing it, exists only to guarantee it against the abuse of power which renders it illusory.

5. Liberty is the power which belongs to man to exercise at his will all his faculties; it has justice for rule, the rights of others for limits, nature for principle, and the law for safeguard.

6. The right to assemble peaceably, the right to express one's opinions, either by means of the press or in any other manner, are such necessary consequences of the principle of the liberty of man, that the necessity to enunciate them supposes either the presence or the fresh recollection of despotism.

7. The law can forbid only that which is injurious to society; it can order only that which is useful.

8. Every law which violates the imprescriptible rights of man is essentially unjust and tyrannical; it is not a law.

9. Property is the right which each citizen has, to enjoy and dispose of the portion of goods which the law guarantees to him.

10. The right of property is restricted, as are all the others, by the obligation to respect the possessions of others.

11. It cannot prejudice the security, nor the liberty, nor the existence, nor the property of our fellow creatures.

12. All traffic which violates this principle is essentially illicit and immoral.

13. Society is under obligation to provide for the support of all its members either by procuring work for them or by assuring the means of existence to those who are not in condition to work.

14. The relief indispensable for those who lack the necessities of life is a debt of those who possess a superfluity; it belongs to the law to determine the manner in which this debt must be discharged.

15. The citizens whose incomes do not exceed what is necessary for their subsistence are exempted from contributing to the public expenses; the others shall support them progressively, according to the extent of their fortunes.

16. Society ought to favor with all its power the progress of public reason and to put instruction at the door of all the citizens.

17. Law is the free and solemn expression of the will of the people.

18. The people are the sovereign, the government is their creation, the public functionaries are their agents; the people can, when they please, change their government and recall their mandatories.

19. No portion of the people can exercise the power of the entire people; but the opinion which it expresses shall be respected as the opinion of a portion of the people who ought to participate in the formation of the general will. Each section of the assembled sovereign ought to enjoy the right to express its will with entire liberty; it is essentially independ-

ent of all the constituted authorities and is capable of regulating its police and its deliberations.

20. The law ought to be equal for all.

21. All citizens are admissible to all public offices, without any other distinctions than those of their virtues and talents and without any other title than the confidence of the people.

22. All citizens have an equal right to participate in the selection of the mandatories of the people and in the formation of the law.

23. In order that these rights may not be illusory and the equality chimerical, society ought to give salaries to the public functionaries and to provide so that all the citizens who live by their labor can be present in the public assemblies to which the law calls them without compromising their existence or that of their families.

24. Every citizen ought to obey religiously the magistrates and the agents of the government, when they are the organs or the executors of the law.

25. But every act against the liberty, security, or property of a man, committed by anyone whomsoever, even in the name of the law outside of the cases determined by it and the forms which it prescribes, is arbitrary and void; respect for the law even forbids submission to it; and if an attempt is made to execute it by violence, it is permissible to repel it by force.

26. The right to present petitions to the depositories of the public authority belongs to every person. Those to whom they are addressed ought to pass upon the points which are the object thereof; but they can never interdict, nor restrain, nor condition their use.

27. Resistance to oppression is a consequence of the other rights of man and citizen.

28. There is oppression against the social body when one of its members is oppressed. There is oppression against each member of the social body when the social body shall be oppressed.

29. When the government violates the rights of the people, insurrection is for the people and for each portion of the people the most sacred of rights and the most indispensable of duties.

30. When the social guarantee is lacking to a citizen he re-enters into the natural right to defend all his rights himself.

31. In either case, to tie down to legal forms resistance to oppression is the last refinement of tyranny. In every free State the law ought especially to defend public and personal liberty against the abuse of the authority of those who govern: every institution which is not based upon the assumption that the people are good and the magistrate is corruptible is vicious.

32. The public offices cannot be considered as distinctions, nor as rewards, but only as duties.

33. The offences of the mandatories of the people ought to be severely punished. No one has the right to claim for himself more inviolability than other citizens. The people have the right to know all the transactions of their mandatories; these ought to render to them a faithful account of their own administration and to submit to their judgment with respect.

34. Men of all countries are brothers and the different peoples ought to aid one another, according to their power, as if citizens of the same State.

35. The one who oppresses a single nation declares himself the enemy of all.

36. Those who make war on a people in order to arrest the progress of liberty and to destroy the rights of man ought to be pursued by all, not as ordinary enemies, but as assassins and rebellious brigands.

37. Kings, aristocrats, and tyrants, whoever they may be, are slaves in rebellion against the sovereign of the earth, which is mankind, and against the legislator of the universe, which is nature.

JEAN JACQUES ROUSSEAU

(1712-1778)

Was one of the most influential philosophers of all times. Although he died eleven years before the French Revolution started, he was one of its main architects, with his ideas on the rights of the poor and the free and equal citizenship of every member of the state. (He was equally influential in world history with his educational theories.) Yet Rousseau's private life, with its strange and unorthodox adventures and final mania, is a fantastic record. Born in Geneva, the second son of a watchmaker, he lost his mother a fortnight after his birth and spent the first ten years of his life in the company of his father, his nurse and an aunt. His father taught him to read and enjoy the classics and contemporary novels, but after an argument with him Rousseau fled to Lyons, and thereafter led a checkered career. His adventures included being an apprentice to a notary and later to an engraver, a private secretary, sometimes footman, to one Madame de Warens, who was twenty-eight and wealthy and who became Jean's mistress. In 1741 he landed in Paris, where Diderot and his friends helped him to secure the post of secretary to the French Ambassador to Venice. When he returned to Paris, Diderot commissioned him to write articles. In 1742 he married a seamstress, Theresa le Vasseur, "ugly, ignorant, stupid and a detestable mother" (he reports in his *Confessions*), with whom he had five children, each left on the steps of the foundling hospital "to save expense"—yet this genius made most impressive contributions to the education of children. His first fame was achieved with a prize essay for the Dijon Academy: *Has the Progress of the Arts and Sciences Helped to Corrupt or to Purify Morals?* (1750). His next success was the production of *Le Devin du Village,* an operetta, which secured him a pension and a position at the Royal Court. Yet he refused both pension and appointment. Then he published *What Is the Origin of Inequality Among Man, and Is It Authorized by Natural Law?* (1754), in which he presented his ideas on the state of nature and on the evils resulting from civilization. (Some political doctrines were also treated in the *Emile,* 1762, his work on education.) *Du Contrat Social* (1762) appeared in Amsterdam, for safety reasons. In this work he based all government on the consent, direct and implied, of the governed; the basis of society is an original compact by which each member surrenders his will to the will of all on condition that he receives protection in return. Rousseau also favored a republic with universal suffrage and put forward the citizen's claims to liberty, equality and fraternity (the battle cry of the French Revolution). Threatened with arrest because of *Emile,* he fled to Switzerland, and attacked his attackers in *Lettres de la Montagne* (1763). This forced him to flee to England, where he asked David Hume for help. (His wife was escorted by James Boswell!) England received him as a celebrity and by royal command a performance was given at Drury Lane in his honor. Hume sheltered him at Wootton (Derbyshire) where he wrote most of his *Confessions;* but an argument with his host forced him to return to France, where he moved from one patron to another, quarreling with them all, as he finished his *Confessions* and *Dialogues.* On July 2, 1778, he was found dead, whether of apoplexy or suicide, the doctors were unable to decide.

It is still debated whether or not Rousseau's work represents an affirmation of rational sentiments against reason. But he did influence Kant and, through Kant, Fichte and Hegel, and thus the rise of German Idealism—and ultimately the most threatening present form of totalitarianism, Communism, which derives in large measure from Hegel. In summary, Rousseau claimed that civilization is a moral sham because the appearance of virtue without the possession of freedom is hypocrisy, and therefore a vice. Since freedom, the prerequisite to virtue, is absent in civilization, and since its loss is the result of "progress," the process of civilization instead of improving man tends to corrupt him further. The closer man remained to his original state, the better he was. Man is naturally good, and civilization represents man's development from original goodness to present depravity and lack of freedom. Man, in order to be moral, must be free and under law. Freedom implies the absence of a superior, while law implies the existence of a superior—but these can be combined if man himself is the lawgiver. Thus man is free when he obeys a self-imposed law; for a self-imposed law must not merely be the expression of natural wants; it must also be a restatement of the laws of Nature. Man's departure from his original happiness is the consequence of the continued operations of the laws of Nature; men did not deliberately foresake their freedom, but were deprived of it by the necessity of their actions. Gradually developing inequality is the outcome of the actual differences produced by the division of law and the consequent inequality in power and wealth. The state is the result of a compact; but because the state represents the codification of inequality, it makes morality impossible. The social contract restores equality through each surrendering to all and through the cession of all possessions to the community, which can then return them to the individuals. The social contract, further, is a self-imposed law and the universal intention to live under law represents the "general will." All power resides within the general will, and sovereignty cannot, therefore, be abused. Unanimous consent is required to the original contract; after the state is formed, the will of the majority must be taken as the general will. Thus Rousseau transferred the concept of absolute and individual sovereignty from monarchy (Bodin, Hobbes) to popular control. Government is created, not by contract (Hobbes) but by the act of the sovereign people, and may be changed at their pleasure for it is merely their agent.

Rousseau's ideas were adopted in the French Revolution and in the Declaration of the Rights of Man (1789), and his ideas of liberty, equality and popular sovereignty have become the core of political discussions ever since and have been expressed in numberless constitutions. His thoughts stimulated Jefferson, and his theory of social contract (as well as that of Hobbes and Locke) was recognized in the Declaration of Independence and in nearly all the bills of rights of the American state constitutions. Kant and Fichte accepted this theory as a working hypothesis.

*The Social Contract**

Subject of the First Book

MAN IS BORN FREE; and everywhere he is in chains. One believes himself the master of others, yet remains a greater slave than they. How did this change occur? I do not know. What can render it legitimate? I think I can answer that question.

If I considered only force, and the effects derived therefrom, I should say: "As long as a people is forced to obey, and it obeys, it does well; as soon as it can shake off the yoke, and it shakes it off, it does still better; for, in recovering its liberty by the same right by which it was removed, either it is justified in regaining it, or there was no justification for those who took it away." But the social order is a sacred right which is the basis of all the others. Nevertheless, this right does not come from nature, it is founded on conventions....

The Right of the Strongest

The strongest is never strong enough always to be the master, if he fails to transform strength into right, and obedience into duty. Hence the right of the strongest, which right, though to all appearances meant ironically, is really established as a principle. But are we never to have an explanation of this phrase? Might is physical power; I cannot see what moral effects it can have. To yield to might is an act of necessity, not of will; at the most, it is an act of prudence. In what sense can it be a duty?

Suppose for a moment the existence of this so-called right. I say that the only result is inexplicable nonsense, for, if might makes right, the effect changes with the cause; every

* This excerpt taken from Jean Jacques Rousseau, *Du Contrat Social,* Paris, 1903, quoted from *Readings in Western Civilization,* edited by George H. Knoles and Rixford K. Snyder, J. P. Lippincott Co., Philadelphia and New York, 1951.

force that is greater than the first succeeds to its right. As soon as it is possible to disobey with impunity, one does so legitimately; and, the strongest always being in the right, needs only to act so as to become the strongest. But what kind of right is that which perishes when might fails? If we must obey by force, there is no need to obey because we ought; and if we are not forced to obey, we are not obliged to do so. Clearly the word *right* adds nothing to force; here, it means absolutely nothing.

Obey the powers that be. If this means: yield to force, the precept is good, but superfluous; I reply that it will never be violated. All power comes from God, I admit; so does all sickness. Does that mean that we are forbidden to call the doctor? A robber surprises me at the edge of the forest: Must I not merely give up my purse on compulsion; but, even if I could keep it, am I in conscience obliged to give it up? Certainly the pistol he holds is also a power.

Let us then admit that might does not create right, and that we are only obliged to obey legitimate powers. In that case, my original question recurs. . . .

THE SOCIAL CONTRACT

I suppose men to have reached that point where the obstacle to their preservation in the state of nature reveals their resistance to be greater than the resources available to each individual for his maintenance in that state. Then that primitive condition can subsist no longer; and the human race would perish unless it changed its way of being.

But, as men cannot engender new forces, but only unite and direct existing ones, they have no other means of preserving themselves, save the formation, by aggregation, of a sum of forces great enough to overcome the resistance; these they must imitate by means of a single motive power, and cause to act in concert.

This sum of forces can arise only when several persons

come together; but, since the force and the liberty of each man constitute the principal instruments of his self-preservation, how can he pledge them without hurting his own interests and neglecting the care which he owes himself? This difficulty in its bearing on my subject, may be stated in these terms:

"Find a form of association which defends and protects with the whole force of the community the person and the goods of each associate, and in which each, while uniting with all, may still obey himself alone, and remain as free as before." This is the fundamental problem of which the *Social Contract* offers the solution.

The clauses of this contract are so determined by the nature of the act, that the slightest modification would render them vain and of no effect; so that, although they have perhaps never been formally announced, they are always the same and everywhere tacitly admitted and announced, and, when the social compact is violated, each regains his original rights and regains his natural liberty while losing the conventional liberty for which he renounced it.

These clauses, properly understood, may be reduced to a single one—the total alienation of each associate with all his rights to the whole community; for, in the first place, as each gives himself entirely, the conditions are equal for all, and, the condition being equal for all, no one has an interest in making them burdensome to the others.

Moreover, the alienation being without reserve, the union is as perfect as it can be, and no associate has anything to demand: for, if the individuals retained certain rights in particular, as there would be no common superior to decide between them and the public, each, being on one point his own judge, would ask to be so on all; the state of nature would continue, and the association would necessarily become tyrannical or useless.

Finally, each in giving himself to all, gives himself to no one; and as there is no associate over whom he does not gain the same right as he grants to others over himself, he gains the equivalent for all that he loses, and a greater force for the conservation of what he has.

If then we discard from the social compact what is not of its essence, we shall find that it reduces itself to the following terms:

"Each of us puts his person and all his power in common under the supreme direction of the general will, and as in a body, we receive each member as an indivisible part of the whole."

At once, in place of the individual personality of each contracting party, this act of association produces a moral and collective body, composed of as many members as the assembly contains votes, and which receives from this same act its unity, its common identity, its life and its will. This public person, so formed by the union of all the others, formerly took the name of *city,* and now takes that of *Republic,* or *body politic.* It is called by its members, *State,* when it is passive; *Sovereign,* when it is active; and *Power,* when compared with others like itself. Respecting the associates, they take collectively the name of *people,* and are called *citizens,* as participating in the sovereign power, and *subjects,* as being under the laws of the State. But these terms are often confused and taken the one for the other; it is sufficient to know how to distinguish them when they are used with precision. . . .

CLAUDE HENRI, COMTE DE SAINT-SIMON

(1760-1825)

Was a French philosopher and social reformer, whose social doctrines were developed by his disciples into a system called "Saint-Simonianism," which demands that all property be owned by the state, the worker sharing in it according to the amount and quality of his work. In his works, *L'Industrie* (1817) and *Le Nouveau Christanisme* (1825), he stated that the goal of social activity is "the exploitation of the globe by association." Believing that politics was primarily the science of production, and that it would ultimately be absorbed into the field of economics, he judged the French Revolution a class war. He was the first to denounce "exploitation of men by their fellow-men," and to prognosticate the increasing concentration of capital and industry; but he was also one of those "wicked speculators" who were branded by Robespierre, and narrowly escaped execution. Although he amassed a large fortune during the French Revolution, he died in poverty. More than a hundred years before the Young Plan, he asked for an international bank, and his most faithful disciples became founders of joint-stock societies and constructors of canals and railroads, which, according to Saint-Simon, are necessary for the organization of human welfare and the realization of the ideals of human solidarity. His dominant idea was that the social system must be an application of a philosophical system, and that the function of philosophy is a prevalently social one. After ten years of studying physics, astronomy and chemistry, he turned to the study of human society and concluded that philosophical changes cause social changes, and that philosophy, as he conceived it, must found a new society, a new religion and a new evaluation of men. He stressed especially the belief that in modern times the industrial worker had become of far greater importance than the nobleman, the soldier and the priest, and that, consequently, he must occupy a higher social position than those former dignitaries. To industrial workers, scholars and bankers he entrusted the organization of his new social system, which may be characterized as a kind of technocratic socialism. But the form of government was, in his opinion, of lesser importance than the problem of administration. Therefore, he was not radically opposed to monarchism. After his death he became world-famous, due to the propagandistic ardor of his pupils; he especially influenced Goethe, Carlyle, Auguste Comte, B. P. Enfantin, St. A. Bazard and Karl Marx.

---

*The New Social Order**

THE CRISIS wherein the body politic has been involved for thirty years has its basic source in the complete change of the social system, that at this time tends, among the most civilized nations, to produce, as a final result, all the modifications that the old political order has successively experienced up to the present. To be more precise, this crisis consists essentially in the passing of the feudal and theocratic system to the industrial and scientific system. It will inevitably persist, until the formation of the new system is in full swing.

These fundamental truths have been, up to the present, and are still, equally unknown to the governed and to the governing class: or rather, they have not been and are not realized, by either class, except vaguely and incompletely, and quite insufficiently. The nineteenth century is still dominated by the critical nature of the eighteenth. It has not yet, to any degree, assumed the organizing character that must be peculiar to it. Such is the true first cause of the horrifying prolongation of the crisis and of the frightful storms that have so far attended it. But this crisis will cease necessarily, or at least will change into a simple moral movement, once

* This excerpt taken from Henri de Saint-Simon, *Système industriel,* translated by H. E. Wedeck.

we have attained the eminent position that the advance of civilization assigns us, once the temporal and spiritual forces that must begin to function have emerged from their inactivity.

The philosophical task, of which I now offer the public a first glimpse, will aim, in a general sense, to develop the important propositions that have just been summarily enunciated: to direct, to the utmost degree, the general attention on the true character of the great social reorganization reserved for the nineteenth century: to demonstrate that this reorganization, gradually prepared by all the progress that civilization has made so far, has in our time reached its full maturity, and that it cannot be deferred without the most serious consequences: to indicate, clearly and precisely, the course to be pursued in order to direct it calmly, with assurance and promptitude, despite the actual obstacles: in short, to strive, in so far as philosophy may, to determine the formation of the industrial and scientific system, whose establishment alone can put an end to the present social agony.

The industrial doctrine—I venture to postulate this boldly —would readily be understood and accepted with little effort, were the majority of men's minds adjusted to the proper viewpoint for the purpose of comprehending and judging it. Unfortunately, this is not the case. Defective and deeply rooted mental habits challenge the comprehension of this doctrine under every category. Bacon's *tabula rasa* would be infinitely more necessary for political concepts than for the others: and, by that same token, it must experience, relatively to this type of ideas, much more difficulty.

The difficulty that the learned have felt in adapting to the true spirit of astronomy and chemistry minds previously accustomed to consider these sciences from an astrological and alchemical angle, is today evident with respect to politics, to which the problem is to effect submission of an analogous change: passing from conjecture to assertion, from metaphysics to physics.

Forced to struggle against indurated and universally extensive habits, I believe that it is advisable to oppose them, and to anticipate to some extent a part of my task by explaining here, in a brief, general way, the influence that the vague, metaphysical doctrines have achieved and maintain in politics: the mistake that leads one to accept them as political truth, and, lastly, the need to abandon them now.

The industrial and scientific system arose and developed under the domination of the feudal and theocratic system. Now this simple relationship is sufficient to make one realize that between two systems so diametrically antagonistic, there must have existed a sort of indeterminate, intermediate system, solely designed to modify the old system so as to permit of the development of the new system, and, later, of the implementation of the transition. It is the simplest general historical fact to deduce from the data that I have presented. No change can take place except by degrees, in a temporal as in a spiritual direction. Here, the change was so great, and on the other hand, the feudal and theocratic system was so at variance, by its very nature, with all the modifications that, if they were to take place, the special action was necessary, persistent for several centuries, of particular classes stemming from the old system, but distinct from it, and up to a certain point independent of it: classes that, consequently, by the very fact of their political existence, must have constituted in the heart of society what I term by abstraction an intermediate and transitory system. These classes have been, in a temporal sense, legislators, and in a spiritual sense metaphysicians, who formed a close association in their political actions, as feudalism and theocracy, as industry and the physical sciences.

The general fact that I have just noted is of the utmost importance. It is one of the fundamental data that must serve as a basis for the positive theory of politics. It is this theory that it is most important at this time to clarify to the utmost, for the vagueness and obscurity that have enveloped it hitherto are what now causes the greatest confusion in political concepts, and almost every kind of divagation.

It would be quite unphilosophical not to recognize the useful and notable influence exercised by the legislators and the metaphysicians, in modifying the feudal and theocratic system and preventing it from crushing the industrial and scientific system, from the moment of its first development. The abolition of feudal justice, the establishment of a less oppressive and more controlled jurisprudence, are due to the legislators. How often has the action of the parliaments in France not helped to safeguard industry against feudalism! To make the ambition of these bodies a reproach is to lay the blame on the inevitable effects resulting from a useful, reasonable, and necessary cause: it is a way of evading the issue. As for the metaphysicians, it is to them that we owe the reform of the sixteenth century, and the establishment of the principle of freedom of conscience that sapped the roots of theocratic power.

I should exceed the limits of a preface if I went on insisting on observations that every sound intelligence will readily develop, in accordance with the foregoing indications. Speaking for myself, I assert that I have no idea whatever how the old system could have been modified and the new system developed but for the intervention of the legislators and the metaphysicians.

On the other hand, if it is absurd to deny the special and useful share contributed by the legislators and the metaphysicians in the advancement of civilization, it is very hazardous to exaggerate this usefulness, or, rather, to misconceive its true character. By the very fact of its direction, the political influence of the legislators and the metaphysicians was limited to a transitory existence, since it was merely of a modifying and passing character, and in no way an organizing influence. It had fulfilled its entire natural function, from the moment that the old system lost the major part of its power, and the forces of the new system became really preponderant in society, in a temporal and a spiritual sense. Apart from this point that has been completely attained since the middle of last century, the political career of the legislators and the metaphysicians would not have ceased its honorable usefulness, whereas it effectively became totally harmful, having exceeded its natural limitation.

When the French Revolution broke out, there was no question any longer of modifying the feudal and theocratic system, that had already lost almost all its real force. It was a question of organizing the industrial and scientific system, called by the state of civilization to replace it. It was, consequently, the industrialists and the theoreticians who had to occupy the political scene, each in his natural role. Instead, the legislators placed themselves at the head of the Revolution, directed it with the aid of the doctrines of the metaphysicians. It is superfluous to recall what remarkable divagations followed as a result, and what evils issued from these divagations. But it must be carefully observed that, despite this vast experience, the legislators and the metaphysicians still remained uninterruptedly at the head of affairs, and that they alone today direct all political discussion.

This experience, however costly it may have been, and however decisive it may actually be, would remain abortive, on account of its complexity, if we did not point out, by direct analysis, the absolute necessity for withdrawing from the legislators and the metaphysicians the universal political influence that is assigned to them, and that depends only on the presumed opinion of the excellence of their doctrines. But it is very easy to prove that the doctrines of the legislators and the metaphysicians are today, by their nature, altogether unfit to direct political action acceptably, whether in the case of the governing class or the governed. This obstacle is so formidable that is obscures, as it were, the advantage that the individual capacities can offer, however brilliant they may be.

The more enlightened spirits realize quite well today the need for a general reshaping of the social system. This need has become so imminent that it must indubitably be felt. But the capital mistake that is generally made in this respect consists in believing that the new system to be built must have as a foundation the principles of the legislators and the metaphysicians. This mistake persists only because we do not go far enough back in the series of political observations, and because the general facts are not examined with sufficient thoroughness, or, rather, because we do not yet base political reasoning on the general historical facts. But for that, one could not make a mistake to the point of taking a modification of the social system, a modification that has already produced its entire effect and can no longer play any part, for a real change of this system.

The legislators and the metaphysicians are prone to take the form for the substance, and words for things. Hence, the generally accepted idea of the almost infinite multiplicity of political systems. But as a fact, there are, and there can be, two systems only of really distinct social organization: the feudal or military system, and the industrial system: and, in a spiritual respect, a system of beliefs and a system of positive demonstrations. The entire possible duration of civilized mankind is necessarily divided between these two great systems of society. In fact, for a nation as for an individual, there are only two purposes for action: either conquest or work, to which either blind beliefs correspond spiritually, or the scientific demonstrations; that is, changes in form and not in system. Metaphysics alone can make us view things differently by means of the fatal cunning it endows us with in merging together what must be separate, and in separating what must be fused together.

Society has been organized clearly and characteristically, while the feudal or military system has been in full vigor, because it then had a clear-cut and definite purpose, namely, to produce a great war-like activity; a purpose for which all the parts of the body politic were coordinated. It also tends to organization today in a more perfect fashion, and not less clear and characteristic, for the purpose of industrial action, toward which all the social forces will equally be directed cooperatively. But since the decadence of the feudal or military system until the present time, society has not really been organized, because, as the two objectives have been at cross purposes, the political order has had only a mongrel character. Now, what was useful and even necessary as a transitory and preparatory state of things, would evidently become absurd as a permanent system, now that the transition is really finished in its main respects. To such a point nevertheless do the doctrines of the legislators and the metaphysicians lead.

GEORGE SOREL

(1847-1922)

The French syndicalist, is often considered a direct forerunner (and causative factor) of both Fascism and Bolshevism. In fact, at one time or another, his ideas have fallen into step with groups marching in very different directions: Marxists, anarchists, militant trade unionists, Fascists, Bolsheviks and *Action Française* royalists—all attracted to him by what they had in common: the rejection of bourgeois democracy as corrupt, hypocritical and decadent, and aspirations toward a healthier, or at least a more heroic, new order. Sorel turned to social and economic studies only after his fortieth year, following a career as an engineer and a very bourgeois life. From 1893 to 1897, he adopted Marx's ideas; thereafter, he expressed animosity not only toward Marx but also toward democracy, rationalism and intellectualism, in his principal books, *The Decomposition of Marxism* (1908), *Reflections on Violence* (1908, 1950) and *Illusions of Progress* (1911). Inspired by Henri Bergson, whom he respected despite his animosity toward Jews, he heralded the "Myth of the General Strike," and distinguished carefully between the Utopia and the myth (the image of a fictitious, even unrealizable future which expresses the sentiments of the revolutionary masses and incites them to revolutionary action). "Violence" was proclaimed by Sorel as the way to power; by "violence," Sorel protested, he did not mean "Jacobinic" action but "psychic warfare" whose means are sabotage, strike and the boycott of workers who decline to participate in that warfare. Sorel succeeded, for a while, in winning over the French syndicalists; but the militant workers soon turned against him when he negotiated with the royalist Charles Maurras, the leader of the *Action Française*. After World War I, Sorel built his hopes upon Bolshevism, but Lenin rebuked him in his polemics against empiriocriticism. Mussolini frequently proclaimed his indebtedness to him.

Basically, Sorel was not interested in socialism, Communism or in any other politicoeconomic system but in the increase of industrial production to the highest possible degree. His experiences as an engineer had convinced him that capitalists or industrial entrepreneurs would be unable to reach this goal; he therefore entrusted its fulfillment to the employees and workers. His thinking impressed Thorstein Veblen, who expressed similar views on the incompetency of capitalists. Sorel's theories of myth and violence and terror are an integral part of the Soviet system. Fascism and Nazism owe him their concepts of totalitarian propaganda, whose chief characteristic is not always the distortion of truth, but the substitution of an entirely new concept of truth; the belief that the end for which the lies are propounded justifies the means, that the masses can think properly only when the mass mind is "liberated" from facts and is offered simple statements which look like facts. This approach was used by Hitler and can be found in Marx's myth of a class struggle.

---

*Class War and Violence**

EVERYBODY complains that discussions about Socialism are generally exceedingly obscure. This obscurity is due, for the most part, to the fact that contemporary Socialists use a terminology which no longer corresponds to their ideas. The best known among the people who call themselves *revisionists* do not wish to appear to be abandoning certain phrases, which have served for a very long time as a label to characterise Socialist literature. When Bernstein, perceiving the enormous contradiction between the language of social democracy and the true nature of its activity, urged his German comrades to have the courage to appear what they were in

* These excerpts taken from George Sorel, authorized translation by T. E. Hulme, *Reflections on Violence,* London: George Allen & Unwin, Ruskin House, 1925, pp. 52-53; 100-103.

reality, and to revise a doctrine that had become mendacious, there was a universal outburst of indignation at his audacity; and the reformists themselves were not the least eager of the defenders of the ancient formula. I remember hearing well-known French Socialists say that they found it easier to accept the tactics of Millerand than the arguments of Bernstein.

This idolatry of words plays a large part in the history of all ideologies; the preservation of a Marxist vocabulary by people who have become completely estranged from the thought of Marx constitutes a great misfortune for Socialism. The expression "class war," for example, is employed in the most improper manner; and until a precise meaning can be given to this term, we must give up all hope of a reasonable exposition of Socialism.

Prejudices Against Violence

The ideas current among the outside public on the subject of proletarian violence are not founded on observation of contemporary facts, and on a rational interpretation of the present Syndicalist movement; they are derived from a comparison of the present with the past—an infinitely simpler mental process; they are shaped by the memories which the word *revolution* evokes almost automatically. It is supposed that the Syndicalists, merely because they call themselves revolutionaries, wish to reproduce the history of the revolutionaries of '93. The Blanquists, who look upon themselves as the legitimate owners of the Terrorist tradition, consider that for this very reason they are called upon to direct the proletarian movement; they display much more condescension to the Syndicalists than the other Parliamentary Socialists; they are inclined to assert that the workers' organisations will come to understand in the end that they cannot do better than to put themselves under their tuition. It seems to me that Jaurès himself, when writing the *Histoire so-*

cialiste of '93, thought more than once of the teachings which this past, a thousand times dead, might yield to him for the conduct of the present.

Proper attention has not always been given to the great changes which have taken place since 1870 in the way people judge the revolution; yet these changes must be considered if we wish to understand contemporary ideas relative to violence.

For a very long time the Revolution appeared to be essentially a succession of glorious wars, which a people famished for liberty and carried away by the noblest passions had maintained against a coalition of all the powers of oppression and error. Riots and *coups d'état,* the struggles between parties often destitute of any scruple and the banishment of the vanquished, the Parliamentary debates and the adventures of illustrious men, in a word, all the events of its political history were in the eyes of our fathers only very secondary accessories to the wars of liberty.

For about twenty-five years the form of government in France had been at issue; after campaigns before which the memories of Caesar and Alexander paled the charter of 1814 had definitely incorporated in the national tradition, the Parliamentary system, Napoleonic legislation, and the Church established by the Concordat; war had given an irrevocable judgment whose preambles, as Proudhon said, had been dated from Valmy, from Jemmapes, and from fifty other battlefields, and whose conclusions had been received at Saint-Ouen by Louis XVIII. Protected by the prestige of the wars of liberty, the new institutions had become inviolable, and the ideology which was built up to explain them became a faith which seemed for a long time to have for the French the value which the revelation of Jesus has for the Catholics.

From time to time eloquent writers have thought that they could set up a current of reaction against these doctrines, and the Church had hopes that it might get the better of what it called the *error of liberalism.* A long period of admiration for medieval art and of contempt for the period of Voltaire seemed to threaten the new ideology with ruin; but all these attempts to return to the past left no trace except in literary history. There were times when those in power governed in the least liberal manner, but the principles of the modern régime were never seriously threatened.

Parliamentary Socialists cannot understand the ends pursued by the *new school;* they imagine that ultimately all Socialism can be reduced to the pursuit of the means of getting into power. Is it possible that they think the followers of the *new school* wish to make a higher bid for the confidence of simple electors and cheat the Socialists of the seats provided for them? Again, the apologia of violence might have the very unfortunate result of disgusting the workers with electoral politics, and this would tend to destroy the chances of the Socialist candidates by multiplying the abstentions from voting! Do you wish to revive civil war? they ask. To our great statesmen that seems mad.

Civil war has become very difficult since the discovery of the new firearms, and since the cutting of rectilinear streets in the capital towns. The recent troubles in Russia seem to have shown that Governments can count much more than was supposed on the energy of their officers. Nearly all French politicians had prophesied the imminent fall of Czarism at the time of the Manchurian defeats, but the Russian army in the presence of rioting did not manifest the weakness shown by the French army during our revolutions; nearly everywhere repression was rapid, efficacious, and even pitiless. The discussions which took place at the congress of social democrats at Jena show that the Parliamentary Socialists no longer rely upon an armed struggle to obtain possession of the State.

Does this mean that they are utterly opposed to violence? It would not be in their interest for the people to be quite calm; a certain amount of agitation suits them, but this agitation must be contained within well-defined limits and controlled by politicians. When he considers it useful for his own interests, Jaurès makes advances to the Confédération Générale du Travail; sometimes he instructs his peaceable clerks to fill his paper with revolutionary phrases; he is past master in the art of utilising popular anger. A cunningly conducted agitation is extremely useful to Parliamentary Socialists, who boast before the Government and the rich middle class of their ability to moderate revolution; they can thus arrange the success of the financial affairs in which they are interested, obtain minor favors for many influential electors, and get social laws voted in order to appear important in the eyes of the blockheads who imagine that these Socialists are great reformers of the law. In order that all this may come off there must always be a certain amount of movement, and the middle class must always be kept in a state of fear.

It is conceivable that a regular system of diplomacy might be established between the Socialist party and the State each time an economic conflict arose between workers and employers; the *two powers* would settle the particular difference. In Germany the Government enters into negotiations with the Church each time the clericals stand in the way of the administration. Socialists have even been urged to imitate Parnell, who so often found a means of imposing his will on England. This resemblance is all the greater in that Parnell's authority did not rest only on the number of votes at his disposal, but mainly upon the terror which every Englishman felt at the bare announcement of agrarian trouble in Ireland. A few acts of violence controlled by a Parliamentary group were exceedingly useful to the Parnellian policy, just as they are useful to the policy of Jaurès. In both cases a Parliamentary group *sells peace of mind to the Conservatives,* who dare not use the force they command.

This kind of diplomacy is difficult to conduct, and the Irish after the death of Parnell do not seem to have succeeded in carrying it on with the same success as in his time. In France it presents particular difficulty, because in no other country perhaps are the workers more difficult to manage: it is easy enough to arouse popular anger, but it is not easy to stifle it. As long as there are no very rich and strongly centralized trade unions whose leaders are in continuous relationship with political men, so long will it be impossible to say exactly to what lengths violence will go. Jaurès would very much like to see such associations of workers in existence, for his prestige will disappear at once when the general public perceives that he is not in a position to moderate revolution.

Everything becomes a question of valuation, accurate estimation, and opportunism; much skill, tact, and calm audacity are necessary to carry on such a diplomacy, *e.g.*, to make the workers believe that you are carrying the flag of revolution, the middle class that you are arresting the danger which threatens them. . . .

OSWALD SPENGLER

(1880-1936)

Was a German philosopher, whose major work, *The Decline of the West* (1918-1922), was translated into many languages and caused great controversy in the United States (1926-28). It constituted a deterministic morphology of history and predicted a phase of "Caesarism" in the future development of Western civilization. Spengler's ideas became very popular with the Nazis, but he refused to enter into the persecution of the Jews, and managed to exist, being independently wealthy, in Germany, somewhat under a cloud, till the end of his life. With the rise of capitalism, Germany, according to Spengler, had acquired wealth and power by repressing all vital impulses "except those that served directly [Germany's] will-to-power." There are two kinds of people in the world: those who merely live and those who enact history. The first exist before the cultural cycle begins, and are mere vegetables; their life is directionless; they endure on a timeless level of pure being. As for the "actors," they experience "Destiny," and pass from a state of culture, in which life is bound up with a common soil and a deep intuitive sense of the importance of blood and race and caste, to a state of civilization, where their waking consciousness transcends their more instinctive earlier life; they become cosmopolitan in extension, highly urbanized and increasingly indifferent to the vital elements and the reign of the mechanical, the desiccated, men in the earlier period. Rationalism and humanitarianism devitalize their will-to-power; pacifism gives rise to passivism. In the state of civilization, the sap sinks to the roots, the stems and leaves become brittle and the whole structure of the organism becomes incapable of further growth. In Spengler's opinion, Western Europe was about to enter the frigid state of winter; civilization meant the deliberate abdication of the organic and vital elements and the reign of the mechanical, the desiccated, the devitalized. The region was shriveling to a point: the world city, megalopolis. What remained of life, if one could call it life, belonged to the engineer; the businessman, the soldier. Life, in short, was to reassert itself as brutality, the sole energy left centered on destruction. The notion that human history moves in ever-recurring cycles dates back to Plato, and Spengler's book was the most influential contemporary revival of this doctrine. It combined the cyclical theory of historical development, a wholehearted acceptance of the organismic theory of society and social evolution, and the Romanticist idea of a culture-soul which dominates the traits and activities of any people. Each great historic social unity constitutes what Spengler calls a "Culture"; each culture has an all-pervading culture-soul of which any people are a unit and their historic achievement a direct product. All great historic cultures pass through the inevitable stages of the life cycle of any organism: birth, youth, maturity and old age (or—as Spengler sometimes expresses it —spring, summer, autumn and winter). Spengler's ideas of a dominant culture-soul, the overwhelming power of Destiny and his denial of any causality in history are akin to the views of the Romanticist philosophers of history of the late eighteenth and early nineteenth centuries. But his philosophy attained great popularity because of the general pessimism following World War I; and there may be some validity in his contention that the Western era is in its terminal stages.

---

*State and Power**

A PEOPLE is *as* State, a kindred is *as* family, "in form"—that is, as we have seen, the difference between political and cosmic history, public and private life, *res publica* and *res privata.* And both, moreover, are symbols of caste. The woman *is* world-history. By conceiving and giving birth she cares for the perpetuation of the blood. The mother with the child at

* This excerpt taken from Oswald Spengler, *The Decline of the West,* New York: Alfred A. Knopf, Inc., 1932, pp. 362-367.

her breast is the grand emblem of cosmic life. Under this aspect, the life of man and woman is "in form" as marriage. The man, however, *makes* history, which is an unending battle for the preservation of that other life. Maternal care is supplemented and paralleled by paternal. The man with weapon in hand is the other grand emblem of the will-to-duration. A people "in condition" is originally a band warriorhood, a deep and intimately felt community of men fit for arms. State is the affair of man, it is Care for the preservation of the whole (including the spiritual self-preservation called honor and self-respect), the thwarting of attacks, the foreseeing of dangers, and, above all, the positive aggressiveness which is natural and self-evident to every life that has begun to soar.

If all life were *one* uniform being-stream, the words "people," "state," "war," "policy," "constitution," would never have been heard of. But the eternal forceful stream of life, which the creative power of the Culture elevates to the highest standards, is a fact, and historically we have no choice but to accept it as such, with all that flows therefrom. Plant-life is only plant-life in relation to animal life, nobility and priesthood reciprocally condition one another. *A people is only really such in relation to other peoples,* and the substance of this actuality comes out in natural and ineradicable oppositions, in attack and defence, hostility and war. War is the creator of all great things. All that is meaningful in the stream of life has emerged through victory and defeat.

A people shapes history inasmuch as it is "in condition" for the task of doing so. It livingly experiences an inward history—which gets it into this "condition," in which alone it becomes creative—and an outward history, which *consists* in this creation. Peoples as State, then, are the real forces of all human happening. In the world-as-history there is nothing beyond them. They *are* Destiny.

Res publica, the public life, the "sword side" of human being-currents, is in actuality invisible. The alien sees merely the men and not their inner connexion, for indeed this resides very deep in the stream of life, and even there is felt rather than understood. Similarly, we do not in actuality see the family, but only certain persons, whose cohesion in a perfectly definite sense we know and grasp by way of our own inward experience. But for each such mental picture there exists a group of constituent persons who are bound together as a life-unit by a like constitution of outer and inner being. This form in the flow of existence is called *customary ethic (Sitte)* when it arises of itself in the beat and march and is unconscious before it is conscious; and *law (Recht)* when it is *deliberately stated* and put forth for *acceptance.*

Law—irrespective of whether its authority derives from the feelings and impulse (unwritten law, customary law, English "equity") or has been abstracted by reflection, probed, and brought into system as Statute Law *(Gesetz)*—is the *willed* form of Being. The jural facts that it embraces are of the two kinds, though both possess time-symbolism—Care in two modes, prevision and provision—but, from the very difference in the proportions of consciousness that they respectively contain, it follows that throughout real history there must be two laws in opposition—the law of the fathers, of tradition, the inherited, grown, and well-tried law, sacrosanct because immemorially old, derived from the experience of the blood and therefore dependable; and the thought and planned law of reason, nature, and broad humanity, the product of reflection and therefore first cousin to mathematics, a law that may not be very workable, but at any rate "just." It is in these two orders of law that the opposition between land-life and city-life, life-experience and study-experience, ripens till it bursts out in that revolutionary embitterment in which men take a law instead of being given it, and break a law that will not yield.

A law that has been laid down by a community expresses a *duty* for every member, but it is no proof of every member's *power*. On the contrary, it is a question of Destiny, who makes the law and for whom it is made. There are subjects and there are objects in the *making* of laws, although everyone is an object as to the validity thereof—and this holds good without distinction for the inner law of families, guilds, estates, and states. But for the State, which is the highest law-subject existing in historical actuality, there is besides, an external law that it imposes upon aliens by hostilities. Ordinarily, civil law is a case of the first kind, a peace treaty of the second. But in all cases, the law of the stronger is the law of the weaker also. To "have the right" is an expression of power. This is a historical fact that every moment confirms, but is not acknowledged in the realm of truth, which is not of this world. In their conceptions of right, therefore, as in other things, being and waking—being, Destiny and Causality, stand implacably opposed. To the priestly and idealistic moral of good and evil belongs the *moral distinction of right and wrong,* but in the race-moral of good and bad the distinction is between those who give and those who receive the law. An abstract idea of justice pervades the minds and writings of all those whose spirit is noble and strong and whose blood is weak, pervades all religions and all philosophies—but the fact-world of history knows only the *success* which turns the law of the stronger into the law of all. Over ideals it marches without pity, and if ever a man or a people renounces its power of the moment in order to remain righteous—then, certainly, his or its theoretical fame is assured in the second world of thought and truth, but assured also is the coming of a moment in which it will succumb to another life-power that has better understood realities.

So long as a historical power is so superior to its constituent units—as the State or the estate so often is to families and calling-classes, or the head of the family to its children—a just law *between* the weaker is possible as a gift from the all-powerful hand of the disinterested. But Estates seldom, and states almost never, feel a power of this magnitude over themselves, and consequently between them the law of the stronger acts with immediate force—as is seen in a victor's treaty, unilateral in terms and still more so in interpretation and observance. That is the difference between the *internal* and the *external* rights of historical life-units. In the first the will of an arbiter to be impartial and just can be effective—although we are apt to deceive ourselves badly as to the degree of effective impartiality even in the best codes of history, even in those which call themselves "civil" or "būrgerlich," for the very adjective indicates that *an estate* has possessed the superior force to impose them on everyone. Internal laws are the result of strict logical-causal thought centering upon truths, but for that very reason their validity is ever dependent upon the material power of their author, be this Estate or State. A revolution that annihilates this power annihilates all these laws—they remain true, but they are no longer actual. External laws on the other hand, such as all peace treaties, are essentially never true and always actual—indeed appallingly so. They set up no pretension whatever of being just—it is quite enough that they are valid. Out of them speaks *Life,* which possesses no causal and moral logic, but is organically all the more consistent and consequent for the lack of it. Its will is to possess validity *itself;* it feels with an inward certainty what is required to that end and, seeing that, knows what is law for itself and *has to be made* law for others. This logic is seen in every family, and particularly in old true-born families as soon as authority is shattered and someone other than the head tries to determine "what is." It appears in every state, as soon as one party therein dominates the position. Every feudal age is filled with the contests between lords and vassals over the "right to rights." In the Classical world this conflict ended almost everywhere with the unconditional victory of the First Estate, which deprived the kingship of its legislative powers and made it an object of its own law-making—as the origin and significance of the Archons in Athens and the Ephors in Sparta prove beyond doubt. But the same happened in the Western field too—for a moment in France (institution of the States-General, 1302), and for good in England, where in 1215 the Norman baronage and the higher clergy imposed Magna Charta and thus sowed the seed that was to ripen into the effective sovereignty of Parliament. Hence it was that the old Norman law of the Estates here remained permanently valid. In Germany, on the contrary, the weak Imperial power, hard-pressed by the claims of the great feudatories, called in the "Roman" law of Justinian (that is, the law of the unlimited central power) to aid it against the early German land-laws.[1]

The Draconian Constitution, the πατρίος πολιτεία of the Oligarchs, was dictated by the nobility like the strictly patrician law of the Twelve Tables in Rome; but by then the Late period of the Culture was well under way and the power of the city and of money were already fully developed, so that laws directed against these powers necessarily gave way very promptly to laws of the Third Estate (Solon, the Tribunate). Yet these, too, were estate-founded laws not less than their predecessors. The struggle between the two primary estates for the right of law-making has filled the entire history of the West, from the early Gothic conflict of secular and canon law for supremacy, to the controversy (not ended even to-day) concerning civil marriage.[2] And, for that matter, what are the constitutional conflicts that have occurred since the end of the eighteenth century but the acquisition by the *Tiers État* (which, according to Sieyès's famous remark in 1789, "was nothing, but could be all") of the right to legislate bindingly upon all, producing a law that is just as much burghers' law as ever Gothic was nobles' law. The nakedest

[1] The corresponding attempt of the absolutist Stuarts to introduce Roman Law into England was defeated chiefly by the Puritan jurist Coke (d. 1634) —yet another proof that the spirit of laws is always a party-spirit.

[2] Above all in connection with divorce, in which the civil and the ecclesiastical views *both* hold good, literally side by side.

form in which right appears as the expression of might is in interstate treaty-making, in peace treaties, and in that Law of Nations of which already Mirabeau could say it is the law of the strong of which the observance is imposed upon the weak. A large part of the decisions of world-history is contained in laws of this kind. They are the constitution under which militant history progresses, so long as it does not revert to the original form of the armed conflict—original, and also basic; for every treaty that is valid and is meant to have real effects is an intellectual continuation thereof. If policy is war by other means, the "right to give the law" is the spoil of the unsuccessful party.

II

It is clear, then, that on the heights of history two such life-forms, Estate and State, contend for supremacy, both being-streams of great inward form and symbolic force, each resolved to make its own destiny the Destiny of the whole. *That*— if we try to understand the matter and unreservedly put aside our everyday conceptions of people, economy, society, and politics—*is the meaning of the opposition between the social and the political conduct of events.* Social and political ideas do not begin to be differentiated till a great Culture has dawned, or even till feudalism is declining and the lord-vassal relation represents the social, and the king-people relation the political, side. But the social powers of the latter (money and mind)—and the vocational groups of the craftsmen and officials and workers, too, as they were rising to their power in the growing cities—sought, each for itself, to subordinate the State-ideal to its own Estate-ideal, or more usually to its estate interests. And so there arose, at all planes from that of the national unit to that of the individual consciousness, a fight over the respective limits and claims each—the result of which, in extreme cases, is that the one element succeeds so completely as to make the other its tool.[3]

In all cases, however, it is the State that determines the *external* position, and therefore the historical relations between peoples are always of *a political and of a social nature.* In domestic politics, on the contrary, the situation is so dominated by class-oppositions that at first sight social and political tactics appear inseparable, and indeed, in the thought of people who (as, for example, bourgeoisie) equate their own class-ideal with historical actuality—and frequently cannot think in external politics at all—identical. In the external battle the State seeks alliances with other States, in the internal it is always in alliance with one or another Estate—the sixth-century Tyrannis, for instance, rested upon the combination of the State-idea with the interests of a Third Estate *vis-à-vis* the ancient noble oligarchy, and the French Revolution became inevitable from the moment that the *Tiers*—that is, intellect and money—left its friend the Crown in the lurch and joined the two other estates (from the Assembly of Notables, 1787). We are thoroughly right therefore in feeling a

[3] Thus come about the much satirized forms of the "patrol-" or "barrack-state," as opponents call it with an unintelligent scorn. Similar points of view appear also in Chinese and Greek constitutional theories [O. Franke, *Studien zur Geschichte des komfuzianischen Dogmas* (1920), pp. 211, et seq.; Pohlmann, *Geschichte der sozialen Frage und der Sozialismous in der antiken Welt* (1912)]. On the other hand, the political tastes of, for example, Wilhelm von Humboldt, who as a Classicist opposed the individual to the States, belong, not to political history at all, but to literature. For what he looked at was, not the capacity of the State to thrive in the real State-world around it, but its private existence within itself, without regard to the fact that such an ideal could not endure for an instant in the face of a neglected outer situation. It is a basic error of the ideologues that, in concentrating on the private life and referring to it the whole inner structure of the State, they entirely ignore the latter's position in point of outward power, though this in fact completely conditions its form for the inward development. The difference between the French and the German Revolution, for example, consists in the fact that the one commanded the external situation and *therewith* internal also, while the other commanded neither and was foredoomed to farce.

distinction between State-history and class-history,[4] between political (horizontal) and social (vertical) history, war and revolution.[5] But it is a grave error of modern doctrinaires to regard the spirit of domestic history as that of history in general. *World-history is, and always will be, State-history.* An inner constitution of a nation aims always at being *"in condition"* for the outer fight (diplomatic, military, or economic) and anyone who treats a nation's constitution as an aim and ideal in itself is merely ruining the nation's value. But, from the other point of view, it falls to the inner-political pulse-beat of a ruling stratum (whether belonging to the First or to the Fourth state) so to manage the internal class-oppositions that the focus and ideas of the nation are not tied up in party conflict, nor treason to the country thought of as an ace of trumps.

And here it becomes manifest that *the State and the first Estate* are cognate down to the roots—akin, not merely by reason of their symbolism of Time and care, their common relation to race and the facts of genealogical succession, to the family and to the primary impulses of all peasantry (on which in the last analysis every State and every nobility is supported)—not merely in their relation to the soil, the clan-domain (be this heritable estate or fatherland), which even in nations of the Magian style is lowered in significance only because there the dignity of orthodoxy so completely surpasses everything else. . . .

---

4 Which is most definitely *not* identical with economic history in the sense of the materialist historian.

5 It is to be noted that the author uses the terms "horizontal" and "vertical" here in the realistic sense to that in which they commonly figure in present-day *political* literature, although in other works the usage is the same as that of the text.—*Tr.*

BENEDICT DE SPINOZA
(1632-1677)

Ranks very high among the philosophers who have contributed to the liberation of the human mind. Born in Amsterdam of Jewish parents who had fled from Portugal to the Netherlands in order to escape persecution by the Catholic Church, he was schooled under rabbinical tutors who familiarized him with the Talmud and the philosophic ideas of the leading scholars of Jewry. As a pupil, also, of the brilliant but erratic Franz van den Ende, a physician, Spinoza learned Latin as well as got an introduction to the natural sciences from a definitely materialistic point of view. His knowledge of Latin unlocked for him the whole field of philosophy and science; he devoured the writings of Descartes (French mathematician and philosopher, founder of "Cartesianism" and father of modern thought through his belief in the possibility of mathematical exactitude in metaphysical reasoning). His desertion of rabbinical theology eventually led to his expulsion from the society of his people; when his means of livelihood was thus cut off (since official and professional careers were closed to Jews), he supported himself comfortably by lens-grinding, while gradually becoming the leader of a school of thought. In his *Tractatus Theologica-Politicus* (1670), *Tractatus Politicus* (1677) and *Ethics* (1677) he stated that knowledge of ultimate reality involves the norm of human action and implies the measure of personal perfection; unlike Hobbes, he believed that it was possible to combine realism with morality. Like Locke, he took a utilitarian view of society and put a new sanction behind it. Religious toleration, liberty of thought, responsibility of government to the governed he gave a philosophic basis, although his was a mystical and original interpretation which looked beyond his own age and had little contemporary influence; but it foreshadowed a great tradition. He assumed that the divine order is not a geometrical pattern "laid up in Heaven," and admits that the order of nature does not reflect human standards; like Hobbes, he justified sovereign power as the price of order. Men obey not because they instinctively do their duty by the light of natural law and right reason, but because they must unite to get themselves out of the state of nature in which no civilized values can live. But unlike Hobbes, Spinoza believed that it is possible to preserve intellectual and political liberty within the framework of a utilitarian state and he did not despair of humanity. Mutual aid is as natural to men as pride and fear; the aim of society is the extension of human awareness and power. He complained that philosophers "conceive men, not as they are, but as they would wish them to be." Thus "they have written satire instead of ethics," and he states, with excellent brevity, that he intends "not to laugh at men or weep over them or hate them, but to understand them." Man can only realize his higher qualities when cooperating for some higher good; the community alone is the medium through which this can be done (a reflection of Aristotle). The best means of attaining concord in society are not through the baser appetites of interest and greed; it is rather the higher faculties which make possible and secure the existence of ordered government. Thus government is an expression of the impulse to mutual aid instinctive to mankind. Spinoza defines the power of the state as "the power of the common people when they are led and determined by a single mind," and it unites men, not through the lowest common factors of fear and pride, but through the sociable instinct for the promoting of the good life of intellectual and spiritual awareness, which can be achieved only where there are liberty and security. The aim of the state is the fullest realization of its own being, and the state's authority is valid only if it promotes the good of its citizens. "The true aim of government is liberty." This thesis is the antithesis of the fear of life expressed in Calvin or St. Augustine; Spinoza accepts evil as part of the incomprehensible nature of things, but was not cowed into a denial of life, into crying for salvation.

Spinoza's ideas became a landmark in the assumption of scientific values, in the acceptance and glorification of life. They embittered Catholics, Protestants, Jews and Freethinkers alike; even David Hume branded him as "*infame.*" Moses Mendelssohn, the affable advocate of tolerance, was horrified when he heard that his friend Lessing had adopted Spinoza's doctrine. A great change in the attitude to Spinoza was inaugurated by Herder and Goethe, who became Spinozists and revered him as a saint; so did Heinrich Heine. Post-Kantian philosophers and Romantic poets in Germany were deeply influenced by Spinoza's conception of nature. Locke was probably influenced by him, and many of his ideas were developed by Rousseau, thus becoming a part of the later European revolutionary upheavals.

---

*On the Right of Supreme Authorities**

UNDER every dominion the state is said to be Civil; but the entire body subject to a dominion is called a Commonwealth (*Civitas*) and the general business of the dominion, subject to the direction of him that holds it, has the name of Affairs of State *(Res publica)*. Next we call men Citizens, as far as they enjoy by the civil law all the advantages of the commonwealth, and Subjects, as far as they are bound to obey its ordinances or laws. Lastly, we have already said that, of the civil state, there are three kinds—democracy, aristocracy, and monarchy. Now, before I begin to treat of each kind separately, I will first deduce all the properties of the civil state (*status civilis*) in general. And of these, first of all comes to be considered the supreme right of the commonwealth, or the right of the supreme authorities.

2. It is clear that the right of the supreme authorities is nothing else than natural right itself, limited, indeed, by the power, not of every individual, but of the multitude, which is guided, as it were, by one mind—that is, on each individual in the state of nature, so the body and mind of a dominion have as much right as they have power. And thus each citizen

---

* This excerpt taken from *The Chief Works of Benedict de Spinoza,* the *Tractatus Politicus,* translated by R. H. Elwes, London, 1883.

or subject has the less right, the more the commonwealth exceeds him in power, and each citizen consequently does and has nothing, but what he may by the general decree of the commonwealth defend.

3. If the commonwealth grant to any man the right, and therewith the authority (for else it is but a gift of words) to live after his own mind, by that very act it abandons its own right, and transfers the same to him, to whom it has given such authority. But if it has given this authority to two or more, I mean authority to live each after his own mind, by that very act it has divided the dominion, and if, lastly, it has given this same authority to every citizen, it has thereby destroyed itself, and there remains no more a commonwealth, but everything returns to the state of nature; all of which is very manifest from what goes before. And thus it follows, that it can by no means be conceived, that every citizen should by the ordinance of the commonwealth live after his mind, and accordingly this natural right of being one's own judge ceases in the civil state. I say expressly "by the ordinance of the commonwealth," for, if we weigh the matter aright, the natural right of every man does not cease in the civil state. For man, alike in the natural and in the civil state, acts according to the laws of his own nature, and consults his own interest. Man, I say, in each state is led by fear or hope to do or leave undone this or that; but the main difference between the two states is this, that in the civil state all fear the same things, and all have the same ground of security, and manner of life; and this certainly does not do away with the individual's faculty of judgment. For he that is minded to obey all the commonwealth's orders, whether through fear of its power or through love of quiet, certainly consults after his own heart his own safety and interest.

4. Moreover, we cannot even conceive, that every citizen should be allowed to interpret the commonwealth's decrees or laws. For were every citizen allowed this, he would thereby be his own judge, because each would easily be able to give a

colour of right to his own deeds, which by the last section is absurd.

5. We see then, that every citizen depends not on himself, but on the commonwealth, all whose commands he is bound to execute, and has no right to decide, what is equitable or iniquitous, just or unjust. But on the contrary, as the body of the dominion should, so to speak, be guided by one mind, and consequently the will of the commonwealth must be taken to be the will of all; what the state decides to be just and good must be held to be so decided by every individual. And so, however iniquitous the subject may think the commonwealth's decisions, he is none the less bound to execute them.

6. But (it may be objected) is it not to the contrary to the dictate of reason to subject one's self wholly to the judgment of another, and consequently, is not the civil state repugnant to reason? Whence it would follow, that the civil state is irrational, and could only be created by men destitute of reason, not at all by such as are led by it. But since reason teaches nothing contrary to nature, sound reason cannot therefore dictate, that every one should remain independent, so long as men are liable to passions, that is, reason pronounces against such independence. Besides, reason altogether teaches to seek peace, and peace cannot be maintained, unless the commonwealth's general laws be kept unbroken. And so, the more a man is guided by reason, that is, the more he is free, the more constantly he will keep the laws of the commonwealth, and execute the commands of the supreme authority, whose subject he is. Furthermore, the civil state is naturally ordained to remove general fear, and prevent general sufferings, and therefore pursues above everything the very end, after which everyone, who is led by reason, strives, but in the natural state strives vainly. Wherefore, if a man who is led by reason, has sometimes to do by the commonwealth's order what he knows to be repugnant to reason, that harm is far compensated by the good, which he derives

from the existence of a civil state. For it is reason's own law, to choose the less of two evils; and accordingly we may conclude, that no one is acting against the dictates of his own reason, so far as he does what by the law of the commonwealth is to be done. And this anyone will more easily grant us, after we have explained, how far the power and consequently the right of the commonwealth extends.

7. For, first of all, it must be considered, that, as in the state of nature the man who is led by reason is most powerful and most independent, so too that commonwealth will be most powerful and most independent, which is founded and guided by reason. For the right of the commonwealth is determined by the power of the multitude, which is led, as it were, by one mind. But this unity of mind can in no wise be conceived, unless the commonwealth pursues chiefly the very end, which sound reason teaches is to the interest of all men.

JOSEPH VISSARIONOVITCH STALIN

(1879-1953)

Soviet Russia's dictator after Lenin's death, can be described within two frameworks: One was the Stalin described by the man himself and his sycophants and henchmen, including Khrushchev (until his ascendancy to power and attack on "the cult of personality") — "a beloved leader and man of genius, wise, kind, infallible and all-knowing." The other was the Stalin known to the non-Communist world and to the Communist world after 1956 (Khrushchev's unpublished speech of February 25, 1956) and especially in 1961, when the 22nd Communist Party Congress, following Khrushchev's speech, voted, on October 30, to oust Stalin's body from the huge mausoleum that stands on Red Square beneath the towers of the Kremlin, because he had been a brutal and ruthless dictator who ruled the largest land on earth by terror and mass suppression. This physically unprepossessing, under-five-foot-six, and bulky (190 pounds) man, with a harsh face, heavy brown eyes, straggling mustache, ominous chin and withered left arm, was one of the most cunning men of the age, the most modern of Machiavellians. He was born Joseph Vissarionovitch Dzugashvili in the village of Gori (in Georgia, an Asiatic state). His father was a drunken cobbler who used to beat him, his mother a devout woman who wanted her son, nicknamed "Soso," to be a priest. In 1893, he enrolled in a religious seminary, the Tiflis Theological School, but was expelled as the head of a secret Marxist cell there; he was given the paid job of an agitator by the illegal Social Democratic Workers' party in 1898 and helped the cause by robbing banks. When the Social Democrats split into the Mensheviks and the Bolsheviks under Lenin's urgings, he went with Lenin, who made him one of his "trusted lieutenants" (although he came to mistrust him before his death). Imprisoned six times, he escaped five times and wrote pamphlets under the name Stalin—"Man of Steel." The sixth time he did not escape, and spent four years in far-off Turkistan, keeping himself in good shape there. When the Bolsheviks seized power in October, 1917, he became People's Commissar of Nationalities; in 1922, he was made Secretary of the Central Committee of the Communist party. His rise to power had actually begun in March, 1917, when he was one of the first Bolsheviks to reach revolutionary Petrograd. As a member of the party's Central Committee, he outranked all other Bolsheviks and set the course for party activities by laying down as party goals the achievement of a democratic republic, land for the peasants, and the protection of labor by the state. His views were near those expounded by the minority faction of the Mensheviks, and a few weeks later, Lenin condemned them as mere "rubbish," and reversed Stalin's policy in favor of a radical policy aimed at the overthrow of the provisional government. Stalin immediately changed his ideas and became a vociferous Leninist. Upon Lenin's death, Stalin suppressed Lenin's will: "Comrade Stalin, having become general secretary of the party, has concentrated tremendous power in his hands, and I am not sure he always knows how to use that power with sufficient caution. . . . Stalin is rude. . . . I propose that the comrades find a way of removing Stalin." But Stalin eliminated, step by step, his rivals (especially Trotsky) and eventually became the greatest despot in history. Probably the two greatest changes which occurred in the U.S.S.R. after Stalin had become her undisputed ruler were industrialization and collectivization; both were the products of other minds, but it was Stalin who implemented them. He had close to ten million small landowners cold-bloodedly killed in the 1920's for objecting to the collectivization of farmlands; he had untold millions (about ten) sent to barbaric prison camps in Siberia for the slightest criticism of his regime, instituted controls of press, speech, science and art and tightened his hold by an omnipresent spy system. In 1937 he had thousands of officers and hundreds of thousands of their friends shot. Officially, he was Premier of the Russian government, and Generalissimo of the Soviet Armies during World War II, but actually he was the sole dictator, as General Secretary of the Communist party and through his power over the Politburo. In 1939, he signed a pact with his archenemy, Hitler, and when Hitler attacked his country a year later, he was saved with Western help. He showed superb skill in negotiating with Churchill and Roosevelt at Yalta, and with President Truman at Potsdam.

Stalin's reputation as a Marxist theoretician had been poor until the late 1920's, when events were rewritten to suit this autocrat's wishes. His essay, *Marxism and the Nationalities,* suggested and checked by Lenin, increased his prestige, however. His theorizing is exaggerated, his hair-splitting goes drearily on, and his massing of illogicalities is astounding. Later Stalin became famous for his doctrine of "Socialism in One Country" and his views on revolution. In *Problems of Leninism,* a series of lectures delivered at the Sverdlov University, Moscow in April, 1924, (and in *Problems of Leninism*), Stalin concluded that it was possible to create socialism in one country even if the world remained capitalist. This was a departure from Lenin's ideas; the state could not wither away, because of "capitalist encirclement," and he linked internal troubles with capitalist encirclement. Thus Stalin corrected not only Marx and Engels but also Lenin, stating that Lenin had intended to enunciate the new doctrine in a second volume of his *State and Revolution.* In the present imperialist stage of capitalism "wars cannot be averted," and Soviet Russia must be the "base for the overthrow of imperialism in all countries," and he approvingly quotes Lenin that "it is inconceivable that the Soviet Republic should continue to exist for a long period side by side with imperialist states. Ultimately one or the other must conquer." After 1931, Stalin supported the rise of Russian nationalism (clearly opposing Marxian views), and during the war made the appeal, "Your motherland needs you," and resuscitated old Russian heroes (Dimitri Donskoi, Peter the Great, Suvarov). In 1950 he proclaimed the doctrine of the superiority of the Great Russians to all other nationalities. All in all, Stalin was but a pale imitator of Lenin's theories; he developed Lenin's mixed heritage into a one-man dictatorship, altered the Marxist concept of the state to conform to this circumstance and reshaped the whole pattern of Soviet social and cultural life, including its operative standards of value. While Marx conceived the state as the servant of a ruling class, Stalin conceived of himself and the state he ran as the makers of "historically objective" conditions (thus reverting to Hegel), and featured the U.S.S.R. as a base for future world revolution, encircled by a capitalistic world. This, in turn, justified his domestic policy of postponing improvements in welfare, his secret police, and Russia's isolation from the Western world. He also stressed the elite character of the party: "The party must be, first of all, the vanguard of the working class." "The party has a monopoly of leadership; it guides and directs the whole machinery of state; it does not test its policies in elections; it mobilizes and enforces consent." This was the highest form of democracy.

---

*Rule by the Party**

THERE is a necessity for a new party, a militant party, a revolutionary party, one bold enough to lead the proletarians in the struggle for power, sufficiently experienced to find its bearings amidst the complex conditions of a revolutionary situation, and sufficiently flexible to steer clear of all submerged rocks in the path to its goal.

Without such a party it is useless even to think of overthrowing imperialism and achieving the dictatorship of the proletariat.

This new party is the party of Leninism.

What are the specific features of this new party?

The Party as the Vanguard of the Working Class. The Party must be, first of all, the *vanguard* of the working class. The Party must absorb all the best elements of the working class, their experience, their revolutionary spirit, their selfless devotion to the cause of the proletariat. But in order that it may really be the vanguard, the Party must be armed with revolutionary theory, with a knowledge of the laws of revolution. Without this it will be incapable of directing the

* Excerpt from Joseph Stalin, *Problems of Leninism,* Moscow: Foreign Languages Publishing House, 1953, pp. 97-99, 100, 102-108.

struggle of the proletariat, of leading the proletariat. The Party cannot be a real party if it limits itself to registering what the masses of the working class feel and think, if it drags at the tail of the spontaneous movement, if it is unable to overcome the inertness and the political indifference of the spontaneous movement, if it is unable to rise above the momentary interests of the proletariat, if it is unable to elevate the masses to the understanding of the class interests of the proletariat. The Party must stand at the head of the working class; it must see farther than the working class; it must lead the proletariat, and not follow in the tail of the spontaneous movement. . . . Only a party which realizes that it is the vanguard of the proletariat and is able to elevate the masses to the understanding of the class interests of the proletariat—only such a party can divert the working class from the path of trade unionism and convert it into an independent political force.

The Party is the political leader of the working class.

I have already spoken of the difficulties of the struggle of the working class, of the complicated conditions of the struggle, of strategy and tactics, of reserves and maneuvering, of attack and retreat. These conditions are no less complicated, if not more so, than the conditions of war. Who can see clearly in these conditions, who can give correct guidance to the proletarian millions? No army at war can dispense with an experienced General Staff if it does not want to be doomed to certain defeat. Is it not clear that the proletariat can still less dispense with such a General Staff if it does not want to give itself up to be devoured by its mortal enemies? But where is this General Staff? Only the revolutionary party of the proletariat can serve as this General Staff. The working class without a revolutionary party is an army without a General Staff.

The Party is the General Staff of the proletariat.

But the Party cannot be only a *vanguard* detachment. It must at the same time be a detachment of the *class,* part of the class, closely bound up with it by all the fibres of its being. The distinction between the vanguard and the main body of the working class, between Party members and non-Party people, cannot disappear until classes disappear; it will exist as long as the ranks of the proletariat continue to be replenished with newcomers from other classes, as long as the working class as a whole is not in a position to rise to the level of the vanguard. But the Party would cease to be a party if this distinction were widened into a gap, if it shut itself up in its own shell and became divorced from the non-Party masses. The Party cannot lead the class if it is not connected with the non-Party masses, if there is no bond between the Party and the non-Party masses, if these masses do not accept its leadership, if the Party enjoys no moral and political credit among the masses. . . .

The Party as the Organized Detachment of the Working class. The Party is not only the *vanguard* detachment of the working class. If it desires really to direct the struggle of the class it must at the same time be the *organized* detachment of its class. The Party's tasks under the conditions of capitalism are immense and extremely varied. The Party must direct the struggle of the proletariat under the exceptionally difficult conditions of internal and external development; it must lead the proletariat in the offensive when the situation calls for an offensive; it must lead the proletariat in retreat when the situation calls for retreat in order to ward off the blows of a powerful enemy; it must imbue the millions of unorganized non-Party workers with the spirit of discipline and system in the struggle, with the spirit of organization and endurance. But the Party can fulfill these tasks only if it is itself the embodiment of discipline and organization, if it is itself the *organized* detachment of the proletariat. Without these conditions there can be no talk of the Party really leading the proletarian millions. . . .

The principle of the minority submitting to the majority,

the principle of directing Party work from a centre, not infrequently gives rise to attacks on the part of wavering elements, to accusations of "bureaucracy," "formalism," etc. It need hardly be proved that systematic work by the Party, as one whole, and the directing of the struggle of the working class would have been impossible if these principles had not been adhered to. Leninism in the organizational question means unswerving application of these principles. Lenin terms the fight against these principles "Russian nihilism" and "aristocratic anarchism," deserving only of being ridiculed and swept aside. . . .

The Party as the Highest Form of Class Organization of the Proletariat. The Party is the organized detachment of the working class. But the Party is not the only organization of the working class. The proletariat has also a number of other organizations, without which it cannot properly wage the struggle against capital: trade unions, cooperative societies, factory organizations, parliamentary groups, non-Party women's associations, the press, cultural and educational organizations, youth leagues, revolutionary fighting organizations (in times of open revolutionary action), Soviets of deputies as the form of state organization (if the proletariat is in power), etc. The overwhelming majority of these organizations are non-Party, and only some of them adhere directly to the Party, or represent its offshoots. All these organizations, under certain conditions, are absolutely necessary for the working class, for without them it would be impossible to consolidate the class positions of the proletariat in the diverse spheres of struggle; for without them it would be impossible to steel the proletariat as the force whose mission it is to replace the bourgeois order by the socialist order. But how can single leadership be exercised with such an abundance of organizations? What guarantee is there that this multiplicity of organizations will not lead to divergency in leadership? It might be argued that each of these organizations carries on its work in its own special field, and that therefore these organizations cannot hinder one another. This, of course, is true. But it is also true that all these organizations should work in one direction for they serve *one* class, the class of the proletarians. The question then arises: who is to determine the line, the general direction, along which the work of all these organizations is to be conducted? Where is that central organization which is not only able, because it has the necessary experience, to work out such a general line, but, in addition, is in a position, because it has sufficient prestige, to induce all these organizations to carry out this line, so as to attain unity of leadership and to preclude the possibility of working at cross purposes?

This organization is the Party of the proletariat.

The Party possesses all the necessary qualifications for this because, in the first place, it is the rallying centre of the finest elements in the working class, who have direct connections with the non-Party organizations of the proletariat and very frequently lead them; because, secondly, the Party, as the rallying centre of the finest members of the working class, is the best school for training leaders of the working class, capable of directing every form of organization of their class; because, thirdly, the Party, as the best school for training leaders of the working class, is, by reason of its experience and prestige, the only organization capable of centralizing the leadership of the struggle of the proletariat, thus transforming each and every non-Party organization of the working class into an auxiliary body and transmission belt linking the Party with the class.

The Party is the highest form of class organization of the proletariat.

This does not mean, of course, that non-Party organizations, trade unions, cooperative societies, etc., should be officially subordinated to the Party leadership. It only means that the members of the Party who belong to these organizations and are doubtlessly influential in them should do all they can to persuade these non-Party organizations to draw nearer to the Party of the proletariat in their work and to accept voluntarily its political guidance.

That is why Lenin says that the Party is "the *highest* form of proletarian class organization," whose political leadership must extend to every other form of organization of the proletariat. (See Vol. XXV, p. 194)

That is why the opportunist theory of the "independence" and "neutrality" of the non-Party organizations, which breeds *independent* members of parliament and journalists *isolated* from the Party, narrow-minded trade unionists and cooperative-society officials *grown smug and philistine,* is wholly incompatible with the theory and practise of Leninism.

The Party as the Instrument of the Dictatorship of the Proletariat. The Party is the highest form of organization of the proletariat. The Party is the principal guiding force within the class of the proletarians and among the organizations of that class. But it does not by any means follow from this that the Party can be regarded as an end in itself, as a self-sufficient force. The Party is not only the highest form of class association of the proletarians; it is at the same time an *instrument* in the hands of the proletariat *for* achieving the dictatorship when that has not yet been achieved and *for* consolidating and expanding the dictatorship when it has already been achieved. The Party could not have risen so high in importance and could not have overshadowed all other forms of organization of the proletariat, if the latter had not been confronted with the problem of power, if the conditions of imperialism, the inevitability of wars, and the existence of a crisis had not demanded the concentration of all the forces of the proletariat at one point, the gathering of all the threads of the revolutionary movement in one spot in order to overthrow the bourgeoisie and to achieve the dictatorship of the proletariat. The proletariat needs the Party first of all as its General Staff, which it must have for the successful seizure of power. It need hardly be proved that without a Party capable of rallying around itself the mass organizations of the proletariat, and of centralizing the leadership of the entire movement during the progress of the struggle, the proletariat in Russia could never have established its revolutionary dictatorship.

But the proletariat needs the Party not only to achieve the dictatorship; it needs it still more to maintain the dictatorship, to consolidate and expand it in order to achieve the complete victory of socialism.

> "Certainly, almost everyone now realizes," says Lenin, "that the Bolsheviks could not have maintained themselves in power for two-and-a-half months, let alone two-and-a-half years, unless the strictest, truly iron discipline had prevailed in our Party, and unless the latter had been rendered the fullest and unreserved support of the whole mass of the working class, that is, of all its thinking, honest, self-sacrificing and influential elements who are capable of leading or of carrying with them the backward strata." (See Vol. XXV, p 173.)

Now, what does to "maintain" and "expand" the dictatorship mean? It means imbuing the millions of proletarians with the spirit of discipline and organization; it means creating among the proletarian masses a cementing force and a bulwark against the corrosive influences of the petty-bourgeois elements and petty-bourgeois habits; it means enhancing the organizing work of the proletarians in re-educating and remoulding the petty-bourgeois strata; it means helping the masses of the proletarians to educate themselves as a force capable of abolishing classes and of preparing the conditions for the organization of socialist production. But it is impossible to accomplish all this without a party which is strong by reason of its solidarity and discipline.

> "The dictatorship of the proletariat," says Lenin, "is a persistent struggle—bloody and bloodless, violent and peaceful, military and economic, educational and admin-

istrative—against the forces and traditions of the old society. The force of habit of millions and tens of millions is a most terrible force. Without an iron party tempered in the struggle, without a party enjoying the confidence of all that is honest in the given class, without a party capable of watching and influencing the mood of the masses, it is impossible to conduct such a struggle successfully."

The proletariat needs the Party *for* the purpose of achieving and maintaining the dictatorship. The Party is an instrument of the dictatorship of the proletariat.

But from this it follows that when classes disappear and the dictatorship of the proletariat withers away, the Party will also wither away.

The Party as the Embodiment of Unity of Will, Incompatible with the Existence of Factions. The achievement and maintenance of the dictatorship of the proletariat is impossible without a party which is strong by reason of its solidarity and iron discipline. But iron discipline in the Party is inconceivable without unity of will, without complete and absolute unity of action on the part of all members of the Party. This does not mean, of course, that the possibility of contests of opinion within the Party is thereby precluded. On the contrary, iron discipline does not preclude but presupposes criticism and contest of opinion within the Party. Least of all does it mean that discipline must be "blind." On the contrary, iron discipline does not preclude but presupposes conscious and voluntary submission, for only conscious discipline can be truly iron discipline. But after a contest of opinion has been closed, after criticism has been exhausted and a decision has been arrived at, unity of will and unity of action of all Party members are the necessary conditions without which neither Party unity nor iron discipline in the Party is conceivable.

"In the present epoch of acute civil war," says Lenin, "a Communist Party will be able to perform its duty if it

> is organized in the most centralized manner, only if iron discipline bordering on military discipline prevails in it, and if its party center is a powerful and authoritative organ, of the Party."

This is the position in regard to discipline in the Party in the period of struggle preceding the achievement of the dictatorship.

The same, but to an even greater degree, must be said about discipline in the Party after the dictatorship has been achieved.

> "Whoever," says Lenin, "weakens ever so little the iron discipline of the party of the proletariat (especially during the time of its dictatorship), actually aids the bourgeoisie against the proletariat."

But from this it follows that the existence of factions is incompatible either with the Party's unity or with its iron discipline. It need hardly be proved that the existence of factions leads to the existence of a number of centers, and the existence of a number of centers connotes the absence of one common center in the Party, the breaking up of the unity of will, the weakening and disintegration of discipline, the weakening and disintegration of the dictatorship. Of course, the parties of the Second International, which are fighting against the dictatorship of the proletariat and have no desire to lead the proletarians to power, can afford such liberalism as freedom of factions, for they have no need at all for iron discipline. But the parties of the Communist International, whose activities are conditioned by the task of achieving and consolidating the dictatorship of the proletariat, cannot afford to be "liberal" or to permit freedom of factions.

The Party represents unity of will, which precludes all factionalism and division of authority in the Party.

Hence Lenin's warning about the "danger of factionalism from the point of view of Party unity and of effecting the unity of will of the vanguard of the proletariat as the fundamental condition for the success of the dictatorship of the proletariat," which is embodied in the special resolution of the Tenth Congress of our Party "On Party Unity."

Hence Lenin's demand for the "complete elimination of all factionalism" and the "immediate dissolution of all groups, without exception, that had been formed on the basis of various platforms," on pain of unconditional and immediate expulsion from the Party.

SUN YAT-SEN

(Born *Sun Wen* 1866-1925)

Chinese political leader, organized the revolution against the Manchus, and was President of China (1921-1922). This son of a Christian smallholder was educated in American and British schools at Honolulu and Hong Kong, became a doctor and practiced at Macao and Canton, founded a Chinese republican organization (1895) and was forced to flee abroad. He organized the Kuomintang, the revolutionary Chinese nationalist party (1905) with the help of the Chinese communities in America and other foreign countries. He was exiled again after the abortive "second revolution" of 1912, in which he had been proclaimed President of the Republic at Nanking. In 1917 he returned to take command of the South China revolutionaries, set up a South Chinese government at Nanking, and was proclaimed its President. He reorganized the Kuomintang with the help of the Soviet Russian adviser, Borodin, and sympathized with the Communists. His mausoleum at Nanking was a national shrine of China before the Japanese occupation. He provided the Chinese nationalist movement with its program and ideology; his famous Three Principles (nationalism, democracy, people's livelihood) formed the platform of the Kuomintang (San Min Chu I, *The Three Principles of People,* Shanghai, 1927; Leonard S. Hsu, *Sun Yat-sen, His Political and Social Ideals,* 1933; H. B. Restavich, *Sun Yat-sen, Liberator of China,* 1931).

On his deathbed, in March, 1925, Sun Yat-sen addressed the following letter to the Central Executive Committee of the Union of Soviet Socialist Republics:

Sun Yat-Sen

*A Message to Soviet Russia**

Dear Comrades:

While I lie here in a malady against which men are powerless, my thoughts are turned toward you and toward the fate of my party and my country.

You are the head of the union of free republics—that heritage left to the oppressed peoples of the world by the immortal Lenin. With the aid of that heritage the victims of imperialism will inevitably achieve emancipation from that international regime whose foundations have been rooted for ages in slavery, wars, and injustice.

I leave behind me a party which, as I always hoped, will be bound up with you in the historic work of the final liberation of China and other exploited countries from the yoke of imperialism. By the will of fate I must leave my work unfinished, and hand it over to those who, remaining faithful to the principles and teachings of the party, will thereby be my true followers.

Therefore I charge the Kuomintang to continue the work of the revolutionary nationalist movement, so that China, reduced by the imperialists to the position of a semicolonial country, shall become free.

With this object I have instructed the party to be in constant contact with you. I firmly believe in the continuance of the support which you have hitherto accorded to my country.

Taking my leave of you, dear comrades, I want to express the hope that the day will come when the U.S.S.R. will welcome a friend and ally in a mighty, free China, and that in the great struggle for the liberation of the oppressed peoples of the world both those allies will go forward to victory hand in hand.

With fraternal greetings,

Sun Yat-sen

*** The *New York Times,* May 24, 1925; reprinted by permission.**

*History of the Chinese Revolution**
(Written on January 29, 1923)

FOLLOWING China's war with France (1883-1884) I made up my mind to devote myself to the revolution. In 1895 I started the first insurrection in Canton and the revolution of 1911 culminated in the establishment of the Republic. Up to the present the task of revolution, however, has not yet been completed. A span of thirty-seven years of my revolutionary work is to be chronicled by future historians from all manner of facts and incidents. An outline sketch is given below.

1. Principles of Revolution

The term *Kemin,* or revolution, was first used by Confucius. Incidents of a revolutionary nature repeatedly happened in Chinese history after Tang (founder of the Shang Dynasty, B.C. 1766) and Wu (founder of the Chou Dynasty, B.C. 1122). In Europe revolutionary tides surged in the seventeenth and eighteenth centuries and they have since spread over the whole world. In due course they created republics; they conferred constitutions on monarchies. The principles which I have held in promoting the Chinese revolution were in some cases from our traditional ideals, in other cases modelled on still others formulated according to original and self-developed theories. They are described as follows:—

1. *Principle of Nationalism.* Revelations of Chinese history prove that the Chinese as a people are independent in spirit and in conduct. Coerced into touch with other peoples, they could at times live in peace with them by maintaining friendly relations and at others assimilate them as the result of propinquity. During the periods when their political and military prowess declined, they could not escape for the time

* Text: Sun Yat-sen, *Fundamentals of National Reconstruction,* Chungking: Chinese Ministry of Information, 1945, pp. 37-41.

from the fate of a conquered nation, but they could eventually vigorously reassert themselves. Thus the Mongol rule of China (A.D. 1260-1333), lasting for nearly a hundred years, was finally overthrown by Tai Tsu of the Ming Dynasty and his loyal followers. So in our own time was the Manchu yoke thrown off by the Chinese. Nationalistic ideas in China did not come from a foreign source; they were inherited from our remote forefathers. Upon this legacy is based my principle of nationalism, and where necessary, I have developed it, amplified it and improved upon it. No vengeance has been inflicted on the Manchus and we have endeavored to live side by side with them on an equal footing. This is the nationalistic policy toward the races within our national boundaries. Externally, we should strive to maintain independence in the family of nations, and to spread our indigenous civilization as well as to enrich it by absorbing what is best in world civilization, with the hope that we may forge ahead with other nations toward the goal of ideal brotherhood.

2. *Principle of Democracy.* In ancient China we had Emperor Yao (B.C. 2357-2258) and Emperor Shun (B.C. 2258-2206) who departed from the hereditary system and chose their successors. We also had Tang and Wu who overthrew kingdoms by revolution. Preserved in our books are such sayings as "Heaven sees as the people see. Heaven hears as the people hear." "We have heard of a person named Chou having been slain, we have not heard of a monarch having been murdered." "The people are most important, while the king is of the least importance." All these sayings ring with democratic sentiments. Since we have had only ideas about popular rights, and no democratic system has been evolved, we have to go to Europe and America for a republican form of government. There some countries have become republics and others have adopted constitutional monarchism, under which royal power has shrunk in the face of the

rising demand for popular rights. Though hereditary monarchs have not yet disappeared, they are but vestiges and shadows of their former selves.

All through my revolutionary career I have held the view that China must be made a republic. There are three reasons. First, from a theoretical point of view, there is no ground for preserving a monarchical form of government, since it is widely recognized that the people constitute the foundation of a nation and they are all equal in their own country. In the second place, under Manchu occupation the Chinese people were forced into the position of the vanquished, and suffered oppression for more than two hundred and sixty years. While a constitutional monarchy may not arouse deep resentment in other countries and can maintain itself for the time being, it will be an impossibility in China. This is from a historical point of view. A third reason may be advanced with an eye on the future of the nation. That in China a prolonged period of disorder usually followed a revolution was due to the desire of every insurgent to be a king and to his subsequent contention for the throne. If a republican government is adopted, there will be no contention. For these three reasons, I have decided for the republican form of government in order to realize the principle of democracy.

My second decision is that a constitution must be adopted to ensure good government. The true meaning of constitutionalism was discovered by Montesquieu. The threefold separation of the legislative, judicial, and executive powers as advocated by him was accepted in every constitutional country in Europe. On a tour of Europe and America I made a close study of their governments and laws and took note of their shortcomings as well as their advantages. The shortcomings of election, for instance, are not incurable. In the past China had two significant systems of examination and censoring and they can be of avail where the Western system of government and law falls short. I therefore advocate that the examinative and censorial powers should be placed on the same level with legislative, judicial and executive, thereby resulting in the fivefold separation of powers. On top of that, the system of the people's direct political powers should be adopted in order that the provision that the sovereign power is vested in the people may become a reality. In this way my principle of democracy may be carried out satisfactorily.

3. *Principle of Livelihood.* With the invention of modern machines, the phenomenon of uneven distribution of wealth in the West has become all the more marked. Intensified by cross-currents, economic revolution was flaring up more ferociously than political revolution. This situation was scarcely noticed by our fellow-countrymen thirty years ago. On my tour of Europe and America, I saw with my own eyes the instability of their economic structure and the deep concern of their leaders in groping for a solution. I felt that, although the disparity of wealth under our economic organization is not so great as in the West, the difference is only in degree, not in character. The situation will become more acute when the West extends its economic influence to China. We must form plans beforehand in order to cope with the situation. After comparing various schools of economic thought, I have come to the realization that the principle of state ownership is most profound, reliable and practical. Moreover, it will forestall in China difficulties which have already caused much anxiety in the West. I have therefore decided to enforce the principle of the people's livelihood simultaneously with the principles of nationalism and democracy, with the hope to achieve our political objective and to nip economic unrest in the bud.

To sum up, my revolutionary principles in a nutshell consist in the Three Principles of the People and the Five-Power Constitution. Those who have a clear knowledge of the general tendency of the world and the conditions in China will agree that my views are practical and must be put in practice.

II. *Fundamentals of Revolution*

In the age of autocracy, the masses of the people were fettered in spirit and body so that emancipation seemed impossible. Those who worked for the welfare of the people and were willing to sacrifice themselves for the success of revolution not only did not receive assistance from the people but were also ridiculed and disparaged. Much as they desired to be the guides of the people, they proceeded without followers. Much as they desired to be the vanguards, they advanced without reinforcement. It becomes necessary that, apart from destroying enemy influence, those engaged in revolution should take care to develop the constructive ability of the people. A revolutionary program is therefore indispensable. . . . The progress of our revolution should be regulated and divided into three stages: First, military rule; second, political tutelage; third, constitutional government. The first stage is a period of destruction, during which military rule is installed. The revolutionary army is to break down (as it did) Manchu despotism, sweep away official corruptions, and reform vicious customs.

The second stage is a transitional period, during which a provisional constitution (not the present one) will be promulgated. Its object is to build a local self-government system for the development of democracy. The *hsein* or district will be a unit of self-government. When disbanded troops are disposed of and fighting ceases, every district should accept the provisional constitution, which will regulate the rights and duties of the people and the administrative powers of the revolutionary government. It will be in force for three years, at the end of which the people will choose their district magistrates. . . .

ALEXIS DE TOCQUEVILLE
(1805-1859)

A French aristocrat, jurist and member of the French parliament, after a visit of the United States wrote *Democracy in America* (two volumes, 1835 and 1840) as a summary of his observations and the conclusions he derived from them. This was the first full-length study of politics and society in the New World. Though he believed democracy was inevitable for all nations of the West, he tried to be as objective as possible in his analysis of the cultural patterns and ideals of America and pointed out what he considered the failures as well as the successes of democracy. Though he saw the possible tyranny of the majority, he believed in democracy because he saw that its freedom was productive of general well-being and a high standard of living. He was thus intellectually democratic but instinctively aristocratic, an admirer of American democracy but fearful of its egalitarian tendencies, and an opponent of government centralization. A wholly civilized man, he believed above all in the dignity of man and could give no more than two cheers for democracy or any other form of government. After an active life he set to work on a history of the French Revolution; only the first volume—another masterpiece—had been completed when he died. It was his genius that, by patient enumeration and analysis, he made the French chaos clear. In the end, the ground tone of his analysis of revolutionary causes lies in his statement: "Every Frenchman felt he was being victimized; his personal freedom, his money, his self-respect, and the amenities of his daily life were constantly being tampered with on the strength of some ancient law, some medieval usage." (*The Old Regime and the French Revolution,* translated by Stuart Gilbert, Anchor, New York, 1955). This is political science in the grand manner.

*Why the People May Strictly Be Said to Govern in the United States**

In America the people appoints the legislative and the executive power, and furnishes the jurors who punish all offences against the laws. The American institutions are democratic, not only in their principle but in all their consequences; and the people elects its representatives *directly,* and for the most part *annually,* in order to ensure their dependence. The people is therefore the real directing power; and although the form of government is representative, it is evident that the opinions, the prejudices, the interests, and even the passions of the community are hindered by no durable obstacles from exercising a perpetual influence on society. In the United States the majority governs in the name of the people, as is in the case in all the countries in which the people is supreme. This majority is principally composed of peaceable citizens, who, either by inclination or by interest, are sincerely desirous of the welfare of their country. But they are surrounded by the incessant agitation of parties, which attempt to gain their co-operation and to avail themselves of their support. . . .

Philosophical Method Among the Americans

I think that in no country in the civilized world is less attention paid to philosophy than in the United States. The Americans have no philosophical school of their own; and they care but little for all the schools into which Europe is divided, the very names of which are scarcely known to them.

Nevertheless it is easy to perceive that almost all the inhabitants of the United States conduct their understanding in the same manner, and govern it by the same rules; that is to

* This excerpt taken from Alexis de Tocqueville, *The Republic of the United States of America, and Its Political Institutions, Reviewed and Examined,* as translated by Henry Reeves, New York, 1856.

say, that without ever having taken the trouble to define the rules of a philosophical method, they are in possession of one, common to the whole people.

To evade the bondage of system and habit, of family maxims, class-opinions, and, in some degree, of national prejudices; to accept tradition only as a means of information, and existing facts only as a lesson used in doing otherwise and doing better, to seek the reason of things for oneself, and in oneself alone, to tend to results without being bound to means, and to aim at the substance through the form;—such are the principal characteristics of what I shall call the philosophical method of the Americans.

But if I go further, and if I seek among these characteristics that which predominates over and includes almost all the rest, I discover, that in most of the operations of the mind, each American appeals to the individual exercise of his own understanding alone.

America is therefore one of the countries in the world where philosophy is least studied, and where the precepts of Descartes are best applied. Nor is this surprising. The Americans do not read the works of Descartes, because their social condition deters them from speculative studies; but they follow his maxims, because this very social condition naturally disposes their understanding to adopt them.

In the midst of the continual movement which agitates a democratic community, the tie which unites one generation to another is relaxed or broken; every man readily loses the trace of the ideas of his forefathers or takes no care about them.

Nor can men living in this state of society derive their belief from the opinions of the class to which they belong; for, so to speak, there are no longer any classes, or those which still exist are composed of such mobile elements, that their body can never exercise a real control over its members. . . .

GEORGE WASHINGTON
(1732-1799)

The first President of the United States (1789-1797), Commander-in-Chief of the colonial armies in the American Revolution, called the Father of his Country, has been one of the most famous and quoted figures in American and world history; innumerable books and articles have been written about him, including those "debunking" him. (There is a respectable school of thought which contends that Washington was not the first president of the United States, and that a distinguished gentleman named John Hanson was. Hanson was the first President of the Continental Congress after Lord Cornwallis' surrender at Yorktown; but this was under the old Articles of Confederation, which were replaced by the U.S. Constitution in 1789.) Born in Westmoreland County, Virginia, one of four sons of well-to-do planter Augustine Washington by his second wife, he had little formal education, but he taught himself considerable mathematics. At the age of sixteen, he was hired by Lord Fairfax to survey the British nobleman's Virginia properties, and became a public surveyor. He served with great gallantry on the staff of British General Edward Braddock in the French and Indian War (1755-1763)—particularly at the scene of Braddock's disastrous defeat by the French near Fort Duquesne (now Pittsburgh) on July 9, 1755—and helped capture Duquesne in 1758. He inherited considerable property and was a shrewd real estate investor; in 1759 he married the wealthy widow Martha Dandridge Custis; hence, when the American Revolution began, he was one of the richest men in the American colonies. Yet he did not hesitate to risk everything he had, including his neck, by accepting the appointment of Commander-in-Chief of the Continental Army by the Continental Congress on June 1, 1775. The story of the Revolution is one of numerous early defeats for the Americans, with a few important victories, plus eventual help from France, with General Washington winning the last round when Cornwallis surrendered on October 19, 1781. Throughout this fierce conflict, Washington was the greatest single source of inspiration and encouragement to soldiers and civilians alike; this can be attributed to his courage, devotion to the cause, love of country, absolute honesty and ability to rise above the backbiting of politicians and the plotting of lesser officers. As Chairman of the Constitutional Convention (Philadelphia, 1787) he was elected and re-elected President (1789, 1792) by unanimous vote of the Electoral College; no President since has had this honor. He refused a third term. As President, he oversaw Alexander Hamilton's fashioning of sound financial policies for the new nation, and stood like a rock for U.S. neutrality in the British-French war which began in 1793. This experience convinced him that Europe's endless family fights were no proper concern of the North American Republic—a conviction which he set forth in detail in his great Farewell Address of September 17, 1796. That policy of friendliness toward all nations and entangling alliances with none lasted until President Woodrow Wilson in 1917 persuaded Congress that the United States must come to the rescue of Britain and France, then hard-pressed by Kaiser Wilhelm's Germany. In retirement on his Mount Vernon estate, Washington on a dour December day in 1799 took a long horseback ride in a snowstorm; he contracted laryngitis, which was beyond the skill of physicians in Washington's time. The great General and President died on December 14, 1799—and was described five days later, in a Congressional resolution written by John Marshall (later Chief Justice), as "first in war, first in peace, and first in the hearts of his countrymen."

*Farewell Address**

THE UNITY of government which constitutes you one people,

* This excerpt taken from Newton Fred Scott, ed., *Webster's First Bunker Hill Oration and Washington's Farewell Address,* New York: Longmans, Green, and Co., 1905, pp. 80-81, 92-94.

is now dear to you. It is justly so; for it is a main pillar in the edifice of your real independence; the support of your tranquillity at home; your peace abroad; of your safety; of your prosperity in every shape; of that very liberty, which you so highly prize. But, as it is easy to foresee that from different causes and from different quarters much pains will be taken, many artifices employed, to weaken in your minds the conviction of this truth as this is the point in your political fortress against which the batteries of internal and external enemies will be most constantly and actively (though often covertly and insidiously) directed; it is of infinite moment that you should properly estimate the immense value of your national union to your collective and individual happiness; that you should cherish a cordial, habitual, and immovable attachment to it; accustoming yourselves to think and speak of it as of the Palladium of your political safety and prosperity; watching for its preservation with jealous anxiety; discountenancing whatever may suggest even a suspicion that it can in any event be abandoned; and indignantly frowning upon the first dawning of every attempt to alienate any portion of our country from the rest, or to enfeeble the sacred ties which now link together the various parts.

For this you have every inducement of sympathy and interest. Citizens by birth or choice of a common country, that country has a right to concentrate your affections. The name of American, which belongs to you in your national capacity, must always exalt the just pride of patriotism more than any appellation derived from local discriminations. With slight shades of difference, you have the same religion, manners, habits, and political principles. You have in common cause fought and triumphed together. The independence and liberty you possess are the work of joint councils and joint efforts, of common dangers, sufferings, and successes.

But these considerations, however powerfully they address themselves to your sensibility, are greatly outweighed by those which apply more immediately to your interest. Here every portion of our country finds the most commanding motives for carefully guarding and preserving the union of the whole.

The North in an unrestrained intercourse with the South, protected by the equal laws of a common government, finds in the productions of the latter great additional resources of maritime and commercial enterprise and precious materials of manufacturing industry. The South, in the same intercourse, benefiting by the agency of the North, sees its agriculture grow and its commerce expand. Turning partly into its own channels the seamen of the North, it finds its particular navigation invigorated; and while it contributes in different ways to nourish and increase the general mass of the national navigation, it looks forward to the production of a maritime strength to which itself is unequally adapted. The East, in a like intercourse with the West, already finds, and in the progressive improvement of interior communications by land and water will more and more find, a valuable vent for the commodities which it brings from abroad or manufactures at home. The West derives from the East supplies requisite to its growth and comfort, and what is perhaps of still greater consequence, it must of necessity owe the secure enjoyment of indispensable outlets for its own productions to the weight, influence, and the future maritime strength of the Atlantic side of the union, directed by an indissoluble community of interest, as one Nation. . . . to betray or sacrifice the interests of their own country without odium, sometimes even with popularity; gilding with the appearances of a virtuous sense of obligation, a commendable deference for public opinion, or a laudable zeal for public good, the base or foolish compliances of ambition, corruption, or infatuation.

As avenues to foreign influence in innumerable ways, such attachments are particularly alarming to the truly enlightened and independent patriot. How many opportunities do they afford to tamper with domestic factions, to practise the arts of seduction, to mislead public opinion, to influence or awe the public councils! Such an attachment of a small or weak towards a great and powerful nation, dooms the former to be the satellite of the latter.

Against the insidious wiles of foreign influence, I conjure you to believe me, fellow-citizens, the jealousy of a free people ought to be constantly awake, since history and experience prove that foreign influence is one of the most baneful foes of republican government. But that jealousy, to be useful, must be impartial; else it becomes the instrument of the very influence to be avoided, instead of a defence against it. Excessive partiality for one foreign nation and excessive dislike of another, cause those whom they actuate to see danger only on one side, and serve to veil and often second the arts of influence on the other. Real patriots, who may resist the intrigues of the favourite, are liable to become suspected and odious; while its tools and dupes usurp the applause and confidence of the people, to surrender their interests.

The great rule of conduct for us, in regard to foreign nations, is, in extending our commercial relations, to have with them as little political connection as possible. So far as we have already formed engagements, let them be fulfilled with perfect good faith. Here let us stop.

Europe has a set of primary interests which to us have none, or a very remote relation. Hence she must be engaged in frequent controversies, the causes of which are essentially foreign to our concerns. Hence therefore it must be unwise in us to implicate ourselves by artificial ties in the ordinary vicissitudes of her politics, or the ordinary combinations and collisions of her friendships or enmities.

Our detached and distant situation invites and enables us to pursue a different course. If we remain one people, under an efficient government, the period is not far off when we may defy material injury from external annoyance; when we may take such an attitude as will cause the neutrality we may at any time resolve upon to be scrupulously respected; when belligerent nations, under the impossibility of making acquisitions upon us, will not lightly hazard the giving us provocation; when we may choose peace or war, as our interest guided by our justice shall counsel.

Why forego the advantages of so peculiar a situation? Why quit our own to stand upon foreign ground? Why, by interweaving our destiny with that of any part of Europe, entangle our peace and prosperity in the toils of European ambition, rivalship, interest, humor, or caprice?

'Tis our true policy to steer clear of permanent alliances with any portion of the foreign world; so far, I mean, as we are now at liberty to do it; for let me not be understood as capable of patronizing infidelity to existing engagements. (I hold the maxim no less applicable to public than to private affairs, that honesty is always the best policy.) I repeat it, therefore, let those engagements be observed in their genuine sense. But in my opinion it is unnecessary and would be unwise to extend them.

Taking care always to keep ourselves, by suitable establishments, on a respectable defensive posture, we may safely trust to temporary alliances for extraordinary emergencies.

Harmony, liberal intercourse with all nations, are recommended by policy, humanity, and interest. But even our commercial policy should hold an equal and impartial hand; neither seeking nor granting exclusive favours or preferences; consulting the natural course of things; diffusing and diversifying by gentle means the streams of commerce, but forcing nothing; establishing with powers so disposed—in order to give trade a stable course, to define the rights of our merchants, and to enable the government to support them—conventional rules of intercourse, the best that present circumstances and mutual opinion will permit; but temporary, and liable to be from time to time abandoned or varied, as experience and circumstance shall dictate; constantly keeping in view that it is folly in one nation to look for disinterested favours from another; that it must pay with a portion of its independence for whatever it may accept under that character; that by such acceptance, it may place itself in the condition of having given equivalents for nominal favours, and yet of being reproached with ingratitude for not giving more. There can be no greater error than to expect or calculate upon real favors from nation to nation. 'Tis an illusion which experience must cure, which a just pride ought to discard.

In offering to you, my countrymen, these counsels of an old and affectionate friend, I dare not hope they will make the strong and lasting impression I could wish; that they will control the usual current of the passions, or prevent our nation from running the course which has hitherto marked the destiny of nations. . . .

MAX WEBER
(1864-1920)

One of the greatest and most influential sociologists, especially in the field of political sociology, was born at Erfurt, Germany, and educated at the University of Heidelberg and later at Berlin and Göttingen. He taught in Berlin, then at Freiburg and Heidelberg. After publishing a work on Roman agricultural history (1891), he established himself as a jurist and participated in state examinations for lawyers, did consultative work for governmental agencies and made special studies for private groups on the stock exchange and the estates in Eastern Germany. In 1898 on a trip to Spain he developed a fever and a psychic malady. After this, throughout his life he suffered alternately from severe depressions and manic spurts of intense intellectual work and travel. Following a few years in a mental institution, in 1902 he resumed teaching at Heidelberg and plunged headlong into history, economics and politics (*Gesammelte Politische Schriften,* 1921; *Gesammelte Aufsaetze zur Religionsoziologie,* 1922-23; *Gesammelte Aufsaetze zur Sociologie und Sozialpolitik,* 1924). In 1904 he published his famous *Protestant Ethics and the Spirit of Capitalism;* that year he also visited the U.S., and noted especially the role of a bureaucracy in a democracy and observed that machine politics were indispensable in a modern mass democracy, resulting in the management of politics by professionals, disciplined party organization and streamlined propaganda.

For Weber, sociology is "concerned with the social activities of human beings; that is, with activities oriented to those of others." It is the study of the concrete facts of society (Durkheim's approach). But among social facts he included the motives, intentions and attitudes which explain human behavior, to be distinguished from the observer's own value judgments about them. In sociological theory he made special studies of economic corporate groups, of the social division of labor, and of authority (legal, traditional and "charismatic"—by which he meant the manifestation by an individual of exceptional qualities of power over others, such as is possessed by chieftains, kings and priests). He made several studies in each of the several branches of his classification of sociology: the sociology of religion, the sociology of economic life, the sociology of law, and the sociology of political life, in which he paid special attention to bureaucracy, traditions and "charisma." In the area of politics, he was partly influenced by Marx, to whose economic materialism he added a political and military materialism, though he wanted to keep political power distinct from the economic. But he was also the foremost revisionist of Marx's ideas, as well as a major critic of high capitalism. In America, his influence has given rise to the study of politics "as is."

---

*The Concept of Legitimate Authority**

Conduct, especially social conduct, and more particularly a social relationship, can be oriented on the part of the individuals to what constitutes their "idea" of the existence of a *legitimate authority*. The probability that such orientation actually occurs shall be called the "validity" of the authority in question.

1. That an authority assumes "validity" must therefore mean more than the mere regularity of social conduct as determined by custom or self-interest. The fact that furniture movers advertise their services regularly about the time that leases expire is caused quite clearly by their desire to exploit an opportunity in their self-interest. The fact that a peddler regularly visits a certain customer on a certain day of the week or month is either the result of long habit or of

* Excerpts taken from Max Weber, *Basic Concepts in Sociology*, trans. & with an introduction by H. P. Secher, Philosophical Library, New York, 1962, pp. 71-73.

self-interest (e.g. the turnover in his district). When a civil servant shows up at his office every day at the same time, it may be determined not only by custom or self-interest, since he can hold on to that as he pleases, but it may be partly the result of his abiding by office regulations which impose certain duties on him and which he may be loath to violate, since such conduct would not only be disadvantageous to him but may be also abhorrent to his "sense of duty," which, to a greater or lesser extent, represents for him an absolute value.

2. Only then will the content of a social relationship represent "authority," if its conduct can be oriented approximately toward certain recognizable axioms. Only then will such authority acquire "validity," if the orientation toward these axioms includes at least the recognition that they are binding on the individual or the corresponding behavior constitutes a model worthy of imitation. Indeed, conduct may be orientated toward an authority for a variety of motives. But the fact that along with other motives the authority is also held by at least some of the other individuals as being worthy of imitation or binding naturally increases to a very considerable degree the probability that conduct will in fact conform to it. An authority which is obeyed for the sole reason of expedience is generally much less stable than one which is upheld on a purely customary basis. The latter attitude toward authority is much the most common one. But even more stable is the type of conduct oriented toward custom, which enjoys the prestige of being considered exemplary or binding, or possesses what is known as "legitimacy." Of course, the transition from a goal- or tradition-oriented conduct to one motivated by a belief in its legitimacy is extremely gradual.

3. There can be orientation toward valid authority even where its meaning (as generally understood) is not necessarily obeyed. The probability that the authority is to some extent held as a valid norm can also have its effect on behav-

ior even where its meaning is evaded or deliberately violated. This may be true at first even on the basis of sheer expediency. Thus the thief's behavior exemplifies the validity of the criminal law merely by the fact that he tries to conceal his conduct. The very fact that an authority is valid within a particular group makes it necessary for him to practice concealment. This is, of course, a marginal case and frequently the authority is violated partially only in one or another respect or its violation is sought to be passed off as legitimate with a varying measure of good faith. Or there may coexist various interpretations of the meaning of authority alongside of each other. In that case the sociologist will regard each one as valid exactly insofar as it actually shapes the course of behavior. It is no great difficulty for the sociologist to recognize within the same social group the existence of several, possibly mutually contradictory, valid systems of authority. Indeed it is possible even for the same individual to orient his behavior to mutually contradictory systems of authority. This can take place not only in short succession, as can be observed daily, but even in the case of the same conduct. A person who engages in a duel orients his behavior toward the observance of the honor code; but he also orients his conduct toward the criminal law by keeping the duel a secret or, conversely, by voluntarily appearing in court. Where, however, evasion or violation of the system of authority in its generally understood meaning has become the rule, such authority can be said to be "valid" only in a limited sense or has ceased to be valid altogether. For the jurist a system of authority is either valid or it is not; for the sociologist no such choice exists. Rather, there is a gradual transition between the two extremes of validity and non-validity and it is possible for mutually contradictory systems of authority to coexist validly. Each one is valid precisely in proportion to the probability that behavior will be actually oriented toward it.

Max Weber

The Concepts of Power and Domination*

BY *power* is meant that opportunity existing within a social relationship which permits one to carry out one's own will even against resistance and regardless of the basis on which this opportunity rests.

By *domination* is meant the opportunity to have a command of a given specified content obeyed by a given group of persons. By "discipline" will be meant the opportunity to obtain prompt, and automatic obedience in a predictable form from a given group of persons because of their practiced orientation toward a command.

1. The concept of power is sociologically amorphous. Every conceivable quality of a person and every conceivable combination of circumstance may put someone in a situation where he can demand compliance with his will. The sociological concept of domination consequently must be more precise and can only mean the probability that a *command* will be obeyed.

2. The concept of "discipline" includes the "practiced nature" of uncritical and unresisting mass obedience.

The fact of the matter is that domination depends only on the actual presence of one person successfully issuing commands to another; it does not necessarily imply either the existence of an administrative staff or, for that matter, of a corporate group. Usually, however, it is associated with at least one of these. To the extent that the members of a corporate group are subject to the legitimate exercise of such domination it will be called "corporate domination."

3. The head of a household dominates without an administrative staff. A Bedouin chief who receives tribute from caravans, persons, and shipments of goods which pass through his mountain fastness dominates all those changing and indeterminate individuals who, without being associated

* Excerpt taken from Secher, *op. cit.*, pp. 127-128.

with each other, happen to have stumbled into a particular situation. He is able to do this by virtue of his loyal retainers, who act, if the occasion demands it, as his administrative staff in enforcing his will. Theoretically, such domination would be conceivable also by one person alone without the help of any administrative staff.

4. If a corporate group possesses an administrative staff, it is always to a certain extent engaged in corporate domination. But the concept is relative. Normally corporate domination is at the same time also an administrative organization. The nature of a corporate group is determined by a variety of factors: the manner in which the administration is carried out, the character of personnel, the objects over which it exercises control, and the extent of effective jurisdiction of its domination. The first two factors in particular are dependent in the highest degree on the way in which authority is legitimized.

Acknowledgments

Acknowledgment is gratefully made to the following for permission to reprint from their publications:

George Allen & Unwin, London, *Reflections on Violence* by George Sorel, translated by T. E. Hulme, 1925.

Cambridge University Press, New York, "The Doctrine of Fascism" by Benito Mussolini, in *The Social and Political Doctrines of Contemporary Europe* by Michael Oakeshott, 1939.

Cassell & Company, Ltd., London, *The Sinews of Peace: Postwar Speeches* by Sir Winston Churchill, edited by Randolph S. Churchill.

Columbia University Press, New York, *Perpetual Peace* by Immanuel Kant, with an introduction by Nicholas Murray Butler, 1932; copyright 1932, U.S. Library Association, Inc.

Ginn & Company, Boston, "Proclamation, 19th Brumaire" by Napoleon Bonaparte, in *Readings in Modern European History* by James Harvey Robinson and Charles A. Beard, 1908.

Alfred A. Knopf, Inc., *The Decline of the West* by Oswald Spengler, 1932.

Harvard University Press, Cambridge, *The Writings and Speeches of Oliver Cromwell,* edited by Wilbur Cortez Abbott, 1945.

J. B. Lippincott Company, New York and Philadelphia, "The Social Contract" by Jean Jacques Rousseau, in *Readings in Western Civilization,* selected and edited by George H. Knoles and Rixford K. Snyder, 1951.

Longmans, Green & Company, New York, *The Living Thought of Confucius,* edited by Alfred O. Mendel, published by David McKay Company, 1950.

McGraw-Hill Book Company, New York, *The Ruling Class* by Gaetano Mosca, translated by Hannah D. Kahn, edited and revised by Arthur Livingston, 1939.

The Navajivan Trust, Ahmedabad, India, *All Men Are*

Acknowledgments

Brothers by Mahatma Gandhi, published by UNESCO and Columbia University Press, 1958.

Oxford University Press, London, *The Speeches of Adolf Hitler, April 1922-August 1939,* edited by Norman H. Baynes, 1942.

The Pareto Fund, San Francisco, *The Mind and Society* by Wilfredo Pareto, published by Harcourt Brace, 1935.

The Philadelphia Yearly Meeting, Philadelphia, *Fruits of an Active Life* by William Penn, edited by William Wistar Comfort.

The Pontifical Institute of Mediaeval Studies, Toronto, *On Kingship* by St. Thomas Aquinas, translated by Gerald B. Pheland, revised with introduction and notes by I. T. Eschmann, 1949.